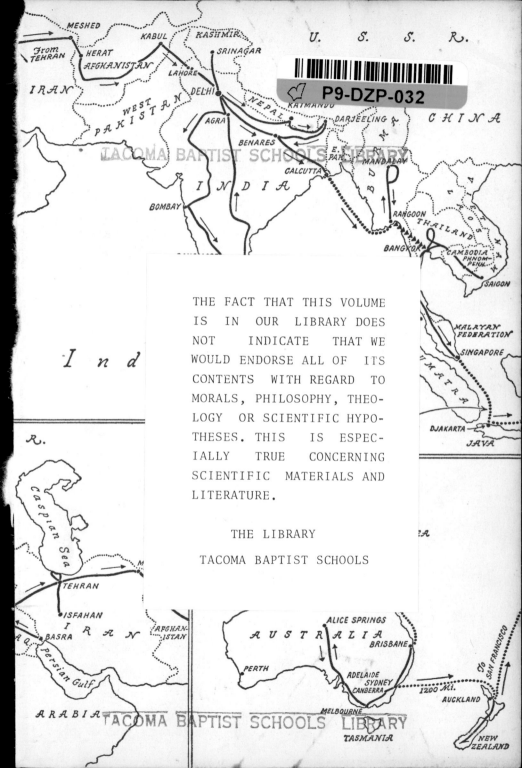

WALK THE WIDE WORLD

WALK THE WIDE WORLD

BY DONALD KNIES

ILLUSTRATED WITH PHOTOGRAPHS

DODD, MEAD & COMPANY

NEW YORK · 1958

TO MY MOTHER, AND TO THE MANY PEOPLE, NAMED AND
UNNAMED, WITHOUT WHOSE HELP MY TRIP WOULD NEVER
HAVE BEEN POSSIBLE

Printed in the United States of America
by Vail-Ballou Press, Inc., Binghamton, N. Y.

FOREWORD

AFTER TWO YEARS of sitting behind a desk in San Francisco I'd had enough! Perhaps I should not have been dissatisfied. Standard Oil Company of California was a benevolent and paternal employer, and my job gave me plenty of leisure in which to dream. I liked my co-workers, had many friends and loved San Francisco with a sort of blind frenzy.

But how could I completely surrender to daily routine when I closed my eyes and could see the pilgrims swarming into the Ganges and smell a sheep roasting in a Bedouin encampment and hear the drums throbbing in Marrakech? My feet itched and I had a great desire to see the world.

I had always loved to wander and already had seen a large part of the United States. Several of my trips had been by hitchhiking and this rather unorthodox method of traveling appealed to me. I enjoyed starting out in the morning not knowing where I would be that night, whom I might meet or what I would learn along the way. The challenge of uncertainty, the spark of adventure in every ride, the close contact with all types of people—these enticements far outweighed the delays and minor discomforts in hitchhiking.

Transportation, of course, is the biggest expense on most trips. Since I wanted to see as much of the world as possible on the money I had saved, what method of traveling could be cheaper than hitchhiking? Twenty-six months of vagabonding cost me seven hundred dollars.

My brother Rich and I had toured Europe several summers before in an all too brief seven-week whirl. I observed then that hitchhiking among Europeans themselves was a widely practiced and apparently successful way to see the Continent. As for the rest of the world, I decided the only way to find out if hitchhiking was practical was to try.

The greatest drawback to hitchhiking is the uncertainty of time, so that travel plans must be very flexible. Most people on ordinary vacations prefer to follow a schedule. But I had all the time that was needed. No one expected me to be back on a certain date. I was twenty-five years old, single, with few responsibilities, in good health—and liked to walk. My curiosity was unlimited. I had studied history and political science at St. Lawrence University and Stanford, a good background for this kind of trip. I didn't mind sleeping in a field and was not particular about what I ate—as long as there was enough of it.

Making a clean break from my very ordinary daily existence was the most difficult step of my whole journey. But once I had resigned from my job, paid for a boat ticket to North Africa and kissed my girl good-by, the future seemed easy. I was free . . . and the world was waiting to be seen.

During the year that I made definite plans, I searched for a traveling companion. My friends were interested, but time was the big obstacle for them. No one else could afford to spend two years on the road.

In retrospect I'm convinced that it was far better to make the trip alone. Hitchhiking, particularly in the Asian countries where there is so little traffic, is much easier for one person. A loaded car or truck can usually fit one more aboard somewhere, but two is very often a physical impossibility. People are able to offer more hospitality to a lone traveler. And even two close friends are certain to have differences of opinion when traveling. One person can go wherever he wants, can stay as long or short a time as he likes and has no one else's plans to merge with his own.

Frequently I have been asked, "Weren't you lonely?"

I met so many friends along the way that there was no time to be lonely. Instead of being alone, I often had more people than I could handle trying to do things for me.

"How did you talk to all those people?", many have inquired in amazement when hearing of the territory I covered.

Language is really not a barrier when people are trying to be friendly. It's amazing how much conversation is possible with a few words, a map and gestures. English is the international language today. Anywhere in the former British Empire it is widely spoken; the colonial rulers never learned the local languages, so the people were obliged to learn English. In even the most isolated countries the students study English and are eager to practice. Anyone who can interpret for the crowd enhances his prestige and at the same time satisfies his own curiosity. I spoke a sort of pidgin French, most of which I picked up in North Africa and Europe. French is widely understood and is the second-best language for traveling. My high-school Spanish helped in Spain. And finally I tried to learn a few key words in each country so that I could at least say "hello" and "thank you."

Amused by my shaggy appearance on my return, my family and friends wanted to know why I grew a beard.

I stopped shaving purely for convenience, to save myself time and trouble. But as my whiskers grew, I realized that a beard was a definite asset: it marked me as a traveler and added to my curiosity value.

"What kind of food did you eat?" is a question gourmets and hypochondriacs ask me.

I ate and drank whatever the local people ate and drank. When someone invited me home for dinner, I could not offend my host by refusing to eat whatever was served. And besides, after a day spent outdoors, I was hungry. The fact that an American would share their food, no matter how simple or highly seasoned, was appreciated by my hosts. In Asia Western meals were expensive and often unavailable. Rice and curry was very cheap and filling. My diet was sometimes monotonous, but frequently fascinating. I tried to enjoy everything, and was sick only in India.

People who also would like to travel light and free invariably want to know what I took with me.

I bought a wooden-framed, canvas "Yukon pack," better

for my purpose than a conventional rucksack. Into it I stuffed about forty-three pounds of gear—two sport shirts, a pair of blue jeans and a pair of khakis, raincoat, leather jacket, wool sweater, a dacron suit with one nylon shirt and one tie, a pair of shoes, two light short-sleeve shirts, two T shirts, two nylon shorts, six pairs of socks, bathing suit, medical kit, toilet kit, one towel, film, maps, canteen, flashlight and a couple of letters stating that I was an American citizen in good standing. Also my two most valuable possessions: a warm and compact sleeping bag weighing only three and a half pounds and a sturdy pair of hiking boots which lasted for two years. Knowing that whatever I brought would be carried on my back helped me hold the weight to a minimum.

I joined the International Youth Hostel Association, took every medical shot possible and renewed my passport. The necessary visas I would pick up from consulates of the different countries as I went along. With my camera in my pocket, a little American flag hung on the back of the pack and my passport and travelers' checks in a money belt around my waist, I was well equipped.

Hitchhiking through forty-eight countries taught me a basic truth about travel which is so simple and obvious, yet is neglected by the great majority of travelers. After the monuments, the museums and the scenery have been seen and admired, the best attraction of each country is its people. The only way to appreciate and understand people, their ideas and their customs, is to live among them. To do this, without actually residing in a foreign country or having relatives or friends there, one must hitchhike. The tourist meets guides and waiters and porters. But the hitch-hiker is taken home to eat and sleep, to talk and perhaps argue with family and friends. He gains an insight into how they live and what they think, and it is an experience that cannot be bought.

A traveler who comes on foot with a pack on his back brings out the best in people. They know he is in their city or village because he wants to be. The Army has not stationed him, he has no mission to preach, no product to sell. And so they accept him wholeheartedly as a friend.

Particularly in the Middle Eastern and Asian countries the hospitality and generosity showered upon me were unbelievable. As I walked down the street someone would approach me—or a vehicle would stop on the road.

"Who are you? Where are you going? Where are you coming from?"

And then after these questions, which became so familiar that I could answer them almost before they were asked—

"Please come to my home for dinner, to spend the night, to stay as long as you wish."

My new-found friends would stop whatever they were doing to entertain me and show me the local sights. If they spoke little or no English, they would send for someone to act as interpreter. Nothing was too much trouble. We were friends; therefore, they helped me. It was as simple as that. So many said, "It is my duty. This is my country and you are my guest. When I visit America, you can do the same for me."

The only trouble I encountered was trying to explain to people why I could stay only a day or two at their homes instead of a week. I had no fixed schedule, but realized that if I were ever to complete the trip there had to be some time limitation. Even in vagabonding there must be a goal; otherwise a person could wander aimlessly for the rest of his life. My twin goals were to explore India as thoroughly as possible and then to reach Australia for the Olympic Games.

I had been warned repeatedly about the dangers of traveling alone among so-called uncivilized and primitive peoples. "You should carry a gun or at least a knife," was the advice of my friends. My cousin gave me a blackjack. Though not knowing what to expect, I still felt quite sure that if I were armed, I would be asking for trouble. But if I went as a friend, I would be accepted as a friend.

This trust, admittedly only a hope at first, proved to be justified beyond my greatest expectations. There were literally hundreds of occasions when my pack might have been stolen or I could have been knocked on the head and robbed of everything I owned. My boots alone would be extremely valuable to a person who had no shoes. Yet nothing was ever taken from me. I was given presents—a hand-engraved Pathan dagger, a silver mirror from Greece, a Burmese shoulder bag, a Malay sarong, a Gurkha kukri (knife)—but did not lose as much as a shoelace.

Unfortunately this fear and distrust of "foreigners" whose ways of life seem strange and different is not confined to Americans, but is prevalent throughout the world. Time after time when I thanked my friends and marveled at the hospitality shown me by their countrymen, they would say, "Yes, the people here are kind to a traveler. But be careful in the next country. Those people cannot be trusted."

And invariably I would find that the ones about whom I had been warned were as fine as or perhaps even more hospitable than the previous group.

Everywhere I found intense curiosity about America and our role in world affairs.

"Do all Americans really own automobiles?"

"Tell us about the skyscrapers in New York."

"Have you ever seen the film stars in Hollywood?"

"Is Chicago controlled by gangsters?"

"How much money does a working man earn?"

Among the dark-skinned peoples of Asia the inevitable question arose, "What about segregation?"

There was widespread apprehension about the terrible destructive power in the hands of what many consider an immature and inexperienced nation.

"Does your government sincerely want peace or are you likely to blunder into another war?"

"Do your scientists really understand the effects of these hydrogen bombs?"

"Are you making genuine efforts to ease tensions with Russia?"

Many of my friends heatedly attacked the motives and methods of American foreign policy, particularly as it affected their own countries. But they never held this anti-American feeling against me as an individual. After blaming the U.S.A. for everything from inflated food prices to peculiar weather due to atomic explosions, they would literally give me the shirts off their backs. Perhaps there were some who simply did not like Americans. If so, they stayed away and kept their dislike to themselves. Unfriendly people never bothered me.

Undoubtedly newspaper accounts of riots and demonstrations, as well as frustrating failures in our efforts to help and influence other nations, have given many Americans the uneasy impression that nothing we do overseas is understood or appreciated. They feel we are batting our heads against a stone wall of ignorance, suspicion and ingratitude. I found that America has more friends and supporters than we give ourselves credit for. Other nations may not blindly follow our lead or agree wholeheartedly with our policies; but our ideals have fired the imagination of a large part of the world.

CONTENTS

ILLUSTRATIONS

Photographs follow page 14

A Jewish wedding in an Atlas Mountains village, Morocco; a fatted calf for the feast hangs on the wall

The pig market at Gijón on the north coast of Spain

Portuguese fisherwomen clean and pack sardines on the beach at Nazaré

Yugoslav peasants on the Dalmatian Coast pressing grapes to make wine

The old and the new in Damascus

Sacred cattle roam among the Indian pilgrims who are spending the day in prayer and meditation in a temple courtyard

Indian sadhu (holy man) in a religious trance on a main street in Delhi

Eyes peer from the stupa of a Buddhist shrine in Katmandu valley, Nepal

CHAPTER ONE

MOROCCO

A FANTASTIC PROCESSION of humanity flowed past me as I sat on a curbstone beside the main entrance to the Casablanca Medina, the old Arab quarter. I was spellbound by the crowds: bearded men in hooded burnooses, heads shaved under their turbans; veiled women, occasionally wearing sunglasses or pushing baby carriages; ebony Negroes with scarred faces, from Central Africa. Jewish patriarchs in black robes marched along in stately solemnity, their heads framed by skullcaps and long beards. Pretty French girls hurried over the cobblestones in their high heels. Children wore anything from miniature burnooses to nothing at all. The businessmen, in blue suits and red fezzes, were pursued by whining, ragged beggars. Berber soldiers from the mountains carried bolt-action rifles and needle bayonets; red-and-black-striped robes were worn over their khaki uniforms and cartridge belts crisscrossed their chests.

· I

My first day ashore in Morocco was a colorful beginning for my trip. I had sailed from New York on a cold, rainy February afternoon ten days before. The *Queen Frederika* was a Greek ship, the cheapest passage I could find. She was fifty feet shorter than when built, from being torpedoed during the war, and in a rough sea she rode like a cork. The first-class passengers were old, fat and dull. I slept in a dormitory deep in the hold of the ship, and my roommates were enjoyable companions—Greeks and Italians returning to the Old Country. There were no unmarried girls between fourteen and forty on board, but this did not prevent the men from doing rousing folk dances at night.

We spent one day in Funchal on the Portuguese island of Madeira. Small rowboats converged on our ship and peddlers swarmed aboard, turning the decks into a bazaar. They hawked embroidery, straw hats, the famous Madeira wine, canaries, dead turtles and French postcards. Funchal is a mountain-encircled town of cobblestone streets, mosaic sidewalks, pastel houses, open-air markets, persistent peddlers, peasant women in black shawls and police who carry bayonets.

And then came the eagerly awaited landing in Casablanca. From the modern docks to the business center around the Place de France the overall impression was that of a European city. But approaching the Medina I stepped suddenly into a new and different world, ancient and Eastern, which was quite overwhelming.

Walking through the twisting alleys of the Medina, I felt dizzy from trying to look in every direction at once. There were more sights, sounds and smells than I could absorb. Water peddlers carried goatskins full of water slung over their backs. Men drank tea in dingy cafés or played checkers in the street. Children sat on the floor of a Moslem school, reciting in singsong unison their lessons from the Koran. Metalworkers transformed empty tin cans into funnels, pipes and lanterns. Workmen pounded stones into the mud to repair the streets. Smells of broiling food and rotting garbage blended in a pungent aroma.

Hawkers bellowed their wares and haggled with customers in animated, guttural Arabic. The shops, niches in the walls, were so tiny that the owners could sit in the center of them and reach any object without moving. All kinds of food were sold, as well as rags, clothes, empty bottles, tin cans, rope, rusty scrap iron, firewood and baskets.

With a few alterations, this might have been a scene some thousand years ago.

My first night was spent at a youth hostel in the Medina which cost twenty-seven cents. The following afternoon I started south and was picked up by the first truck to come along, a good omen for hitchhiking. The coastal plateau was green, sprinkled with white flowers and palm trees. Farmers plowed their fields with camels and mules harnessed together, and shepherd boys tended flocks of sheep and goats. Along the side of the road lanky Arabs rode tiny donkeys, their feet trailing on the ground, while the women trudged behind, balancing bundles on their heads.

In Mazagan, a sixteenth-century Portuguese trading port, the city walls are still intact and guarded by rusty cannon. Outside the City Hall several hundred Moroccans squatted sullenly on the ground for a police interrogation. A Jewish funeral procession moved slowly toward the cemetery, the bearded mourners chanting and carrying the casket from which the deceased's feet protruded. After an involved discussion with half the local population, none of whom could understand my faltering French, an Arab G.I. guided me to the youth hostel. The little old lady was overjoyed to see me.

"Monsieur, you are my first guest this year."

Properly awed by this honor, I slept for ten hours.

En route to Mogador with a traveling salesman and his dog, we drove through areas which had been hard hit by the locust plague. At times the locusts, some four inches long, filled the air and peppered the car windshield. Farmers gathered the insects into sacks, beat them to death and piled the dead ones on the ground to be used as fertilizer. The locusts destroy the crops, stripping fields and orchards bare, so the Arabs, philosophically perhaps, roast the locusts and eat them.

Mogador is another Portuguese walled town. I sat on the ramparts, ate bread and cheese and watched the waves beating on the rocks below. Wherever I looked there was something of interest. Cobblers stitched sandals, tailors sat cross-legged on the ground sewing while small boys wound the thread, and blacksmiths hammered in their tiny holes in the wall while more small boys pumped the bellows. In an outdoor grain market merchants lay on the ground amid sacks of wheat while women squatted in groups tossing the grain into the air to let the chaff blow away. A chanting holy man wandered from shop to shop with his incense burner. Butchers sold not only pieces of meat and whole carcasses—but also items like a sheep's head or half a cow's head. Everything from a handful of tea to coal and firewood was purchased by weight on hand scales. In the harbor Arabs repaired a barge by pounding pieces of green lumber into the damaged side. Nails were not necessary. A Frenchman was building a fishing boat alone and by hand. Workmen carried sacks of wheat on their shoulders from carts to dockside.

That evening there was a carnival in Mogador. Several games of chance, a shooting gallery and a derelict merry-go-round were the whole show, but this modest offering drew a wildly enthusiastic crowd. An energetic Negro tap dancer and a bored girl who danced listless, clumsy flamenco provided the come-on for the spinning wheels. The Algerian lottery did a booming business. Moroccan men walked in pairs, holding hands, a custom which is prevalent throughout the East.

Next afternoon I caught a truck to Agadir with three Arabs, who insisted that I get in front while one of them rode on top. There was not much conversation but lots of smiles and meditation. We stopped for lunch in a small, dark café and ate stew out of one big bowl, using pieces of bread as spoons. Flies buzzed incessantly and Arabic music blared from the radio. One of my friends produced a teapot and brewed sweet mint tea on a charcoal brazier.

Agadir is the coastal resort of Southern Morocco. The new part of town is very modern and has several plush hotels, gleaming apartments and shops, a beautiful beach and parks full of trees and flowers. High on a hill above Agadir is the Casbah, the Arab fortress town built long ago. I climbed up the cliffs to the Casbah, past the ruins of a small fort and two fifty-year-old French naval guns overlooking the bay. Completely encircled by a great wall with only one narrow entrance, the Casbah must have been impregnable in its day. Now it is partly in ruins and partly inhabited. I walked around the walls, looking down at the activity in the courtyards and on the roof tops. From the tower of the mosque echoed the evening cry summoning the Faithful to prayers.

I saw my first Foreign Legionnaires, dressed like regular French soldiers except for their distinctive white kepis and red epaulets. There were turbaned Moroccan infantrymen and more of the deadly Berbers, the silent, knife-wielding Goums. French conscripts were rare; these were mostly tough professional soldiers.

Tiznit is an oasis town on the edge of the Sahara, as far south as I went in Morocco. The country is flat and arid, green only during the winter rains. Neighboring villages, even individual farmhouses, are built like miniature forts protected by stone walls topped with natural barbed wire of thorns and brush. Tiznit itself is completely surrounded by red mud walls with great wooden nail-studded doors at each gate. The only French people were the police and the hotel keeper, who cut his price in half when he saw my pack.

Two itinerant musicians drifted from shop to shop playing mandolin-type instruments and singing loudly and off key until they were paid to move on. A Moslem Billy Graham conducted a rousing revival meeting in the town square. First he preached to the crowd with repeated references to his Koran and prayer beads. Then he started the people clapping and he sang while they kept time and chanted the chorus. Except for language and costume it could have been a Georgia tent meeting. Outside the walls the locusts were so thick they looked like clouds of dust rising from the ground.

I rode to Taroudant with Guy Phelipon, a French farmer, who invited me to stay at his home. His sister-in-law, a pretty blonde who had been to college in New Orleans, was a granddaughter of "Tiger" Clemenceau.

They showed me their mechanized and irrigated farm. "Before we settled this land it was all dry scrub brush—worthless," Guy told me. "Now we raise tomatoes and oranges for the winter market in France. We have eighty Arabs working for us, forty adults, the rest boys and girls."

"Do you have any trouble with the Arabs?" I asked.

"Not really," said Guy, "but we must watch them all the time. They are like children, have never done anything to help themselves. Actually, the young ones are better than their parents. An Arab is all right until he grows up. Then he gets big ideas and doesn't want to work."

I liked Guy and his family but couldn't accept their idea that the Arabs were completely hopeless. It sounded like the old, familiar apology for colonialism—"The 'natives' are incapable of handling their own affairs. They need the Great White Father to look after them."

And, incidentally, reap the benefits.

Morocco was changing before my eyes and would soon erupt in bloody revolution; yet the French settlers clung stubbornly and blindly to the past.

Sunday was market day in Taroudant and the square was thronged with people, scrawny cattle, pathetic little donkeys, lumbering camels, black-faced sheep and long-horned goats. Women kept their faces demurely veiled but calmly opened their dresses to feed their babies. A farmer pedaled his bike down the street with a fat sheep wrapped around his shoulders. A snake charmer struggled to arouse his apathetic cobra.

Guy found an Arab friend to show me around. We visited an old man who carved curious figures out of stone, talked to rug merchants and pottery-makers and walked through private courtyards and hidden streets.

About noon I was standing outside the Foreign Legion post and spoke to the Italian sentry on duty at the gate.

"*Americano?*" He seemed startled. Then urgently, "*Momento, momento,*" and disappeared. He returned with a pair of Legionnaires who greeted me like a long-lost brother. George was a Londoner and Joe claimed to be an American. Actually I think Joe was a Hungarian who had spent some time in Chicago. Both were nearing the end of their five-year enlistments and, after service in Indo-China and Sahara outposts, were overjoyed to meet someone who spoke English. The French don't associate with the Legionnaires and foreign travelers are rare in Taroudant.

"Let's have a party," said George.

Maurice, a happy-go-lucky Belgian, joined us with a large suitcase full of bottled beer and we set off. First we stopped to eat at the local hotel. My friends would not let me pay for anything. As we sat talking, an Arab came in and the landlady scornfully refused to serve him. When he protested, she shouted for the police and the unfortunate fellow was taken away by two gendarmes.

George was disgusted. "The French will never learn. In Indo-China it was the same. Someday they will be sorry."

Accompanied by a young Arab who joined us somewhere along the line, we retired to a secluded garden behind high mud walls. We propped ourselves up against palm trees and drank the contents of our suitcase. As the afternoon progressed we became musical. Maurice spoke no English but sang "Old Man River" quite well. George and I harmonized on tunes like "Tipperary."

Later we accompanied Maurice while he visited his Arab girl friend. George and I sat cross-legged on floor mats while several girls, none of whom looked older than fifteen or sixteen, scurried about, overcome with giggles, and served us mint tea and sweet cakes.

Returning to the Legion post, my friends checked to be sure there were no officers around and I slipped through the gate and into their barracks. We sat on the bunks and enjoyed a meal of bread, wine and cold bacon which they sliced with their bayonets.

They invited me to spend the night but after more sober consideration, George decided I should leave.

"If the captain finds you here, there will be no trouble for you. But we would probably be sent to the disciplinary company at Colomb-Béchar. Discipline in the Legion is no joke and that place is a hellhole—Devil's Island in the desert. My time is almost up. I don't want to take a chance."

So I slept instead in the local church, whose padre informed me that he was a friend of Eleanor Roosevelt.

On Monday at the foot of the High Atlas Mountains a truck picked me up and we traveled a total of seventy-two miles during the next eight hours. Abdul, the driver, was a quizzical little fellow in a faded green suit who walked feet out and bowlegged, like Charlie Chaplin.

"I am a very good driver," he told me proudly. "I have driven for the French Army."

"Well, you certainly aren't reckless," I thought as we crawled along.

Abdul had four assistants and was hauling no less than twenty-five cows. The second in command, a grizzled Berber tribesman with tattooed hands and a long curved dagger at his belt, sat beside me, solemn and silent. Mohammed, our bouncy, cheerful mechanic, clung to the top of the cab. The two cattle herders, lowest in the chain of command and understandably morose, rode in back with the cows.

Our stops were frequent—three times to rest the engine while going uphill, at the summit to give thanks that we made it, twice for coffee and then for dinner, and once while one of the herders delivered a bitter tirade against the hapless cows. Our snail's pace gave me time to admire the snow-covered peaks and Biblical stone villages with terraced fields nestled in the gorges.

As we crept downhill the engine repeatedly gasped and choked. Each time Abdul shouted, " 'Hamed, 'Hamed," and Mohammed hopped from his perch to putter under the hood, singing all the while what sounded like the same tune. Abdul did nothing but supervise these repairs, as befitted a man of his position. Before reaching Asni our final stop was to pay a social call on friends who lived beside the road.

The Asni youth hostel boasted a single lantern and had no plumbing. In the morning I washed in the river. A young Berber took me to a Jewish wedding in the village.

"This is the first day," he said. "The marriage takes three days. Everyone in the village joins in the feast. Sometimes the bride's father spends all his money."

"That happens to fathers in my country, too," I said.

The wedding party clustered outside the house, the bridegroom in beret and blue robe passing out drinks to his friends. The married women sang, beat small drums and emitted piercing howls like Indians on the warpath.

"You see the one all covered up?" asked my companion. "She is the bride." A small figure stood motionless beside the door, her head completely wrapped in red cloth. I wondered how she could breathe. She was the only one not having fun.

"You must give them a wedding present. Fifty francs will do," announced my companion.

So I presented fifteen cents to the groom. He gave me a drink of home brew and said, "You are welcome."

The fatted calf decked with flowers was brought forward. A bearded patriarch slit its throat and cut off its head. Two men expertly skinned the carcass and hung it on a peg on the wall. The women began dancing, each in turn holding a bowl above her head and smearing a bit of greenish paste on the foreheads of bride and groom.

"What are they doing?" I asked.

"It is a fertility dance. In the bowl is green barley, the symbol of a fruitful marriage."

One of the guests inquired, "Have you been to Israel?" He seemed disappointed when I admitted that I had not. "Someday all of us here will go to live in Israel."

Soon after the fertility dance everyone went inside to rest and I left.

For the next two days I witnessed what even P. T. Barnum would have admitted was the original "Greatest Show on Earth." The town center of Marrakech—Djemaa El Fna Place—was the scene of the most amazing carnival-

circus every afternoon and evening. Into the square
thronged people who watched snake charmers, Arab bands,
storytellers, magicians, acrobats, dancers, clown acts, fortune tellers and trained-animal acts. One group in particular fascinated me—an even dozen nomads, including one
woman, from the desert. They all beat drums while one
with long bushy hair danced round and round, pounding
a small tom-tom cradled between his head and shoulder.
They worked themselves into a frenzy of savage, primitive
rhythm until the dancer collapsed from exhaustion.

Other musicians wore white robes and played strange
instruments—shrill flutelike horns, small one-sided drums,
stringed instruments bowed like violins. The music was all
Arabic and sometimes resembled American hillbilly, especially the singing, which sounded like Elvis Presley on a
windy night. The acrobats were not particularly clever
or original but drew large crowds. The magicians used
many props such as lizards, pigeons and mysterious bundles.
They hollered and jumped around, but never seemed to
perform any tricks. The snake charmers looked impressive
as they kissed the cobra—until you realized that the snake's
fangs had been removed. The clowns featured a crude slapstick which really convulsed the crowd. Gamblers dealt
cards, spun wheels of chance and played the old shell game.
Storytellers recited their legendary tales to rapt audiences.

In addition to the side shows, hundreds of portable businesses were conducted in the square. Barbers shaved the
heads of their customers; scribes wrote letters; peddlers
sold food, herbs and knick-knacks; medicine men lectured
on tonics and drugs; books, clothes, shoes and food were
spread on the ground; blind beggars operated in groups

chanting and rattling their tin cups in rhythm; restaurants in tents did a thriving business. At night the throbbing drums of Djemaa El Fna could be heard far across the city.

Marrakech is the capital of Southern Morocco and the stronghold of the Berbers. The city sprawls in a vast palm tree oasis, flanked by snow-capped mountains and encircled by ten miles of mud brick wall. Its most famous landmark is the Koutoubia Mosque, a square stone tower built in the twelfth century, a masterpiece of Moslem architecture. Near the youth hostel are the Saadien Tombs, a sixteenth-century cemetery for various sultans, with walls and ceilings a solid mass of delicate stone carvings. The Bahia Palace, built by an ex-slave 150 years ago, has ceilings of carved cedar brilliantly colored by the original vegetable dyes, walls and arches and pillars of scalloped plaster and stone. A large courtyard was the harem for 250 women.

I spent many hours in the *souks,* the most interesting markets in Morocco. The workmen and merchants are grouped according to their trades along winding alleys. In cluttered shops craftsmen fashion by hand gold and silver jewelry, copper and brass trays and utensils, wooden furniture, wicker baskets, leather purses, pipes, carpets, curved daggers in beautifully engraved silver sheaths, and straw-filled saddle mats for animals. Five or six men work in one tiny shop, where up to a dozen may congregate to play cards and gossip. The traffic in the alleys is always intense. Sometimes the continued sidewalk haggling and bargaining plus the congestion caused by animals and carts make it impossible to move at all. The most colorful *souk* is that of the dyers. Wool yarn is dyed brilliant shades in large vats and then hung to dry on poles which crisscross the streets.

The effect is amazing, a splashing rainbow of color against drab, smoke-blackened walls.

Traveling northwest from Marrakech, I stayed in Beni Mellal with a French schoolteacher who had hitchhiked in England. I crossed treeless plateaus inhabited only by nomads living in goat-hair tents. In Azrou storks nested on rooftops and chimneys. There are many storks in Morocco; the Arabs consider them lucky. Azrou was cold, and raw clouds warned of snow. A French engineer brought me out of the Atlas Mountains through green irrigated valleys, which looked like California, to Rabat.

In this city, now the clean and modern capital of Morocco, the Moorish sultans gathered their armies to conquer Spain and threaten all of Europe. The Medina of Rabat was the most prosperous Arab quarter I had seen. Outside the Sultan's palace his Negro bodyguard paraded in scarlet pantaloons and jackets, white cross-belts and blue and white checkered caps. I climbed the Hassan Tower, unfinished twin of the Koutoubia in Marrakech, and explored the ruins of Chellah, a Phoenician settlement which was ancient in the days of Rome.

While visiting Jean Josset, the cousin of a friend in New York, I realized with pride that the French I spoke was becoming recognizable. My ear was tuned to the language and my vocabulary was growing rapidly from continual practice.

En route to Fez, I stopped in Meknes, ate *couscous*, a mixture of meat, vegetables and rice, with an Arab family and slept in a school dormitory. Fez is the cultural and religious center of Morocco with seven *medersas* (Islamic universities) and some two hundred mosques. The streets

Portuguese fisherwomen clean and pack sardines on the beach at Nazaré

A Jewish wedding in an Atlas Mountains village, Morocco;
a fatted calf for the feast hangs on the wall

The pig market at Gijón on the north coast of Spain

Yugoslav peasants on the Dalmatian Coast pressing grapes to make wine

The old and the new in Damascus

Sacred cattle roam among the Indian pilgrims who are spending the day in prayer and meditation in a temple courtyard

Eyes peer from the stupa of a Buddhist shrine in Katmandu valley, Nepal

Indian sadhu (holy man) in a religious trance on a main street in Delhi

The author—outside a Nepali temple

A Nepali woman is carried in a sedan chair over the trail to Katmandu

Basket-weaving villagers in north India

of the old city are too narrow for even small French cars. In the *souks* doorways and public fountains are decorated with carvings and mosaics.

With a German student from the youth hostel I was given the rare privilege of viewing the interior of Moulay Idriss Mosque. Ordinarily, Moroccan mosques are strictly off-limits to non-Moslems. But as we stood by the door a rotund Arab called out, "Come inside. It is all right, we are making repairs, and no one will mind. My name is Ibrahim," he introduced himself, adding modestly, "I am a great artist."

Ibrahim was justifiably proud of his work. Intricate stone carving and bright mosaic covered walls, columns and ceiling. I had never seen such detailed beauty.

In the courtyard an old craftsman laboriously chipped bits of stone for the mosaics.

"Each piece is cut and polished and painted by hand," said Ibrahim. "See how they fit together perfectly in the pattern."

We watched men washing their hands and feet in the courtyard pool before kneeling and prostrating themselves in prayer. Their women sat on the floor and waited patiently.

That night my economical German friend and I bought eggs (three cents each), potatoes and bread and enjoyed a boiled dinner for twenty-five cents apiece. My last ride in Morocco took me across 150 miles of dry, barren plains to Oujda on the Algerian border.

CHAPTER TWO

ALGERIA
AND TUNISIA

MY FIRST ENCOUNTER with frontier officials was a pleasant surprise. The Algerians declined to inspect my pack and brought me coffee, and a burly policeman ordered a passing motorist to give me a lift. So I proceeded to Tlemcen, high in the mountains, and next day on to Sidi-bel-Abbès, the headquarters of the Foreign Legion.

A British Legionnaire, limping from Indo-China wounds, guided me through the Hall of Honor filled with trophies, paintings and battle flags.

"The Legion has more tradition than a British Guards Regiment," he said. "We are the shock troops of the French Army. We ask no questions, just follow orders. In the last war Legionnaires fought on both sides in Syria. There are all nationalities, even five or six Americans, though your government does not approve. Today about seventy-five per cent of the Legion are Germans. Most of the officers are French."

"Is the Legion really a refuge for criminals?" I asked.

"There are some fugitives from the law. But the French police in Marseilles check all recruits carefully. Most Legionnaires are political refugees, professional soldiers, like the Germans, or simply adventurers like me."

A column of trainees tramped along the rain-swept street, marching and singing in slow cadence. Some of them were no older than high-school boys.

I caught a truck to Oran, and in the morning joined a dozen French students for a beach party at Cap Falcon. My friends were bubbling with energy. They danced on the beach and wrestled on the sand dunes while I relaxed with a pretty Corsican girl. They sang beautifully, particularly a haunting Spanish tune called "Los Pastores." I tried to teach them "Swanee River."

One car carried me from Oran to Algiers, a distance of 275 miles and a good ride in any country. The French have been in Algeria for 125 years and their influence is widespread. The towns were like provincial France—ornate buildings with balconies and iron grillwork, cobblestone streets lined with neatly planted trees, the inevitable heroic war memorial, sidewalk cafés, stucco and stone farmhouses. Many Algerian Arabs dressed and looked like Europeans. Their way of life seemed typically French. Yet an undercurrent of discontent, an atmosphere of tension, was apparent. Army units patrolled the countryside and police roadblocks searched vehicles for hidden guns. There had been scattered clashes and sabotage, but the serious trouble had not begun.

The Algiers youth hostel, busy as any hotel and palatial

by my standards, buzzed with the activity of fellow vaga-
bonds. It was reassuring to find other young men with itchy
feet. I had always wanted to roam from one end to the other
of a busy harbor and for a full day in Algiers I did just that.
I inspected every dock and watched an incredible variety
of cargo being loaded and unloaded. There were twenty-
five freighters from a dozen countries in port and I had a
good look at each one. An Italian ship listed precariously
and seemed to be sinking; a small Yugoslav coaster proudly
sported a huge red star on its funnel.

Ogba Kader drove a truck hauling produce to the docks
and earned fifteen dollars for a sixty-hour, six-day week.
He was my age, a darkly handsome Arab.

"You must come tonight and stay at my home. We will
go *promenade* on the boulevards."

Kader lived in the famous Casbah where the streets are
so narrow the houses, leaning outward, almost touch at the
rooftops. With his family we ate fish and vegetables and
my friend's generosity caused me acute embarrassment. He
tried to give me a present of 500 francs and insisted that I
sleep in his bed while he curled up on the floor. At 5:30
A.M. I awoke to the sound of chanting. Kader's father, an
old gentleman in nightgown and turban, was kneeling a
few feet from my bed and saying his morning prayers.

Crossing the mountains south of Algiers I rode with a
farmer who took me home for lunch. Adrien was a Seventh-
Day Adventist, the only Frenchman I've ever known who
didn't drink wine. But on his farm he raised just grapes.
The mountain vineyards were dark splashes of red, black
and green under a cold and rainy sky. That afternoon I
drove as far as Boghari with a carload of Berbers and slept

beside the stove in the police station.

The next morning in the village of Paul Cazelles the entire Arab populace flocked around to examine me. The *Caid* (chief) was a burly ex-sergeant of the Tirailleurs Algeriens with the Croix de Guerre pinned to his jacket. We spoke of the Fellagha, the rebel guerrillas, and I mistakenly used the word *terroriste*.

"Pardon, Monsieur, the Fellagha are nationalists, not terrorists. I fought with the French Army in Tunisia and Italy. But we do not like the French here in Algeria. They treat us very badly and this is our country. We are all nationalists."

"But what of the million Frenchmen who have lived in Algeria all their lives?" I asked. "It is also their country. Will they be forced to leave?"

"No, but they must stay as equal citizens, not rulers."

When a truck appeared the *Caid* sent his boys to flag it down. As I climbed aboard the postmaster came running with my pen which I had forgotten. "I hope no one ever again tries to tell me that the Arabs are thieves and cutthroats," I thought to myself. Perhaps some of them do take advantage of rich tourists or servicemen but, after all, driving a shrewd bargain is an ancient and honorable art among these people. I certainly had no complaints.

Now the fertile mountains were left behind and I was entering Sahara, a vast expanse of rock and dirt, sun and sky and little else. The horizons stretched away to the ends of the earth. Mirages appeared—very real lakes and trees in the shimmering heat. Sand drifted across the ribbon of asphalt, and steel telephone poles marched beside us. I saw herds of camels and nomad sheep herders in the desolate

Oulad Naïl. Horsemen out of *The Arabian Nights* rode on high wooden saddles with great iron stirrups, bright blankets on their prancing Arab ponies. Sahara is more than a land area; it's a silence and an emptiness, a foreboding magic, a way of life.

In a restaurant at Djelfa we ate mutton chops and threw the bones on the floor for the dogs. The driver, of course, would not let me pay for my lunch. We stopped in the Berber village of Aïn El Ibel to visit some relatives. The single room of their mud brick house was furnished with rugs, a couple of trunks, a big brass platter and earthenware jugs, pin-up girls on the wall, fireplace, one bed (the place of honor where I sat) and some cooking utensils. Three men and a woman were playing cards, gambling intently. The men were real desert Berbers—daggers at their belts, flowing turbans, big leather purses slung over their shoulders. The woman wore a brightly colored print dress, jeweled necklace, silver bracelets, dangling earrings, and her hair was bound in an elaborate coiffure. We drank delicious coffee and I tried my first roast locusts, cooked on a charcoal brazier. They were crunchy and spicy and tasted quite good. Our conversation was limited since my friends spoke no French. I pointed to myself and said, "California." Blank stares. I tried, "Hollywood. Cinema." Excited comment. "New York" and "Roosevelt" also drew nods and smiles, but that was about it.

We continued on to Laghouat, a cool palm-tree oasis. There I met *Sergeant Chef* Jody Jiri, a tough Czech Legionnaire who had at least as much authority as a colonel in the American Army. I stayed with Pères Blancs, the White Father missionaries. For the first time missions were not off in some remote corner of the world, but operating right before my eyes. Pères Blancs were dedicated men who exemplified the true spirit of Christianity, teaching and healing among the desert tribes.

"These nomadic Berbers are proud, poor people," Father Pierre told me. "When the water holes dry out, their sheep and goats die and they come into the oases and starve. It is very sad, and we try to help them. In the villages at least one man from each family serves in the Army. The families depend on the military allowance, small as it is, for survival. Often it is their only money income."

I asked a question which had been bothering me. "What is the difference between Arabs and Berbers?"

"The Berbers are the original inhabitants of North Africa. The conquering Arabs drove the Berbers from the coastal plains into the mountains and desert. The Berbers were converted to the Moslem religion and today are greatly outnumbered. But their spirit has never been broken; they scorn the Arab town dwellers."

The police in Laghouat found me a truck going south to Ghardaïa. The driver, a laughing Frenchman with a dust-caked beard and a red scarf knotted around his head, looked like a pirate.

"Come with me to Tamanasset," he boomed. "It is only 1500 kilometers and you will really see Sahara. We will return to Algiers in two, maybe three weeks."

I was tempted—but I had a date in Paris.

Ghardaïa is an old desert citadel built on a hill crowned by the mosque, a tall windowless mud-brick tower. The streets are low, narrow passages like tunnels between the walls of the houses. It must have been an impregnable for-

tress in its day. Little girls in miniature copies of their
mothers' bright costumes were so shy they would run and
hide whenever they saw me.

The Pères Blancs mission was beside a "camel park"
where caravans bringing firewood from the hills congregated. I watched the camels being fed, an intriguing
performance. The drivers fidgeted like mother hens with
their temperamental animals. After much coaxing, four or
five camels were grouped in a circle. The driver sat in the
center and actually fed them dates and hay by hand, all the
while soothing them in a gentle voice. After dinner the
camels bellowed and groaned, complaining bitterly as they
settled down for the night. They sounded like giants belching. Finally all was quiet, the men and animals sleeping together.

Sunday I started retracing my steps to Algiers. Outside
Ghardaïa I attracted a crowd of children and the town
idiot, who was almost run over trying to stop a car for me.
To escape this befuddled well-wisher I walked into the
desert and sat beside what proved to be the caravan route
from the east. Three groups of nomads passed as I waited
for a ride. The men walked in front, old shotguns and rifles
on their backs, leading the camels loaded with tents, carpets,
hay, firewood and small children. The barefoot women followed behind driving the sheep and goats.

A truck came along and carried me all the way to Algiers.

I headed east into the Grand Kabylie, wild mountain
country conspicuously lacking in traffic. I progressed exactly eighteen miles, mostly on foot, in twenty-four hours.
The Fellagha were active and no one was traveling. Finally
admitting defeat, I bought a bus ticket to Bougie.

The Gulf of Bougie is like the Alps, with luxuriant tropical vegetation and the purple-blue Mediterranean thrown in. Palm trees line the road and snow caps the mountains. This coast is called the North African Riviera, but to my eyes it was prettier than the Côte d'Azur.

The schoolteacher in Aokas village asked me to dinner and I bunked in a classroom. The next morning the weather was so perfect, the country so beautiful, that I turned down a ride and walked. I drank coffee with the foreman of a road gang, who showed me pieces of Roman pottery his boys were uncovering in their digging. From Djidjelli the road wound inland through forests of cork trees. A valiant old Model A driven by a distinguished Arab, whose mustache must have measured six inches from tip to tip, brought me to Constantine.

This ancient city is built in a unique position along both sides of the deep, rocky Rhummel River gorge. White-painted buildings line the very edge of the chasm. In Constantine I stayed with a Methodist missionary, Dr. Elmer Douglas, a remarkable and busy man. In addition to supervising a church, mission and home for Arab boys, he conducted an adult literacy program and was doing the first translation of the Bible into the Kabylie Berber language.

Southeast of Constantine I became involved in a social whirl at the Aïn Beïda police club. First a young Arab patrolman took me home for dinner. When we returned to the club a raucous party had developed and the gendarmes insisted that I join them for dinner. So I was obliged to eat again. After numerous glasses of wine a fat corporal escorted me to the military barracks. Pistol in hand, he crept through the streets, peering carefully around each corner and muttering, "Be very quiet. We are not safe."

I couldn't decide if he was just drunk or if Aïn Beïda really was dangerous. But we arrived safely and soon my friend was snoring like a camel.

The police commissioner gave me a lift to Tebessa and arranged for a free bus ride to the Tunisian frontier. With a load of Arab farmers, chickens and sheep our wayward bus struggled along making frequent stops. The man sitting beside me smiled apologetically as the rooster he held in his lap crowed long and loud. An arrogant fellow furiously berated his young wife for letting her veil slip off as she fed their tiny baby. At the border the driver and his assistants shared their lunch of eggs, dates and bread with me.

A French Army captain in a jeep stopped and announced cheerfully, "There are Fellagha in these hills. Sometimes they shoot at cars."

We rocketed along the road, traveling on the theory, I'm sure, that if anyone fired at us we could outrun the bullets. The arid countryside was covered with Roman relics—broken columns and viaducts, remains of houses and paved streets. Ruins are so common in Tunisia that no one pays any attention to them.

At the home of the *Controler Civil* in Gafsa I encountered my first hot running water in North Africa and wallowed happily in the bathtub. A policeman was appointed as my guide around the oasis and the crumbling Turkish fort. The Roman baths, fed by underground springs, had become swimming pools for naked, whooping children.

The absence of traffic in southern Tunisia, of which I had been warned, became painfully apparent. After several hours I had traveled only four kilometers on a motor scooter, so I caught the bus to Gabès. A group of Arab passengers sang gaily until the disgruntled driver slammed on the brakes and shouted, "Shut up or get out!" or Arabic words to that effect. In Gabès the temperature was close to 100°. I swam and slept on a superb white sand beach.

The local Esso salesman offered to take me to Foum Tataouine and we left at six o'clock in a mild sandstorm. Foum Tataouine is the end-of-the-road in Tunisia, a primitive, fly-blown settlement where families live in caves and nothing but desert tracks lead to the south. In the dusty open market sheep and goats were sold and slaughtered while men wrapped in their voluminous robes slept on the ground beside piles of grain. Camels sulked or roared in protest at imagined indignities and women carried water from the well in great earthenware jugs on their backs. I watched the desert patrol departing for the wastelands—bearded French soldiers in baggy pantaloons, and Spahis, with turbans wound around their faces covering all but their eyes.

Returning to Gabès I stopped at Médenine where the houses, called ghorfas, are cut out of rock and look like loaves of bread stacked on top of each other. Some of these apartment-caves are five stories high. In the seaport of Sfax the Arab fishing boats, brightly painted craft with a single red or white sail, raced to the docks and I was almost trampled in the clamor of the fish market.

I tried to sleep at the church, but the old padre didn't understand what I wanted and offered me some money. Disgusted with my "command" of the French language, I went instead to the police station. There I met Mohammed Bah Bah, a skinny little patrolman in a threadbare uniform. Mohammed took me to dinner and was upset when I attempted to pay.

"No, no, you are my guest. I worked for the Americans during the war and they were very kind to me. I am grateful to your countrymen."

Later he said, "I am paid five hundred francs ($1.50) for a twenty-hour tour of duty." Now it was my turn to be upset, so I gave him my second pair of blue jeans, figuring that he needed them more than I did.

Heading north, I admired the giant Roman coliseum standing alone in the grubby Arab village of El Djem on the barren plains. It must have been the center of a great city long ago. The walled town of Sousse was celebrating the opening day of its trade fair with a parade and bicycle race. At nine o'clock in the morning I came upon the red-light district, bustling with activity. Painted ladies lounged in the doorways, crowds milled in the streets and French soldiers patrolled with submachine guns. Was business always so good this early, or was it due to the fair?

I rode to Kairouan with a confused fellow who was learning to drive. His inexperience, however, did not dampen his obvious enthusiasm for stunt driving. Kairouan is a Moslem paradox, the most holy city of North Africa with over two-hundred mosques, yet dirtier, more poverty-stricken and dilapidated than any other Tunisian town. Its medieval atmosphere is similar to that of Marrakech. I visited the Mosque of the Barber, where the hairs of the Prophet's beard are enshrined, and the Grand Mosque, largest in the world, built in the seventh century with hundreds of columns from Roman temples and early Christian churches. Inside the vast prayer room groups of Arab students clustered under dangling light bulbs, reciting the

Koran. Dozens of these classes going on at the same time produced quite a racket. In the *souks* women wove the famous tan and brown Kairouan carpets, and a blindfolded camel drew water from a spring which supposedly flows from Mecca.

The road to Tunis was busy with high-wheeled wooden carts and camel caravans, including one family of nomads who pitched camp right beside me. But no cars or trucks. I walked about six miles until a low-flying Frenchman slowed down enough so that I could jump aboard. The only time we touched the ground was at a spot where the road was flooded and my friend hired some bystanders to push us across.

In Tunis a French detective found me a bed in an Italian boardinghouse and we ate at a Spanish restaurant in the Arab quarter. The proprietor was an exiled Spanish Republican sailor and served an excellent meal, including boiled octopus, for thirty cents. My last two days in North Africa were spent with Thorleif Teigland, a hearty Norwegian missionary, his charming wife and family.

I visited the remains of Carthage on the Gulf of Tunis. Nowhere has a prophesy been fulfilled more completely than the Roman Senate's ominous pronouncement, "Carthage must be destroyed." The city was leveled so thoroughly that the ruins were not particularly impressive. But the sense of history was very strong. I sat on a hill and could visualize Hannibal marching off at the head of his elephants to attack Rome.

On Good Friday I flew to Paris by Air France, in a fat, double-decker Provence. I had been in North Africa for seven weeks and had spent fifty-two dollars.

CHAPTER THREE

THE
GRAND TOUR

"Sorry, Monsieur, we are completely full."

"Do you know where I can find a room?" I asked.

The hotel clerk shrugged. "You must realize this is Easter week end and there are 150,000 visitors in Paris. It is most difficult."

"What a ridiculous situation," I thought to myself. "Here I am on an expense account for the first time and I can't find a place to sleep." The only solution was to revert to my former simpler way of living. I walked to the Gare du Nord and unrolled my sleeping bag on the floor of the waiting room.

I had come to Paris to be tutor and guide for my eleven-year-old cousin Melinda in a six-week family tour of France and Italy. My Aunt Winifred, her husband Charlie, Ken and Katie Mountcastle and Melinda were arriving aboard the *Ile de France*. I was to pick up a Ford station wagon and meet them in Le Havre.

Paris was the Queen of Europe in the spring. Trees bloomed and fountains played along Champs Élysées and Sacré-Coeur shone in the sun. Fishermen dozed on the banks of the Seine, crazy drivers roared around the Étoile and the whole city promenaded on the boulevards. At night the Eiffel Tower glowed like a giant beacon and the obelisk in the Place de la Concorde was a silver column against the sky. I felt exhilarated revisiting familiar places.

At the American Embassy I found a bewildered G.I. farm boy from North Dakota. "I have one day to spend in Paris," he told me, "and all I've seen is the Eiffel Tower. Nobody speaks English and I don't know where to go."

So I did for him what so many have done for me: showed him as much as possible in a few hours. That evening in a café I ran into my mother's best friend, a pleasant surprise for me because I didn't know she was in Europe. Together we went to church on Easter, to Les Halles, the wholesale food market which is the "Belly of Paris," and to the Casino de Paris, where the show was fast and naked.

After an exhausting squabble with French customs to obtain clearance for the station wagon, I drove to Le Havre. Next morning, piling thirteen pieces of luggage on the roof, we launched the grand tour to the Cathedral of Chartres with its breathtaking stained-glass windows, the châteaux along the Loire Valley and the prehistoric cave paintings of Lascoux. The countryside was bright green and intensely cultivated, the solid stone farm buildings and powerful red oxen lending an air of permanence and prosperity. It became easy to understand the French peasant's fierce love of his land. In the fortress town of Carcassone I explored the

ramparts and towers and had the same feeling as at Carthage
—Roman legions, barbarian tribes and French kings were
marching on the plains below.

From Avignon with its famous bridge and palace of the
papal exile we continued to the plush Carlton Hotel at
Cannes. We swam and sunbathed on the Riviera and had
lunch at swank Eden Roc, where three years before, my
brother and I had swum in to avoid paying the admission
charge. How times had changed! We drove to St. Paul de
Vence, a small town perched on top of the world. Coming
down we were caught in the middle of a frantic, hell-for-
leather bicycle race which almost forced us off the road. At
the Casino international society dined and danced and
gambled in a deadly serious atmosphere of artificiality.

Crossing the Italian border, the sheer volume of our baggage dazzled the customs officials, who did not even ask
to look. Over twisting mountain roads we stopped in Pisa
to climb the Leaning Tower. Then on to Rome where our
first sight was a hysterical, arm-waving argument at the
scene of a minor auto collision. Horns squawked, bystanders heckled happily and police struggled to clear the intersection. The Romans are worse drivers than the Parisians,
more flamboyant in their recklessness.

Rome is a magnificent city reflecting the easy charm,
friendliness and excitable nature of the Italian people. For
the first time I began to acquire a real appreciation of great
art. The foreboding "Last Judgment" in the Sistine Chapel,
Michelangelo's fire-breathing statue of Moses, the glowing
paintings by Raphael, the bright perfection of Botticelli,
the statue of Pharaoh's mother, 5,000 years old and as modern as tomorrow, the unsurpassed strength and majesty of

Greek sculpture—these impressed me deeply.

I was determined that Melinda should be soaked in culture and we toured the great monuments, churches, museums and art galleries. But I'm afraid it was a bit too much for an eleven-year-old. Melinda's favorite spots were the zoo and the Fountain of Trevi. She loved animals and befriended every carriage horse in town. We went to the movie *Battle Cry* and discovered that the sound track was in Italian.

"Don't worry," Melinda said brightly, "I've seen this picture twice before and I'll explain it to you."

Fortunately it was one of those Hollywood epics which hardly need dialogue.

On May Day, the traditional Communist holiday, the Christian Democrats staged a massive counterdemonstration. Tens of thousands of Italians marched to St. Peter's with bands and floats, singing and chanting "Viva Papa," to hear the Pope speak.

At the Church of St. Paul a wedding was going on at the main altar, a monk lay in state on one side, visitors wandered about and workmen hammered on the roof. The conflicting activity seemed to bother no one.

One day I came upon a procession of several thousand war veterans marching to protest something or other. It looked interesting so I joined the parade. We arrived at the Piazza Colonna in the center of the city and my comrades began shouting slogans and caused the most awe-inspiring traffic jam I had ever seen. Many *carabinieri* (military police) were standing by but it was all very orderly. After half an hour of quiet agitation everyone went home for lunch.

Adding to the color of flower stalls and sidewalk cafés, street vendors and motor scooters, were the flashy uniforms of Rome—the Vatican's Swiss Guard in blue and gold, soldiers wearing red stocking caps with large blue tassels, the jaunty *Bersagliéri* in plumed hats and *carabinieri* dressed in dark blue with white braid, red stripes on their trousers and swords at their belts.

From Rome we drove south to Naples, Pompeii and Ravello, a small village hanging on the mountainside overlooking the Amalfi Drive. There was a view even from the hotel bathrooms. Capri was idle luxury, basking in the sun at Marina Piccola and watching Neapolitans dance the rousing tarantella.

In Florence, most artistic of all Italian cities, we inspected the Renaissance churches and palaces, galleries and statuary that all good tourists see. At Melinda's urging I made the mistake of renting a Vespa motor scooter. I managed to start out with no trouble, but not being very mechanically minded, could not stop the little monster. We putt-putted across a busy intersection, against the traffic and out of control, while a policeman whistled frantically and pedestrians looked on in amazement. After this incident poor Melinda was quite upset and refused to ride any farther. I returned ignominiously to the hotel, pushing the Vespa, and we hired a horse and buggy.

Across the hills of Tuscany and the Po Valley we drove to Venice. At night a band played on a lantern-lit barge which drifted down the Grand Canal followed by a procession of gondolas. The Piazza San Marcos with its Byzantine cathedral, Campanile and Palace of the Doges is unique among city squares. Café orchestras, clouds of pigeons and throngs of people blend in an ever-changing scene. While in Venice I received a letter from my brother Rich telling of his plans to be married in August. I was very disappointed to miss the wedding; for the first and only time I considered returning home.

Melinda and I drove to Switzerland while the others went by train direct to Paris. The summer tourist rush had not begun in Zermatt and Alpine life was simple and serene in the shadow of the Matterhorn. The local brass band rehearsed in the town hall, shepherds drove their sheep and goats down from the high meadows every evening and peasants climbed the trails with big milk cans on their backs. A stillness enveloped Zermatt, the quiet of a village where there are no automobiles. The townspeople greeted us on the streets and made us feel at home. Melinda shopped for cuckoo clocks and music boxes and I hiked close to the Matterhorn.

We followed the Rhone Valley, Lake Geneva, and turned northwest through the Jura Mountains to Paris. For the next two and a half weeks we were ensconced in the elegant Hotel Plaza-Athenée. I remember most vividly the bright vignettes of Paris: the exquisite stained glass windows of St. Chapelle, the kaleidoscopic flower market behind Notre Dame, the cluttered book stalls of the Left Bank. A young man in a frayed top hat and scarf pounds out ragtime piano in a Montmartre dive. Children play in the Luxembourg Gardens and a fashion model poses in the Place de la Concorde. Bargemen gently pilot their cumbersome craft through the river locks. An hysterical prostitute curses a phlegmatic waiter in a Pigalle café. Inconsolable sorrow is reflected in the blue-lighted figures of soldiers at the tomb of Marshal Foch. A drum and bugle corps shrills under the Arc de Triomphe. The black waters of the Seine swirl beneath the Pont Alexandre late at night. Butchers in blood-soaked aprons and revelers in rumpled evening clothes congregate at dawn in the bistros of Les Halles. Three Algerians gaily sing and play bongo drums and mandolin on the Métro, the city's subway.

The apple orchards were in bloom among the age-old hedgerows and thatch-roofed farmhouses of Normandy. Mont St. Michel was the last stop on our tour. This fairy-tale castle rises up from the solid rock, surrounded on three sides by the sea, with a village encircling its base. Built by the Benedictine monks as a monastary-fortress in the eighth century, Mont St. Michel was impregnable.

On May 26 my traveling companions sailed from Cherbourg and I returned the station wagon to Paris. Our grand tour had been a success, and I hoped that Melinda had learned her arithmetic. Living in unaccustomed comfort and earning money at the same time was a welcome change of pace for me. But I had missed the close and informal contact with people and was looking forward to the open road again.

CHAPTER FOUR

SPAIN
AND PORTUGAL

"WE BASQUES ARE very independent people. The government has never been popular here in Bilbao, but there is nothing we can do to change it."

Luis gazed at me with a sad smile. We were sitting in a murky wine shop drinking *vino* for one and a quarter cents a glass. My companion was a thin sallow student and part-time salesman, an aspiring linguist in a shabby suit.

"What will happen after Franco dies?" I inquired.

"*Quién sabe?*" Luis shrugged. "Perhaps the monarchy will be restored. I hope someday we will have a republic again. But I don't think there will be another Civil War. The people are too tired." The wistful smile broadened. "Never mind. I only tell you these things because you are an American. We must be discreet." (Later I learned that Luis was a political refugee in Belgium.) "And now one more glass of wine and it will be time for dinner."

The time was twelve midnight.

I had left Paris a week before and circled leisurely around the coast of Brittany. In the remote fishing villages of this rocky isolated region many of the Bretons wore wooden shoes and spoke Celtic. Old women were dressed all in black with white lace caps. At a crossroads outside Bordeaux the hitchhiking bogged down and three United States Army officers stationed nearby befriended me. I continued south through pine forests and vineyards to the swank seaside resort of Biarritz and the Spanish border.

From the moment I walked across a bridge into Spain the warm-hearted spontaneous reception I encountered was a preview of what was to come in the Middle East and Asia. In Bilbao, where I met Luis, and every other town on the north coast, it was difficult to walk around the block without making friends with someone. Most Spaniards are very poor but possess a gracious dignity which no amount of money can buy. My wrist watch was being cleaned in Paris, so I fitted nicely into their relaxed, timeless way of life.

From Bilbao I rode an extremely slow train to the fishing village of Ribadesella. Since there was practically no road traffic and third class transportation was so cheap I had decided to alternate train or bus travel with hitchhiking. Ribadesella would be a fisherman's paradise. I stood on the shore and watched big salmon jumping in the bay. No one bothered to catch them. I stayed at a *fonda* where room and fish dinner cost sixty-two cents and planned to take the early and only bus for Gijón. But the landlady forgot to wake me, so I started hiking, flagged a truck and we soon passed the bus, which had broken down. At the market in Gijón little pigs squealed and struggled as they were carried around in sacks. The porkers were spotlessly clean, as if they had been scrubbed with loving care.

Three hours and four rides later I reached Avilés, a distance of only fifteen miles. Then a sympathetic policeman put me aboard a truck and we rattled on until nightfall, when the driver and I curled up under the truck to sleep.

In the morning as I trudged along a grizzled peasant in a floppy straw hat hailed me. His brown face was seamed like a walnut and wreathed in smiles. "It is too hot to walk. Come and stay at my house today and continue tomorrow. My name is Manuel García García."

I accepted his invitation and spent a fascinating day on a Spanish farm. I helped bury a calf which had died of hoof-and-mouth disease, loaded sacks of potatoes on an ox cart, pitched hay and rounded up the cattle shouting "*Ay! Vaca!*" in my best Spanish. Manuel's house was three hundred years old and built of stone. The animals lived downstairs, the family upstairs. My friend raised potatoes and must have consumed most of his own crop. For lunch we ate potato chowder, fried potatoes, black bread and milk. Dinner consisted of more fried potatoes, boiled potatoes, homemade sausage and rice pudding. Fortunately I like potatoes. My only difficulty during meals was preventing the numerous flies from committing suicide in my bowl of milk.

We sat in the kitchen solemnly greeting the neighbors who came to see *el norteamericano*. They spoke only Spanish and I managed to converse quite well except with one elderly woman. She evidently believed that the louder she shouted, the better I would understand. Her continual hollering began to deafen me. I was relieved when Manuel announced, "Now it is time for siesta," and we retired for a couple of hours.

That evening Manuel said, "We have known you for just one day but you will always be our friend."

Third class on a Spanish bus meant riding on the roof. This was an excellent spot for viewing the green coast of Asturias tumbling into the sea but it became uncomfortably exposed during a sudden downpour. I crawled under the tarp with the baggage and brooded about the "rich American" who was the only one traveling third class. Soon the driver climbed up to my damp perch and invited me to come inside with the other passengers. Three of them were law students from the University of Santiago and we stayed together at a pension in La Coruña. The morning train brought us to Santiago de Compostela and my companions guided me through this medieval pilgrimage center, the shrine of St. James the Apostle. The baroque Cathedral was the most ornate I saw in Spain, festooned with statues of saints and angels. Accompanied by several other students we toured the wine cellars. I sampled fried shrimp and octopus, mussels in wine and similar delicacies. Late that afternoon the boys gave me a big send-off on the bus to Vigo. This little seaport snuggles comfortably on a deep fiordlike arm of the sea.

Next day as I bumped along a terrible road on the tail gate of an ox cart, a Buick Roadmaster appeared, awe-inspiring as a royal chariot. The driver, a tough New Yorker, said he had come back to visit the Old Country. A logical explanation, but I pictured him as a deported racketeer living in enforced exile.

I crossed the Portuguese frontier and since it had started

to rain, caught the train for Porto. The peasant women who clambered aboard, balancing great bundles on their heads, were the most raucous crowd I had ever encountered. They shouted, laughed and argued, ate fish and swigged bottles of wine and raised hell in general. These Portuguese women seemed to be the hardest workers in southern Europe so I guess they deserved to make a little noise. In contrast old men wearing high-crowned black hats like American Indians sat in silent meditation. Even groups of young soldiers were strangely subdued.

Porto is a dark and somber city, the shipping center for port wine from the Douro valley. Hoping for traffic on the main road to Lisbon, I tried hitchhiking again. Two rides sandwiching a three-mile walk brought me to the ancient university town of Coimbra. I traveled in a wrecked car behind a tow truck to Leiria where the people were celebrating the Feast of Corpus Christi. Long processions of singing peasants, mostly women in bright bandannas, converged on the cathedral carrying banners and statues. Bands played and bells rang. Black-robed priests shepherded the marchers like army drill sergeants.

The fishing village of Nazaré is, I think, the most colorful spot in Portugal. The entire population fishes for sardines. The men launch their little boats into the surf and plant their nets offshore. Then lines of men, women and children pull the nets up onto the beach. Women clean and pack the fish right on the sand. The only modern note is the use of a tractor instead of oxen to haul the boats to the water. The fishermen wear long stocking caps and both shirts and pants of bright Scottish tartans inherited from Wellington's Highlanders during the Peninsular War. The women dress severely in black and everyone is barefooted.

I unrolled my sleeping bag on the beach. In the morning a jolly innkeeper invited me to breakfast.

"I lived in San Francisco for seven months," he said with a chuckle, "until the immigration people deported me."

"Why did they do that?" I asked.

"Because I had jumped ship and was working as a smuggler." And he roared with laughter.

Lisbon mirrors the character of a nation and its people better than any other European capital. The cobblestone streets of the medieval Alfama district and the Castle of St. George where the Reconquest began reflect Portugal's early history. The peculiar Manuelino architecture of Belém Tower and Jerónimos convent and the mellow grandeur of Black Horse Square evoke memories of exploration and empire. The bustling Avenida da Liberdade is the cosmopolitan heart of the city. Outlying sectors with their pastel and tile houses, flowers in profusion and somberly dressed citizens are facsimiles of any provincial town. This is Portugal in a nutshell.

In the waterfront sheds boxes of fish were auctioned to female peddlers. The chattering, bickering and squabbling would have shamed a North African *souk*. Two old fishwives came to blows and the police rushed in, swinging their clubs to break up the resulting riot.

A tree-lined belt divides the Avenida da Liberdade and this shaded strip is a popular drinking spot for Lisboans. Waiters from the cafés on either side scurried back and forth, incredibly daring and agile with their loaded trays in the rushing traffic. White-uniformed police carried their own protection from the sun, umbrellas stuck into their belts. In a dimly-lit cellar a handsome woman sang the melancholy *fado* to the accompaniment of a plaintive guitar.

Lisbon was celebrating a four-day religious and national holiday climaxed by a Sunday night parade. There were lantern-lit floats carried on men's shoulders, girls in peasant costumes, gilded horse-drawn carriages, Portuguese *campinos* (cowboys), Iberian bagpipes and several bands, each playing the Lisbon anthem. The festivities began at eleven o'clock and lasted until dawn.

I crossed the Tagus River and caught a ride to Setúbal; then came paralysis. After waiting five hours, during which time I fell asleep beside the road, a priest brought me to the next town. Here I enlisted the aid of the police, who found a truck going to Lagos. I spread my sleeping bag in a field outside the town.

Strong Moorish influence is apparent along the south coast of Portugal. The flat-roofed windowless white houses are identical with those in North Africa. Arabic water wheels are turned by blindfolded mules instead of camels.

At Portimão the sardine fleet had just docked and the unloading and selling of fish was a furious scramble on the waterfront.

Stewart Deas, a white-haired Scot, was the unusual proprietor of an inn called the Solar Penguin in Praia da Rocha. "I was born in Aberdeen," he told me, "but the name Deas is really Spanish. One of my ancestors was a shipwrecked sailor from the Spanish Armada. I have traveled all over the world and this is the most restful place I have ever lived."

I was inclined to agree with Mr. Deas. Praia da Rocha was an unspoiled little gem, a sun-baked village on the cliffs overlooking a perfect beach and flanked by huge rocks in the sea. I spent the day swimming and relaxing.

Crossing back into Spain on the Rio Guadiana ferry, I met a retired Polish diplomat and his American wife, who drove me to Seville. Andalusia is the romantic tourist land of Spain and the old Santa Cruz quarter of Seville, formerly the Ghetto, looks like a travel poster. Through the narrow alleys, with their antique street lamps, peddlers led their donkeys. Bored lottery salesmen dozed in the sun, organ grinders played wistful tunes, and monks in robes and sandals scurried about on errands. Flowerpots lined the balconies of whitewashed houses. Beyond wrought iron grillwork gates were cool patios filled with plants, palms and bubbling fountains.

The cathedral which dominates Seville is an enormous gloomy Gothic structure, second in size to St. Peter's. While admiring its lofty Moorish-built Giralda Tower I was joined by a harassed Australian named Jack Melrose.

"G'day, mate, am I glad to see you," he grinned. "I've been hitchhiking with three girls and it's enough to drive a bloke crazy. All they want to do is shop for bloody souvenirs."

Aileen, Beryl and Dawn proved to be cheerful companions, as Aussie girls usually are, in spite of their feminine instinct for collecting junk. The five of us moved into a cramped and inexpensive pension in the Santa Cruz. Seville drowsed in the June heat and we were told that Madrid was the place to see bullfights. The only flamenco we heard was played by a young Frenchman at our pension.

Traveling south I stopped in the wine-producing town

of Jerez de la Frontera. Our word *sherry* is a corruption of the name Jerez. At one of the large *bodegas* (wine cellars) I sampled numerous types of sherry and continued on my way rather lightheaded. As the road winds around the coast a majestic panorama unfolds. Across the Straits lie the mountains of Morocco and straight ahead rises Gibraltar. I took the ferry from Algeciras to the town of Gibraltar. Hundreds of sailors from the aircraft carrier *Ark Royal* were trooping boisterously through the streets. I followed a road up the face of the Rock until soldiers stopped me at a military zone: One must have special permission to visit the fortified galleries. That night I camped on the beach and fell asleep under the sheer wall of the Rock, while the RAF dropped flares over the sea. What better way to feel the spirit of this famous outpost?

From Gibraltar to Málaga and Granada I rode with an interesting assortment of people: a British naval officer and his wife; a retired Victorian couple in a chauffeur-driven Bentley, who told me very definitely that hitchhiking was impossible in Spain; a suave Portuguese businessman who hinted that I must be some peculiar type of smuggler; a worried Frenchman continually warning me that his Renault was about to break down—which it eventually did. I covered the last few miles in an antiquated Spanish ambulance.

Granada is the site of the Alhambra, masterpiece of Moorish architecture and the most intricately designed palace in the world. No one has ever equaled the Arabs for delicate hand-carved ornamentation and the Alhambra is their crowning achievement. Set on a hill overlooking the city, surrounded by gardens, towers and walls, it must be seen to be appreciated. The walls of the rooms are covered with mosaics and carved inscriptions, and the ceilings and arches drip with sculptured stone. The palace of Emperor Carlos V built beside it looks like a dull flophouse in comparison. From the Alhambra you look over a fertile valley to the snow-capped peaks of the Sierra Nevada and across a narrow gorge to the Gypsy caves of Sacromonte.

I walked through the dusty blistered hills of Andalusia, where peasants were cutting wheat by hand. I passed a Gypsy caravan on the move, ate bread, sausage and olives with a bemused villager and rode on a hay wagon. A Model A which made pitiful grinding noises but rolled doggedly on brought me to Jaén, the center of the olive country. Further hitchhiking seemed doubtful, so I took the train to Córdoba. The Great Mosque which was converted into a Christian cathedral is impressive with its hundreds of red-and-white-striped double arches. Córdoba has retained the same medieval atmosphere as Seville. I thought that Cervantes would still feel at home. Between nine and midnight the population poured into the streets to stroll in the nightly *paseo*. No self-respecting Spaniard would eat dinner before ten or eleven o'clock.

The walled city of Toledo, encircled by the Rio Tajo, typifies the dark sun-baked land of Castile. The brown and yellow buildings stand in marked contrast to the brilliant white of Andalusia. The dry eroded countryside has been exhausted from generations of misuse. The Alcazar fortress where Rebel soldiers were besieged by Loyalist militia during the Civil War was being rebuilt as a Fascist shrine. With a group of Spanish students I was conducted through the ruins by a portly one-legged veteran. He spoke eloquently of the heroic defenders fighting for God and country against the hordes of Communist barbarians.

"Were all the Republicans really Reds?" I asked.

"Of course, Señor. Communists and atheists, the scum of the earth."

I thought it best not to argue with this positive opinion.

From the massive Toledo Cathedral, the paintings of El Greco and the little workshops where the famous steel is forged I proceeded north to Madrid. At the bullring on a Sunday afternoon I witnessed an unusual demonstration which had deep implications beyond the normal excitement of the *corrida*. The pageantry and emotion were no different from other fights until the last bull appeared. The picador broke his lance in this animal's neck and failed to cut the neck muscles. With this advantage the enraged and clever beast gored two young matadors in quick succession. At this point I thought that the bull should have been declared the winner. Instead, the brother of one of the wounded men, a spectator on this occasion but also a matador, grabbed a sword and jumped into the arena. He killed the bull to uphold the family honor. The crowd cheered this noble gesture but the police arrested him for unauthorized entry into the bullring. Whereupon the people went beserk. Shouting and cursing, throwing seat cushions and bottles, they poured into the arena, revealing their pent-up hatred of the police. But the demonstration was short-lived. Suddenly soldiers with submachine guns appeared around the top of the stands and armed men cleared the bullring. The angry mob was helpless to do more than protest and soon began to disperse. A riot had been averted, but the frustrated bitterness of Franco's people had broken through the usual Spanish reserve and resignation. Revolutions have been triggered by lesser incidents.

For Spain, although nonaggressive and outwardly peaceful, is still a Fascist state ruled by a dictator and troubled by economic unrest. The controlled press prints no real news, students are pitifully uninformed and misinformed about the world in general and the sole political party is the disreputable Falange. The Civil Guards, in black patent leather hats and green uniforms, patrol the roads, armed with rifles and always in pairs. Heavily guarded prisons still hold thousands of Civil War Republicans. The Church exerts strong influence in state affairs and a few enjoy great wealth while many are poverty-stricken.

In Madrid I saw *jai alai* played by the Basques, who originated the game. I visited the Prado, said to be the world's finest art museum, El Rastro, the thieves' market, and El Escorial, the depressing monastary-palace in the hills where the Hapsburg kings are buried. Goose-stepping Spanish troops in Nazi-style bucket helmets paraded outside the Royal Palace.

The *Rápido* was certainly misnamed, but was faster than most Spanish trains. In Barcelona the Feast of St. Peter was being celebrated with street carnivals, fireworks and much gaiety. About 3:00 A.M. I retired to the soft grass of a park. The following night I treated myself to a thirty-five-cent room, where the bed was no more than three feet long. From Barcelona I hitched slowly but surely into the Pyrenees and walked across the French border. An idiot policeman at Bourg Madame stamped my passport three times —first the wrong date, then *sortie* instead of *entrée* and finally correct but upside down.

The next day I left France for a few hours to detour into

Andorra, the strange, tiny principality perched on the crest of the Pyrenees. There are no customs regulations and most Andorrans are engaged, at least part time, in the flourishing smuggling trade between France and Spain. They are even more ingenious at their profession than the Basques. Upon first crossing the border I had the impression that Andorra was inhabited only by long-haired ponies and herds of cattle. There were no people at all. After awhile I began to see a few off-duty smugglers and they honestly looked the part, disheveled and furtive, though perhaps this was my imagination.

A Frenchman is above all an individual, a delightful mixture of realist and dreamer. Daniel du Genêt, a roadside acquaintance in Limoges, illustrated this paradoxical nature. "I work as a part-time mail carrier," he told me as his wife prepared a lavish meal, "but only to support my family. I am really an artist. I paint, write poetry and play three musical instruments."

His two-room cottage literally overflowed with books, classical records and paintings. We spent several hours discussing philosophy and art.

Daniel's diagnosis of French political difficulties was simple. "No one trusts the politicians. They are associated with. the defeat and disillusion of France since 1940. As soon as a man joins the government coalition, especially if he is premier, the people suspect him. They say 'He is as bad as all the others.' It is impossible for a politician to become a truly popular leader."

That evening I took refuge from the rain in a barn. The peasant owner was suspicious and kept my passport for security until morning. Perhaps he feared that I would steal a cow. I arrived in Paris the following afternoon. After trying to contact three different friends and finding no one at home, I gave up in disgust and slept in the Bois de Boulogne. Early-morning rain forced me out of the woods and into a café where I brooded about being in Paris on the Fourth of July. But soon the sun appeared and I went to the American Embassy and crashed Ambassador Dillon's garden party. My blue jeans and faded shirt provided an interesting contrast to the sleek finery of the other guests but no one seemed to mind. At least the Marine guards did not throw me out.

On the road again, two U. S. Air Force officers spotted the little American flag on my pack and drove me to their base in Germany. Military quarters never looked better. Lieutenant Jack Cannon happened to be mess officer and after feeding me a giant American meal, he packed the biggest lunch I have ever had the pleasure of carrying. Down the Rhine and through the grimy coal mines and steel mills of the Ruhr valley, I reached Bielefeld that evening. Having done so well with the Americans, I decided to try the British Army. At the Eleventh Armored Division barracks I was greeted like a long-lost comrade.

"Corporal, there's a Yank here who wants a place to sleep. Take him to the Sergeants' Mess and the boys will look after him." With a wink at me, "Watch out for those blokes. They have a few pints and go bloody wild."

The Sergeants' Mess is a formidable institution in the British Army and the members need very little excuse for a celebration. My arrival touched off a riotous party which lasted most of the night.

Bright and early I hitched along the *autobahn* to Helmstedt on the East German border but the *Vopos* (People's Police) would not let me go through to Berlin. Americans, British and French must have a special visa; anyone else receives an entry permit within minutes. I watched Dutch, Swedes and Swiss driving in and felt frustrated. So all I saw of East Germany was a big red flag.

I turned back and rode to Hamburg with a busload of German tourists. During the war Hamburg suffered as much bomb damage as all of England. The center of the city is brand-new, and only the medieval town hall escaped destruction. Large areas remain leveled and vacant. The youth hostel, built in 1952, is ultramodern and overlooks the harbor. Leaving Hamburg I crossed the lush farmland of Schleswig-Holstein to the Danish border.

CHAPTER FIVE

SCANDINAVIA

I WONDER IF there has ever been an unenthusiastic visitor to Denmark. This charming well-scrubbed happy little land must impress even the most blasé tourist with its neat brick and wood thatch-roofed houses, fat red cattle and blocks of apartments, each with a flower-decked balcony. There are postmen in scarlet jackets, pipe-smoking men, cute blond children and pretty girls pedaling bicycles with their skirts flying.

I traveled up the west coast of Jutland on the metal baggage rack of a motorcycle and could hardly walk after dismounting. A fisherman and his family gave me a ride and I joined them for a picnic lunch. We were bound for Herning but my friend got completely lost and we wandered aimlessly along the back country roads. It's a funny thing about the Danes—their country is small and the highways are well marked, yet everyone seems confused about directions. Since they try so hard to be helpful, any question leads to a long and involved discussion among the local inhabitants and the concensus of opinion is usually wrong. We finally stumbled on Herning purely by accident. I crossed through the lake district of central Denmark and slept blissfully in a hay field outside Aarhus.

On a Sunday I progressed exactly forty-five miles. Every Dane who owned a car was out for a drive with the family but no one was going anyplace. Like Sunday at home, except that here motorists waved and smiled and sympathized. I swam and took a nap beside the road.

Next morning I breezed into Copenhagen. This is, in my opinion, the best "good time" city in Europe. The night life is varied and exciting, easygoing as the Danes themselves, and costs less than half what it does in Paris. To meet girls in Paris you must either speak fluent French or have plenty of money. But in Copenhagen all you need is a roving eye and a big smile. Half an hour after arriving I met a girl while collecting my mail at the American Express office. Elana was plump and pretty with lustrous brown eyes and a long pigtail. She had been born in Czechoslovakia, lived in San Francisco, Israel, and for the past year in Denmark.

"Can I take you to dinner?" I inquired.

"I have a better idea. Come home with me and I'll cook for you. Then I'll show you the city."

Elana was an excellent guide and knew Copenhagen from its palaces to its back-alley dives. We hired bicycles for seven cents a day, toured the sprawling Carlsberg Brewery whose beer is Denmark's biggest export and spent an evening in the Tivoli, the famous carnival-amusement park. Elana took me to the Club Montmartre to hear a Danish jazz band . . . and who should be playing clarinet but Albert Nicholas, an old acquaintance from New York jam sessions.

"Man, how are things on Fifty-second Street?"

"I wouldn't know, Albert, I haven't been in Jimmy Ryan's for five years."

Another night we went to a party given by Karl Knudsen, a record collector of New Orleans jazz. I hadn't heard so much good music since leaving San Francisco. The guests included a Calypso singer from Trinidad, an English trumpeter and a Danish girl who tried valiantly to sing blues.

I finally tore myself away from Copenhagen and rode off to Hamlet's Castle on another motorcycle, fortunately one with a rear seat. I crossed on the ferry to Sweden and traveled north to Gothenburg with two high school girls. Hitchhiking was slow in Sweden and female companions improved my luck. The Swedes are clever and prosperous, extremely fortunate in their neutrality, proud and reserved. They suffer by comparison with their warm-hearted neighbors, with whom they are not particularly popular. The Swedes who did give me rides were delightful people, but many cars passed by.

Stockholm is a bustling modern metropolis. The old town, built on a cluster of islands bisected by canals, is called the Venice of the North. At the Riksdag (Swedish parliament) I saw how this democratic constitutional monarchy functions. I admired the medieval Riddarholm Church with its delicate wrought-iron steeple and the radically modern design of the Town Hall, pride of Stockholm.

The youth hostel is certainly the most unusual in Europe

—a gleaming white square-rigged sailing ship moored in the harbor. Its location surpasses that of the swank Grand Hotel. The ship is a favorite afternoon tea spot for the people of Stockholm. My first night aboard I sat writing a letter and listening to a discussion in English about America in the next cabin.

"America doesn't need political control of other countries," said a Dutchman. "She wants to gain economic control with her money. The Americans are imperialists posing as humanitarians."

"How can you say that a country which has given away hundreds of millions of dollars is purely selfish?" someone replied. "No other nation has ever tried to rebuild and improve a large part of the world. The Americans are inexperienced and they make mistakes. But I believe their motives are honest and we should give them credit."

A Dane changed the subject to the Cold War. "The Americans don't trust anyone. When they blunder into another war we will all be finished. Why don't they make a real effort to reach some agreement on disarmament with the Russians? An arms race can only end in war."

"Can you give me one good reason why the Americans should trust the Russians? They have been deceived enough to make anyone suspicious. The only country which can prevent the world-wide spread of Communism is the United States. The Russians know this and so do the Americans. The Russians respect strength and perhaps this respect will lead to peace."

I wondered who this defender of American policy could be and joined the argument. Surprisingly, he was an African from Kenya on vacation from an English university. I think the United States has more supporters in unlikely places than we realize.

From Stockholm I traveled deck class on a ship across the Baltic Sea to Turku, Finland. After an all too brief week in this remarkable country I decided that the Finns were the most calm and courageous people I had ever known. They live under the shadow of the "Bear Who Walks like a Man" but they are not afraid. Their hard realistic outlook toward the Russians is born of a thousand years' bitter experience. Because of hardship and economic necessity the Finns have developed a highly socialistic form of government. But they love their freedom and will have nothing to do with Soviet Communism.

Every Finn has a personal reason for hating the Russians. Pekka looked like any American college boy except for his glass eye. He spoke with a fierce intensity. "In 1940 the Reds bombed my village. There were no military targets but they destroyed every house. My mother died and I lost my eye. I was six years old. Look around, my friend. We are Western people like you. If war comes again we will not be neutral, we will fight them as we have always done. They are barbarians."

The only difficulty I had in Finland was explaining to each person who invited me home why I could not stay for several days. I can remember only two cars passing me on the road and one of these had Swedish plates. There was very little traffic, but when a vehicle did appear I knew it would stop and fit me in somewhere. Even drivers going in the opposite direction asked if I would like to change my mind and ride with them.

A Dutch friend from the ship introduced me to a family

in Turku who immediately asked both of us to visit their farm outside town. We swam and fished in an inlet of the Baltic Sea and attended a birthday party for one of the daughters. Next morning on the road to Helsinki a truck loaded with blue mud stopped to give me a lift. As the driver pulled up the mud began pouring over the side, a blue stream coming toward me in slow motion. I tried to jump out of the way but tripped and fell down a bank and was splattered from head to foot. The scene was perfect slapstick comedy. The driver apologized profusely and I could not stop laughing.

Helsinki is a blend of old and new—sturdy timber houses and sleek concrete apartments, domed and turreted Victorian architecture and the futuristic railway station, simple wooden cathedral and impressive Olympic stadium. The open-air market was quiet and dignified compared to the racket and confusion of similar places in southern Europe. Everyone in Helsinki seemed busy. Women were doing heavy manual labor, repairing the streets and digging ditches. Finnish barbers are pretty girls—it was a good place for my badly needed haircut.

In the town of Lahti I went to see Matti Eerala, a fellow passenger on the ship from Stockholm who had extended the usual invitation. His sister cooked a delicious dinner and Matti showed me pictures of his three brothers who had been killed fighting the Russians. In the morning Matti fired the iron stove in a shed behind the house, poured water over heated rocks and we took a *sauna*. The Finnish bath is justly renowned as an invigorating experience. The Finns say it is better in the winter when you run from the steam room outside into the snow, but jumping under cold water was enough of a shock for me. I had never felt so gloriously clean.

I continued north through innumerable lakes and vast tracks of timber, the "Finnish gold." Lumberjacks floated log rafts to the sawmills. Farmers stood like Roman charioteers driving their two-wheeled carts pulled by small stocky Russian ponies. The road was a typical terrible Finnish highway, a rocky dirt track through the woods.

A taxi driver who gave me a lift spoke of being driven from his home in Karelia. "When the Russians occupied Karelia the whole population was evacuated into Finland. Every town and village took a few people. We did not want to live under Russian rule so everyone left."

I trudged through the woods for a couple of hours without seeing a car, and a nice old lady let me sleep in her farmhouse. I walked another five miles before a truck finally appeared and brought me to Jyväskylä. In this lakeside town I was surprised to see a baseball game. The Finns are the only Europeans who play baseball, and in spite of some differences it is basically the same game. At the dance that night the band played American pop tunes; the girls were pretty but very shy.

Outside the industrial town of Tampere a young schoolteacher pulled up. Almost before I was in his car he announced, "You must come home with me and stay for a week. I live in Vammala and the fishing there is very good."

When I explained that I had to catch the ship back to Sweden he gave me a bag of food and waited beside the road to flag the first car bound for Turku. What more could a person do?

I spent another day in Stockholm and traveled across

central Sweden to Oslo. One short ride was with a Finn on a motor scooter so of course I was taken home for lunch. Norway is as scenic as any country in Europe and the Norwegians are as cordial as the Danes. It is an ideal combination. In Oslo the Town Hall with its bold murals, the crowded harbor, rambling palace and statues of Frogner Park were familiar sights from three years before. I stayed with Einar Staff, a friend during my previous visit, and his lovely blond wife. Together we drove north to his mother-in-law's home in Gjövik where I was fed almost to the point of insensibility. The Norwegians understand the lean hungry look of a hitchhiker.

I continued on to Lillehammer, such a restful spot that I stayed an extra day. The modern youth hostel was complete with hot-water showers and a thirty-five-cent *smörgåsbord*. I considered taking an American girl to the Saturday night dance, but she had a date with four Norwegian soldiers. So I went out with her mother. We walked far up into the hills and saw a scene I will never forget: the town of Lillehammer nestled beside the lake, bathed in the light of a full moon and ringed by dark mountains. It looked unreal, like a Nordic fairy tale.

I asked the doctor who brought me to Trondheim about socialized medicine in Norway.

"We have a health insurance plan which covers virtually 100 per cent of the population and gives complete protection against illness. The system is not perfect. There are improvements which should be made but in general the plan works very well."

"American doctors are violently opposed to any form of government health insurance," I said.

"Yes, I know that. But Norwegian doctors earn a good income and most of us approve the idea of medical care for all who need it. I think that our social welfare is more advanced than yours."

"We could learn a great deal from you," I agreed.

Trondheim lies below the Arctic Circle on a line with central Alaska. It is a thriving seaport and fishing center with a distinguished university and a wooden cathedral, nine centuries old, where the medieval kings of Norway were crowned. Coastal steamers loaded a bewildering variety of cargo since the towns to the north receive all their supplies by sea. Trondheim was the northern limit of my travels.

Heading south again I shared a picnic lunch with an elderly couple and was picked up by a jovial building contractor.

"I will take you to the youth hostel at Lom," he said. "It is only fifty kilometers [30 miles] off my route."

Next day while crossing the Jotunheimen, the highest peaks in Norway, I asked the startled driver to let me out in the middle of nowhere. He thought I was crazy. But why ride when you can hike through a glacier-encrusted world of rock and snow with no sign of life to detract from nature's majesty?

By four o'clock I was tired and happy to accept a lift down the hairpin curves to Skjolden. This village is located at the tip of the Sognefiord, longest and most spectacular fiord on the Norwegian coast. The hostel offered a million-dollar view for twenty-eight cents. Waterfalls cascaded down rock walls and farms clung precariously to the mountainsides. The Norwegian farmers manage to culti-

vate the most inaccessible-looking slopes. An Austrian mo-
torcyclist, a Swedish tourist and a three-hour ferry trip
across the heart of the fiord brought me to Gudvangen, a
tiny place on a sliver of land between sheer cliffs. There
were two American girls at the hostel. They were the only
girls I met from the States who had the imagination to
hitchhike through Europe. European women do it, but
most Americans feel they must travel in style.

From Gudvangen to Stalheim is a distance of twelve
kilometers, the last two almost straight up. Since there
would be no cars until the afternoon ferry arrived, I
walked, stopping for an hour in a cave during a heavy
downpour. On top of the pass I sat in a German-built pillbox and watched a string of automobiles crawling along
the floor of the valley. At Voss I stayed in another lovely
all-you-can-eat youth hostel. The Scandinavians provide
unexcelled facilities for impoverished travelers.

I traversed more mountains to reach Bergen. After roam-
ing the waterfront and the fish market, I called on the
father of my Norwegian missionary friend in Tunisia. A
kindly old gentleman, he embarrassed me by insisting that
I accept twenty kroner ($2.80) to treat myself to a big
meal. I left Bergen feeling like a beggar.

CHAPTER SIX

THE
BRITISH ISLES

RAMÓN'S DARK FACE split into a wide grin.

"I have come to England to learn the language," he laughed, "and you who speak English cannot understand. What hope is there for me?"

We were asking directions to the Great North Road and I was baffled by the peculiar Northumberland dialect. For the first time in six months I was in an English-speaking country and could barely understand what was being said.

"Don't blame me, Ramón. I'm only a simple American. I bet lots of Londoners couldn't follow this 'Jordy' accent."

Ramón was the son of a Spanish Republican refugee living in Paris. We had met successively in Stockholm, Trondheim and on board the steamship *Leda* crossing the North Sea from Bergen to Newcastle. The twenty-kroner gift from my friend in Bergen bought a smörgåsbord feast for both of us.

We set off for London in Ramón's tiny, battered Renault, one wheel wobbling so badly that people kept warning us it was about to fall off. After stopping every few miles to rest the engine, we camped that night in what looked like an empty field. A series of ear-splitting roars informed us that our camp site was located on the edge of an RAF jet airbase. We were tired and slept in spite of the racket.

Since leaving home I had been planning to meet Jan, my girl from San Francisco, on August 10 when she arrived in London. She was waiting for me at the Regent Palace Hotel, looking pretty as a picture—if somewhat startled by my vagabond appearance. With Jan's friend Marie, and Clarke, a big genial fellow from Detroit, we toured London. Not wanting them to miss anything, I'm afraid that I walked my friends into a state of exhaustion.

London is still the commercial capital of the world, more cosmopolitan than other cities because the people of every nation come not only as tourists but to live, work, trade and study. For six days we gazed at great landmarks, from Westminster Abbey and the Houses of Parliament to St. Paul's and the Tower of London. We listened to the soapbox orators at Hyde Park Corner—an acid-tongued Scottish Communist, a couple of Africans blasting imperialism and the white man, a discussion of how the Salvation Army spends its money, a crackpot who thought he was Churchill, a vague debate on the soul, an aspiring comedian who simply liked to entertain and several sidewalk preachers. We talked with detectives at Scotland Yard and waited expectantly outside No. 10 Downing Street but saw only the cleaning woman. I watched the changing of the guard

at Buckingham Palace for the third time and ate the worst
meal I've ever had at a Lyons cafeteria. The jokes about
English cooking are no exaggeration.

On my first night in London I took my sleeping bag to
St. James's Park and settled down for a nice rest. But different bobbies kept waking me to ask silly questions.

"Who are you? What are you doing?"

"I'm a Yank trying to sleep," I answered with what I
hoped was biting sarcasm.

"Righto, sorry to bother you," and all was quiet until
the next one appeared. Finally at six o'clock they sent me
off to the Salvation Army for a cup of tea. Two other disturbed sleepers who were bedded down nearby turned out
to be friends I had known in Paris. The three of us joined
a group of destitute men on the Salvation Army dole.

I couldn't see any future in St. James's Park so the next
night I slipped into Clarke's room at the Regent Palace
and bunked on the floor. For the rest of our stay in London
I successfully played hide and seek with the house detective. The hotel employees either thought I was a regular
guest or were too polite to ask questions.

After much feminine confusion about packing, the four
of us left on the night train for Ireland. It was a long trip.
We reached Holyhead at 3:00 A.M. and spent an hour in
the customs line. The Irish Republicans had raided a British
Army depot two days before and the police were determined that the stolen guns would not be smuggled to Ireland. All baggage was carefully searched. Marie, for some
reason known only to herself, had four suitcases and carrying them did not improve our tired spirits. The ship sailed
at 4:30 and the notorious Irish Sea was smooth as glass.

Four hours later we collapsed in a Dublin guest house and slept until late afternoon.

Feeling bright-eyed and bushy-tailed again, we strolled around Dublin to Trinity College, the Abbey Theater and the Guinness Brewery. Jan's cousins had invited us to visit them on Dingle Bay in County Kerry. Gerald Teahan was a husky, soft-spoken Gaelic football player. With his wife, Nellie, her sister Maureen, their father and aunt, Gerald operated a general store between the tiny village of Castlemaine and the tinier village of Inch. This is the storybook Irish countryside, green as the Emerald Isle is supposed to be. Hedges and stone walls cut the land into small fields, barren mountains roll down to Dingle Bay and whitewashed cottages overgrown with flowers line the narrow lanes. Farmers in high boots, rough tweed jackets and cloth caps drive their donkey carts and women wear long black shawls.

Jan discovered that she was related to practically everyone along the road and all the relatives dropped in to say hello. The three Teahan children were so shy they never spoke to us during our four-day visit. We went to Killarney, hired a horse-drawn jaunting cart with a young driver who sang tenor and rode around the famed lakes. The Irish call them "Heaven's Reflex" and nearby are mountains with the quaint name of MacGillicuddy's Reeks. Clarke and I swam in Dingle Bay, but since he had won the hundred-meter free-style at the Helsinki Olympics, we didn't race. Jan and I pedaled bicycles down the coast into a setting sun which splashed the fields with gold and etched the mountains like deep blue crystal against the sky.

In Cork we kissed the Blarney Stone and rented a run-down Austin for three days. We drove to Limerick and despite some difficulty with a flat tire, broken jack and gashed spare, proceded to Galway. O'Connor's pub on Galway Bay was having an amateur night. Accompanied by a willing but tone-deaf accordionist, the customers were performing enthusiastically. They sang sentimental ballads, songs about moving old Ireland to Sydney Bay and fighting the Black and Tan in Dublin, and Joe Fitzpatrick danced the Irish jig. With very little urging we got up and sang "That Good Old Mountain Dew," which brought down the house. But our encore was a blunder. We had been harmonizing on "America" in the car and now sang it unthinkingly. Any idiot should have known it is the same tune as "God Save the Queen," a very touchy subject in the Irish Free State. An embarrassed silence followed the chorus and we apologized for our error. But in spite of the mental lapse it was a fine evening.

After midnight we found a guest house where the landlady obligingly fed us and let me sleep on the floor. Driving west into the country called Connemara we found the mountains bare and rocky, sprinkled with lakes and inlets of the sea. Men cut peat in the bogs and stacked the blocks beside the road to dry. We picnicked on a little bay where sailboats sat on the mud flats at low tide and stopped to watch the sun dissolve in a flaming ball of fire. Travelers who don't have time to enjoy the sunset should not come to Ireland.

From Sligo we returned to Dublin, parted reluctantly with our Austin, caught the train to Belfast and the night boat for Glascow. Early the following morning we steamed up the Firth of Clyde past the greatest concentration of shipyards in the world. For more than an hour all types of vessels in various stages of completion lined the Clyde-banks. The yards work around the clock under batteries of arc lights, riveting and hammering and welding the raw steel hulls. The Queens were built here and you wonder how such giants could have been launched in this narrow waterway.

My friends went by rail to Edinburgh and I hitchhiked, arriving twenty minutes later than the train, having visited a coal mine en route. Edinburgh was in the midst of its Music Festival and the city swarmed with tourists and bag-pipers. The first thing I did was to follow a pipe band the length of Princes Street. Clarke and the girls checked into a guest house and I tagged along. Mrs. Price, the landlady, told me, "You can take a bath, too, and be as clean as every-one else."

I love bagpipe music and hope to hear many pipe bands in the future, but I doubt that I will ever witness a spectacle as colorful and spine-tingling as the Military Tattoo at the castle that night. The massed pipes and drums of the British Commonwealth marched against a backdrop of the floodlit castle—turbaned Punjabis of the Pakistan Army, the Cana-dian Black Watch, regimental bands of the Gordon High-landers, King's Own Scottish Borderers and Argyll and Sutherland Highlanders, plus representatives from Aus-tralia, New Zealand, Northern Ireland, South Africa and two little soldiers of the Gurkha Brigade. In addition to the pipes and drums there were military brass bands, preci-sion drilling by the Scots Guards, Highland dancing, his-torical tableaux of the Scottish regiments and the Tattoo itself, played by a lone piper high on the walls of the castle.

· 65

The Empire may be dead, but pomp and circumstance live on.

Late that night I scaled a fence and slept comfortably in a private park. But in the morning it was embarrassing to climb out while numerous passers-by stopped and stared. Our second day in Edinburgh was spent exploring the castle. High on a rocky promontory, like a crown above the city, it looks the part of a romantic, impregnable fortress. Jan and I joined Peter Gardner, a youth-hosteling friend, and several other Scots for a quick evening on the town. It had to be quick since all the pubs close at eleven o'clock.

We paid four shillings (fifty-six cents) to hear guitarist Andrés Segovia, saw a special exhibition of Gauguin's paintings and listened to the Newmarket Fisherwomen's Choir, funny old ladies singing folk songs. After attending a rally of the Scottish Nationalist party whose kilted speakers demanded independence from England, we returned to the castle for a repeat performance of the Tattoo.

In Edinburgh our happy foursome separated. Clarke departed for Norway and the girls took the boat train for Copenhagen. I was sorry to see them go. They were good traveling companions and we had fun together. I wondered when Jan and I would meet again.

After following the pipe band down Princes Street for the last time, I headed for Perth and across empty moors to Inverness, capital of the Highlands, a clean, very Scottish town built of stone. To my mind one of history's most intriguing episodes is the story of "The Forty-Five," the gallant, tragic rebellion of the Highlanders in 1745. Bonnie Prince Charlie came from France to gather the warlike clans and regain the throne for his father, the exiled Stuart king. His cause was doomed to failure and the final battle was fought at Culloden Moor outside Inverness. The ragged clansmen, outnumbered, armed only with their broadswords and weakened by dissention among their chiefs, charged the English guns and were slaughtered. After his victory "Butcher" Cumberland, the King's general, rode through the Highlands burning and hanging until all trace of rebellion was destroyed. Prince Charlie escaped to the Isle of Skye and sailed back to France, ending "The Forty-Five."

A local resident, guiding me over the battlefield, pointed to a large rock. "From there Cumberland directed his troops. The English claim he stood on top, but we say he was hiding behind the rock. The men of each clan are buried together where they fell under those wee stone markers."

I rode with an old lady in a jeep along the shore of wild Loch Ness. She wasn't sure about the fabled monster but insisted there was some strange creature in the Loch, perhaps a displaced sea lion. I followed the legendary Road to the Isles to Kyle of Lochalsh. The summer had been so dry that water was rationed in this village, an unheard-of procedure in the normally rain-soaked western Highlands.

The Isle of Skye is a sparsely populated land of desolate wind-swept moors, stone and thatch-crofters' cottages, fat black-face sheep, shaggy longhorn Highland cattle and the Cullin Hills, most rugged country in Britain. Skye typifies the harsh, romantic appeal of the Highlands.

Unfortunately the long-expected rain began as I walked along a deserted stretch of the road. There was no shelter of any kind, not even a tree, so I floundered through the downpour wondering morbidly if it was possible to drown in a rainstorm. At last I came to a cottage and inquired if I could sleep in the barn. A lanky, lantern-jawed sheepherder surveyed me thoughtfully and puffed on his pipe.

"You better come inside and have supper with us. My wife will give you dry clothes. We have a spare bed."

My benefactor's name was Kenneth Nicholson and his hospitality was certainly welcome. We sat by the fire and he told me melancholy stories about Skye.

"The MacDonalds and MacLeods own most of this island. In the old days they wanted more grazing land for their sheep and shipped hundreds of tenant families to America. They should be ashamed of themselves. During the Great War Skye lost a higher percentage of men than any other place in Scotland. And today there is no opportunity here. All the young men leave for Glascow or London."

Returning to the mainland, I found the channel so rough that I barely escaped being violently seasick. We landed just in time. With an Australian couple I stopped at Glenfinnan, the spot where Bonnie Prince Charlie raised his standard to begin "The Forty-Five." Then along Loch Lomond to Glascow and through the Lakes District to the walled city of Chester. From the north coast of Wales I embarked on a meandering four-hundred-mile journey to Cornwall with a vacationing actor. We photographed old castles, admired quaint Welsh villages with unpronounceable names, drank potent Devon cider and eventually reached the rolling green and gold countryside of Cornwall. After spending the night in the spare room of a police station, I started back to London riding with a Royal

Marine, a Canadian "spiderman" and an Oxford art professor. While searching for the youth hostel near High Wycombe I inquired at the home of an American engineer who offered his guest room instead.

In London I reorganized for the long haul to India—new soles on my boots, light meter cleaned, pants patched, etc. I contacted Pat Halcox, my trumpeter friend from Copenhagen, and he introduced me to the other members of Chris Barber's Jazz Band. These young Englishmen played excellent jazz in the best George Lewis tradition. They had an authentic New Orleans sound, learned entirely from records, but a distinctive style of their own. I stayed with banjo player Lonnie Donegan and traveled the London Jazz Club circuit with the band.

Jack, Aileen and Beryl, my Australian friends from Seville, were working in London and we spent a week end together. Saturday night we celebrated at the Overseas Visitors' Club, a pseudosophisticated spot full of South Africans, and the rocking, wide-open Down Under Club where the Aussies go to blow off steam. The latter is a colorful joint which would be popular in San Francisco—sawdust on the floor, a loud, off-key combo and a huge picture of Ned Kelly, the notorious "bush ranger" who robbed banks and battled the police wearing a suit of home-made armor. Sunday we went to the Farnborough Air Show, a lavish display of the latest British military and civilian aircraft.

En route to Dover I thought about the difference between the helpful Britons I had known and the stereotype cold Englishman and dour Scot. The Channel ferry reached Dunkirk at the awkward hour of 4:00 A.M. so I curled up

· 69

in a waiting room with some French longshoremen. Dunkirk is still clearing the rubble from the 1940 evacuation. I traveled into Belgium to Bastogne, where the only evidence of the Battle of the Bulge is a Sherman tank in the town square and a big monument near the American cemetery. A cold rain was falling when I found shelter in a hayloft.

"Your soldiers slept in my barn eleven years ago," the farmer told me. "But you are more fortunate. No one is shooting at you."

The next day in Luxembourg a Dutchman came along who was driving to Switzerland. "We will take the longer route through France to Basel," he said. "I saw enough of Germany in a Nazi concentration camp."

Without a single franc in my pocket, by that evening I had been in four countries within the past thirty hours. In Zurich I visited fellow hitchhiker Werner Erne. His mother treated me like her own son and packed a two-day supply of food when I left for Austria. As I climbed Arlberg Pass in an ancient car with a photographer and his wife, the overheated engine set fire to the wooden floor boards. Luckily my canteen was full of Frau Erne's tea and I put out the flames before any serious damage was done.

"You have saved our car with your tea!" said the woman.

"How can we ever thank you?" her husband asked.

"Believe me, I'm very happy to be able to do a favor for someone else for a change."

We packed snow on the charred floorboards and continued into the Tyrol. From Innsbruck I rode with one of the dependable Dutch tourists who invariably stop for hitchhikers, to Salzburg. This venerable city of Mozart boasts one of Europe's finest castles. Along the road to Vienna the crops were being harvested. Peasant families cut hay, dug potatoes and picked fruit. Fresh plums cost four cents a pound; at that price you can eat a lot of plums.

Vienna was like a great lady of the old school who had fallen downstairs—battered but undaunted. In spite of war and occupation she remains a proud city. Her Hapsburg palaces and monuments have survived the bombs, and the clatter of reconstruction echoes on the wide boulevards of the Ringstrasse. The Opera House, symbol of Viennese glory, was preparing for its grand reopening in November. The famed wine gardens and rathskellers offered inexpensive drinks, hearty food and rollicking music. An air of buoyant optimism pervaded most of the city. But across the Danube Canal in the former Russian sector Vienna seemed more dead than alive, as if the war had just ended. In contrast to crowded and noisy streets, here they were quiet and almost deserted. I sensed a strange atmosphere of emptiness and futility. Evidently the people had hesitated to rebuild while the Russians remained in control and it was difficult to shake off ten years of lethargy. My only chance to observe the effects of Soviet occupation was a revealing experience. The Red Army had constructed a garish victory memorial in a square which they renamed Stalinplatz. This monstrosity included a giant, gold-helmeted soldier on a pedestal, a columned arc topped by statues of more soldiers, many hammer and sickle emblems, a tank, graves, trees and noble inscriptions. To the Austrians it served as a constant reminder of their defeat and would undoubtedly be torn down at the first opportunity.

The Vienna youth hostel was a motellike, international

gathering place with hot water showers, my criterion of excellence. As a vagabond information center it had no equal.

"Traveling is very slow in Yugoslavia," a Swiss student returning home from Greece warned me. "The only cars are driven by tourists and there are few trucks. You will need good luck."

I rode across Austria to Villach near the Italian border with a jolly hotel owner. He added two Aussie girls to his already overloaded car and bought steak dinners for the three of us. I crossed the frontier to Tarvisio, joined a group of Italians in their Saturday night songfest and slept in the dining room of the café. The road to Trieste followed a river canyon through the Julian Alps, a military zone patrolled by smartly uniformed Alpine troops in plumed Tyrolean hats.

The long-disputed city of Trieste has been reunited with Italy, thus satisfying the fervent nationalism of its citizens. But political expediency has not solved the economic problems of this seaport, useless to Italy and practically empty of ships. The Italians have erected a memorial cemetery for all Triestinos killed from the time of the Ethiopian campaign to the postwar riots in the city. What makes this memorial unusual is that it commemorates those who fought on both sides. Men who died in the Fascist cause and partisans executed by the Nazis are buried together.

I changed dollars into Yugoslav dinars at double the official rate of exchange and also decided to grow a beard. From the hostel, located in a hillside castle overlooking the city, I took a long last look at the bright lights of Western Europe.

CHAPTER SEVEN

YUGOSLAVIA

COMMUNISM IS a failure. For the first time I could see with my own eyes the basic fallacies of the Marxist system. Yugoslavia is a poor and primitive land, desperately in need of drastic reform. But its problems can never be solved by Communism. The people need an inspiration, an incentive to help themselves, and under the present form of government they just don't care. In theory the workers own all means of production except the smallest one-man shops, yet in practice this ownership gains them nothing except low wages. A factory worker earns about 8,000 dinars ($27 at the official exchange rate) a month. A pair of shoes costs 4,000 dinars, a good wool suit 50,000.

A medical student told me, "A doctor would have to work for fifty-three years to buy a Volkswagen."

An office clerk said, "I am wearing my best suit. The cloth is made of wood fiber." He added wistfully, "Someday I hope to be able to afford a bicycle."

The party officials may not have large bankrolls but they live in plush apartments and drive Mercedes or Buicks. There is as much class consciousness in Yugoslavia as anywhere in Western Europe. Although neither would appreciate the comparison, I found Spain and Yugoslavia amazingly similar in their poverty, inequality, police control and physical appearance. The Yugoslavs are kind and generous people and they deserve a brighter future.

I left Trieste in a garbage truck and walked across scrub brush hills into Tito-land. A citizen in a tiny car gave me a short lift. I thought this a good omen for the future but it was misleading. During the next eighteen days I rode in only one other Yugoslav automobile. A truck driven by a cheerful Italian brought me to Ljubljana, the capital of Slovenia. This city is as modern as any in Yugoslavia, with a handful of new buildings, fairly well-dressed people, paved streets, cyclists and horse-drawn carts, a heroic statue commemorating the Partisans, a picture of Tito in every shop and the omnipresent blue-uniformed police. The merchandise in store windows was limited in quantity, poor in quality and expensive. Every official, including the street cleaner, sported a red star on his cap. I slept in a university dormitory and ate a simple student dinner which cost eight cents at the black-market rate of exchange.

In Ljubljana I learned my first lesson in Communist efficiency. My Italian friend was going to Rijeka and offered me a ride. We drove to a paint factory and spent three and a half hours fiddling around while three men and a woman loaded the truck. The woman did most of the work. I could have completed the job alone in twenty minutes.

These were the workers who "owned" the factory but slave laborers could not have been more indifferent. Finally with the truck half full we drove twenty-five kilometers to pick up more paint but discovered that it was not ready to be shipped. So we returned to Ljubljana and searched the town for a bureaucrat to sign the receipts. After six hours of bungling we departed for Rijeka.

At dusk the road was crowded with Slovenian peasant families homeward bound from the fields. Their narrow wooden wagons overflowed with corn and potatoes, children piled on top, grandmother riding severely on the tail gate and lanterns hanging on the sides. These were the people who resisted the plan for collectivizing their farms so stubbornly that the Communists abandoned the entire program. They had been landowners instead of tenant serfs for only a hundred years and refused to accept a new variation on the old system.

The tallest building in Rijeka had a large red star on the roof and "TITO" emblazoned in giant letters across the front. Antiquated sailing ships in the harbor looked almost Arabic in design. A friend had given me the address of a family there and I found the small apartment. The son Nick was a tall, intense young man, a former student who loved America with a passion. He greeted me excitedly and asked innumerable questions about the United States. Then Nick told me of his own unhappy plight.

"I hate this Communist government and tried to escape to Austria, and perhaps someday, with luck, to America. But I was foolish going alone, not knowing the trails through the woods. The police caught me easily and I spent four months in prison."

"Now what will you do?" I asked.

"What can I do? I have been in political prison so the government will not allow me to work. It is hopeless for me here. I must try to escape again."

"Will you go the same way?"

"Yes, but this time I will be more clever. My months in prison were not all wasted. I learned the name of a man from a border village who guides people across the mountains. I will pay him to lead me to Austria. This time I will succeed."

"I hope you make it, Nick," I thought to myself. "If they catch you a second time I'm afraid you will not have another chance."

This type of situation had always seemed remote and unreal to me, the make-believe plot of a book or film. But suddenly the drama involved a friend and I realized it was a deadly serious business. They were not playing games in Yugoslavia.

After spending two days in Rijeka, I wished Nick good luck and caught the coastal steamer to Split. The peasants on board carried wooden suitcases full of black bread and goat cheese which they shared with me. A group of Macedonian students wanted to know about segregation in America.

"Racial prejudice is probably our most serious problem," I admitted. "Most Americans realize this and relations between Negroes and whites are generally improving. But the quiet changes are not spectacular and don't make stories for the newspapers."

The Macedonians looked skeptical.

In talking of politics, one asked, "What is the difference

between Eisenhower and Stevenson?"

I tried to explain the two-party system.

"But to us the Republicans and Democrats are both the same, conservative and reactionary."

"No, they are not the same. The big difference between our system and yours is that we *do* have a choice. If we disagree with the party in power, we elect the opposition. Whom did you vote for in the last Yugoslav election?"

"We are too young to vote," he answered lamely, but I think he got the point.

Split is an unusual city built in and around the third-century palace of the Roman Emperor Diocletian. To protect themselves from roving tribes and pirates the early inhabitants settled inside the fortified walls. They used the abandoned palace as a quarry so that today the stone houses blend into the remains of imperial temples, columned arcades and courtyards. The city spreads beyond the walls but some 3,000 people still live within the former palace grounds.

I sat for an hour at a lookout point and admired the beauty of the Dalmatian coast. Harsh gray mountains adorned with black pine forests and terraced fields and orchards stretched to the horizon. Sheer cliffs plunged into the blue-green Adriatic, a string of islands floated on the translucent sea. The white-stone and red-tile houses of Split poured down the hillside at my feet.

A busload of American tourists screeched to a halt beside me. They hopped out, exclaiming excitedly,

"Oh, isn't this lovely!"

"Just look at that view!"

"See the hotel, Henry, right over there."

"I'm using a hundredth at 6.3."

Click, click went the cameras. Five minutes later they roared away to the next sight on the itinerary.

Dubrovnik is only 138 miles from Split but the trip took me three and a half days. The first evening I reached Makarska with a German tourist and stayed at the hotel as his guest. The next day I walked without seeing a single vehicle, not even a wagon. It was all hike and no hitch for the first time. But I was in no hurry. The Dalmatians were harvesting grapes and making wine and they invited me to eat and drink with them. The men jumped up and down in large wooden tubs, crushing the juice from the grapes with their bare feet. They left their sandals on the ground before stepping into the tubs.

"I spent ten years in America working hard on the railroads," one of the farmers told me while we sampled his tart new wine. "I came home and bought two houses with all the money I had saved. Then the government accused me of being a landlord and seized my houses. So I am forced to live here on my sister's farm."

And after a pause, "But please don't mention what I've said to anyone else."

As I ate bread and cheese in the next village my host announced, "I remember American razor blades. When I can find one I use it fifty times."

"How many times?" I asked incredulously.

"Fifty, maybe more. It is good steel."

I dug out my three remaining Gillette blades and presented him with what would probably amount to a year's supply. And at the same time I committed myself irrevocably to my fledgling beard.

Another winemaker spoke bitterly as he picked huge bunches of grapes for me. "None of us can make any money. The Yugoslav people have bread to eat but nothing else. The only decent clothes my family has are sent by my wife's cousin in California."

And again the nervous plea, "I hope you will not repeat what I've said."

It is a terrible thing when people are afraid to speak.

That night I stayed in the home of a fellow who had lived in New Zealand for twenty years. He had come back to visit his family, the war began and now he could not return.

After another six hours on the deserted road a truck appeared and took me to Kardeljevo. From here I caught a train which chugged along a river bustling with fat skiffs filled with corn and pumpkins. Most of the passengers rode in box cars, but being a foreigner, I rated space in a decrepit coach. After an hour we had progressed only nine miles so I transferred to a horse-drawn wagon.

The Yugoslavs call Dubrovnik the "Pearl of the Adriatic." A former maritime kingdom and rival of Venice, it is probably the best-preserved medieval town in Europe. Nothing new has been built within the walled city since the eighteenth century. I met Jacky D'Roubaix, a Belgian girl who was hitchhiking to Ethiopia for Haile Selassie's silver jubilee. This sounded like quite a trip for a girl alone —but I discovered that Jacky could take care of herself very well. Together we roamed the fortified ramparts and the twisting alleys between stone houses festooned with flowers and vines. Handmade lace curtains hung at every window. Dubrovnik is the most popular tourist spot in Yugoslavia and the inhabitants look unusually prosperous and well-dressed. Many women wear the colorful red and black Dalmatian costume.

I rode in a truck, perched on sacks of sugar, to the Bay of Kotor. A couple of miles beyond Herzegovina I stopped for dinner in a roadside café. A disheveled young woman sat down beside me and began conversing in French. After the usual questions about who I was, she asked, "Where will you sleep tonight?"

"I don't know."

"Come with me. You can stay at my house but you must be very quiet."

"O.K., lady," I said in English, "lead the way."

She lived in one room of an ugly concrete building. We waited until after dark and sneaked through the back door. An old hag brought us spaghetti and sausages. At dawn I was urgently requested to disappear. I never understood the reason for the cloak-and-dagger performance unless the girl had boy friends who might have been jealous. There was an army camp nearby and perhaps I was lucky to have avoided some giant Slav officer brandishing a sub-machine gun.

Since it was raining I waited in a café for a bus which was expected any minute but didn't arrive for three hours. A stupid policeman interrogated me in Serbian, which I could not understand, and carefully copied information from my passport. The poor fellow had no idea what he was writing, misspelled all the words and got everything completely confused. My name was New York and my birthplace, Donald Knies. But he was doing his job and the questioning kept me occupied.

Titograd, the capital of Montenegro or Crna Gora as it is now called, boasts a modern hotel where a room with bath costs sixty cents. I visited the office of Putnik, the official tourist agency and sole source of information in Yugoslavia. Putnik representatives are invariably most solicitous but at least half of what they tell you is wrong. At the outdoor market men wore red pirate bandannas and women dressed in baggy Turkish pantaloons and embroidered jackets. A peculiar sight in Balkan markets is the peasants continually eating whatever food they are selling. How they can earn any money this way is a mystery.

I caught a truck from Titograd into the wild and primitive Crna Gora mountains. We bounced over one of the worst roads I had ever seen past black, wooden houses with pointed roofs, pigs wallowing in the mud of village streets and ragged children herding bony cattle. We stopped in a smoky café full of fierce-looking mountaineers in fur hats and sheepskin coats. My driver introduced me to the crowd and we solemnly drank a toast to President Roosevelt. One hulking fellow whose mustaches swept across his face in a bold crescent pounded me on the back and bellowed, "Amerika! Dobra [good]!"

I was glad that this one was on my side. He might have been a reincarnation of Black George, the fiery swineherder who led the ancestors of these mountaineers against the Turks and became king of Serbia. This café was the only public place I remember in Yugoslavia without a picture of Tito on the wall. I think Communism has made little impression on these isolated people.

The woods were cold and foggy, and when a peasant

family beckoned me into their home I was only too happy to accept. We sat around the fire eating black bread and potatoes while the old woman carded wool and her son played the *kolo* on his guitar. I slept in an ornately furnished guest room while my hosts retired to the loft.

Next morning a carload of characters from a Hollywood gangster film gave me a ride. They were actually an important party leader and his boys. A tough young thug drove the Buick, a nervous little man acted as personal flunky to the boss and the bodyguard, a hired-killer type in trench coat and snap-brim hat, brooded in cold silence. The big man himself was suave, well-groomed and had recently returned from a diplomatic mission to the United States.

My friend Jacky was waiting at the hotel in Andrijevica. We decided to travel together, and since there was no sign of traffic, bought tickets on the afternoon bus to Peć. Ignoring persistent rumors that a bridge had been washed out and the road was impassable, we set forth.

Just before dark our bus reached a tiny mountain village. The river was flooded, the bridge had collapsed, and vehicles could go no farther. But we were only twelve miles from Peć and it might have been weeks before the Yugoslavs opened the road again. So three of us started walking.

Milan, the leader of our little expedition, was a cool and calm Serb from Belgrade, an ex-Partisan who had fought in these mountains. We managed to climb across the fallen timbers of the bridge but just beyond, a landslide blocked the road. Searching for solid ground in the dark, we floundered into knee-high mud and rushing water up to our waists. The weight of our packs added to Jacky's and my distress as we struggled to free ourselves from the morass which held us like quicksand. Milan helped me pull myself out and together we extracted Jacky. The poor girl was exhausted and half drowned. Our resourceful leader produced a flask of *slivovitz*, cigarettes and rolls of paper from his satchel. After a drink and a smoke we felt better, recrossed the bridge by the light of paper torches and hiked back to the village. A gnarled peasant and his wife took us into their log cabin; the finest hotel could not have looked better. These Good Samaritans gave us food and dry clothes, and as we relaxed by the fire the woman cleaned the mud off our boots and trousers. I slept in a single bed with two stranded truck drivers.

The village where we found refuge was a stone's throw from Albania and inhabited mainly by turbaned Siptars, descendants of fierce Tartars from the Asian steppes. The forests were splashed with color as the leaves turned every shade of red and gold. After waiting patiently for most of the day, we returned to Andrijevica where Milan discovered three cronies from Belgrade. We rode in their truck to the Ivangrad hotel and enjoyed a memorable feast to the accompaniment of exciting Macedonian music played by a Gypsy band. Next morning an English couple had room in their small car for one passenger so I was a gentleman and waved good-by to Jacky. Leaving Ivangrad I noticed that the Communists mark their graves with red stars instead of crosses.

The hills were silent and empty except for an occasional band of woodcutters. I walked for awhile with a peasant and his two mules. He fed me juicy apples and we conversed, each in his own language, with gestures. In Yugoslavia I often spoke a weird mixture of German and Italian words which people, surprisingly enough, seemed to understand. I rode to Rozaje in what must have been the slowest truck in Europe. Louis was a dumpy little fellow with a Hitler mustache, obviously a man of importance, as are all Yugoslav truck and tractor drivers. His raw-boned assistant looked like a cowboy.

"This is Rozaje," Louis announced with as much civic pride as a Texan speaking of Dallas. The object of his admiration contained a large lumber mill, ramshackle wooden houses, several shops and a government office, the sole modern building. Cows wandered in the thick mud of the streets and the residents were bundled in sheepskin coats as protection against the freezing winds. I have never seen a Siberian village but Rozaje fitted my mental picture perfectly.

With Louis and assorted friends I stayed at the local hotel, which had no plumbing of any kind. The nervous proprietor panicked when he saw my passport and called the police. I don't think he had ever coped with a foreign guest. After an involved debate everyone was convinced that I was a tourist and not an enemy of the state. We planned to leave at 7:00 A.M. but four hours later were still waiting for the truck to be loaded. I killed time drinking Turkish coffee and Yugoslav *slivovitz* in a café and was the center of attraction. When we finally departed one old man was overcome with emotion and kissed me on both bearded cheeks.

Continuing at our snail's pace we reached Raska that night. As a welcome change from hitchhiking I took the train to Skopje, capital of Macedonia. The railroad follows the Ibar River through southern Serbia, a poverty-stricken region even by Yugoslav standards. Here I saw my first lumbering water buffalo. A Greek animal buyer told me that the law limiting a man to ownership of not more than fifty sheep had ruined a formerly thriving wool industry.

The Skopje market mirrored the clothing styles of south-eastern Europe. Men wore loose turbans, felt skullcaps or bushy fur hats; tight leggings, sheepskin cloaks and wide sashes or tattered coats and trousers. Macedonian peasant girls were resplendent in embroidered jackets, aprons and bandannas with different colors and designs from each village. Albanian women dressed in white gowns and headdresses, Moslem women in pantaloons and shoes with curled-up toes. There was a wonderful assortment of pigtails, beards and handlebar mustaches.

I discovered the fate of London's red double-decker buses after they are retired from Piccadilly. They cruise the streets of Skopje like proud old ladies who have known better days, complete with their "London Transport" emblems.

Macedonia seemed an unlikely spot to meet a San Francisco family. Mike Chaney, his wife and three-year-old daughter were traveling by Land Rover from London to Dhahran, where he worked for the Arabian-American Oil Company. The road to the Greek border looked like the world's worst highway, but I saw its equal many times later. On the rare occasions when the route was marked, the signs were written in the baffling Cyrillic alphabet. The houses were garlanded with strings of red peppers hung

· 85

out to dry, giving them a carnival air. We passed through villages where all the horses and mules stood saddled and waiting as if the Macedonians momentarily expected a call to arms.

CHAPTER EIGHT

GREECE

COMING FROM Yugoslavia into busy, brightly lighted Salonika was like entering a new world. For the first time since leaving Trieste I could not walk blithely down the middle of a city street and feel perfectly safe. Admittedly not Times Square, at least there were automobiles in Salonika. Terribly battered by the Nazis, civil war and recent earthquakes, Greece has made great progress toward recovery with the help of sincerely appreciated American aid.

Greece is a stark, semi-arid land similar in topography to parts of our Western states. Painted carts creak through villages of whitewashed stone and red tile, and donkeys bray forlornly in the olive groves. Peasants pick cotton, tobacco dries on racks in the sun, and herds of goats browse on the raw hills. The snow-covered triple peaks of Mount Olympus tower above low-lying clouds in the early morning—a proper home for Zeus and his family.

I checked into the Salonika Y.M.C.A. and was promptly invited home for dinner by the secretary. An insurance adjuster gave me a lift to Verroia, a Macedonian town at the foot of faded green hills where St. Paul preached. I rode on the tail gate of a peasant's wagon until a truck came along. In Kozane I slept at a tiny inn whose owner had relatives in California. He refused to accept any payment for my bed and breakfast. I walked through vineyard country, eating grapes until I could hold no more. Every farmer presented huge bunches to me and finally in bloated desperation I began giving the grapes back to the shepherd boys. A brawny motorcycle policeman took me to the nearest village. With a grin, he said, "We will sit in the café and drink coffee. When a car or truck appears I will order them to stop for you."

This was certainly effortless hitchhiking.

In a village near Larissa I watched a wedding procession. Accompanied by clarinetist, violinist and drummer, the bride and groom paraded from the church followed by most of the local population. The musicians played loud and long and the best man sang a serenade. I was invited to join the wedding feast in the courtyard of the groom's house. The villagers performed lively folk dances, shuffling in a sort of chorus line or following the steps of a leader who held a handkerchief in one hand which linked him to the other dancers. The guests toasted one another with *ouzo*, the milky white Greek liquor, and I made a little speech which was translated by the village linguist. When I retired to the schoolhouse floor long after midnight the newlyweds were still dancing and the party showed no sign of ending.

I traveled south on a scooter, a tractor, two wagons, and

then to Athens in a sleek '55 Chrysler driven by a wealthy Turk and his handsome wife. We climbed the tortuous curves over Thermopylae Pass where the Spartans died battling the Persian hordes. To avoid hitting a stray horse we ran off the road and had to be pulled from a ditch by helpful peasants. We also decapitated a turkey. Fast driving in Greece is fraught with animal hazards.

The Mantzouranis family virtually adopted me in Athens. Their son Harry and his wife Koula had been fellow passengers aboard the *Queen Frederika* at the start of my trip. "When you reach Athens, come to see us," Harry had said.

I accepted his invitation and met one of the nicest families I have ever known. They took me to Marathon battlefield, across the narrow canal to ancient Corinth and to Dafni where the Byzantine mosaics in the church are scarred by Turkish bayonets. We spent a week end at their summer house on the Bay of Salamis below the spot where Xerxes, the King of Kings, sat on his throne and watched the Athenian navy destroy his Persian fleet 2,500 years ago. They repaired my pack, washed my clothes and sewed my torn blue jeans. Brother-in-law Steve, an engineer with a phenomenal knowledge of Greek history, showed me the Acropolis. Mrs. Mantzouranis served delicious Greek food —roast lamb, macaroni with ground meat, broiled fish, homemade pastry and a great variety of fruit. I went with Harry and Koula to an Athenian *taverna* where we ate grilled meats, drank *retsina*, the golden wine which tastes strongly of turpentine, and listened to rousing folk music.

Harry told me of the Greek bitterness about Cyprus.

"The British could have prevented all the trouble if they had been wise and accepted the Cypriot demand for self-determination. NATO would have guaranteed a hundred-year lease for their military bases. But instead they have lost our friendship, reopened the old grievances against the Turks and Cyprus will eventually be united with Greece no matter what they do."

"How about the Turkish people of Cyprus?" I asked.

"They have no reason to fear Greek rule. A large Turkish minority has lived in Thrace for over thirty years and they have never been persecuted."

Athens is a city of hot sunshine, palms and flowers, little squares hemmed in by plaster-walled and balconied houses with the shops of craftsmen in the cellars, statues of revolutionary heroes who fought the Turks, black-robed priests of the Greek Orthodox Church with bushy beards and stovepipe hats. The streets and markets are almost deserted at midday but are alive with people in the morning and late afternoon. The guards at the Tomb of the Unknown Soldier wear blue jackets and ruffled skirts, long tassels on their caps and white balls on their shoes. The museum is filled with the peerless Greek sculpture.

But the sight which alone is worth a trip to Athens is the Rock of the Acropolis. Especially when the Parthenon is floodlighted at night, its white marble columns suspended in the black sky, there is no more perfect definition of grandeur. Other architecture cannot match the simple majesty of the Greek temples. Like good sports cars, they are built with smooth, clean lines and no fancy frills.

After six days in Athens I started back to Salonika. Mrs. Mantzouranis packed more food than I could carry and the entire family gave me presents. How could I thank them for all that they had done for me?

In Lamia a car passed me and then turned back. "I thought you were English and was not going to stop," the driver explained. "But then I saw the American flag on your pack."

He was a cotton dealer named George Paspati, bound for Salonika. I bedded down on the floor of a cotton gin while George conferred with business associates. Next morning a procession of peasants unloaded sacks of cotton from their ox-drawn wagons. The gin workers were coated from head to foot with cotton fluff and looked like snowmen.

Greek bus passengers are quiet and orderly, unlike their Yugoslav neighbors who sing, play guitars and celebrate noisily whenever they travel. But the Greek rural buses are startling in their ornamentation. I rode toward Mount Athos on a vehicle painted in multiple colors and decorated with flowers, flags, patriotic slogans, figurines, religious icons and snapshots of the family. The driver could hardly see through the cluttered windshield. Not that it mattered, since the road was so rough we might have been navigating overland by compass. From a high ridge far above the Aegean Sea, we descended to the village of Jerissos. With five Greek companions and seven goats I crawled aboard a fishing boat and we sailed into a unique little monastic world.

Mount Athos is an isolated peninsula, accessible only by trail or by sea, where some 4,000 Eastern Orthodox monks live in medieval seclusion. Women are not allowed on Athos and the female ban extends even to animals. There are no cows or horses, and the monks ride mules. The only exception is hens, the source of eggs. The monasteries scattered around the Holy Mountain are treasuries of Byzantine art. They uphold an ancient tradition of extending hospitality to any visitor and have special guest rooms for this purpose. Some of the more ascetic monks live as hermits in caves and huts on the slopes of the Holy Mountain itself. The peninsula is under special religious jurisdiction and permits to visit must be obtained from the Greek Foreign Ministry.

We landed at Vatopede, the largest and reputedly wealthiest monastery. The abbot proudly displayed priceless paintings and mosaics, silver icons and illustrated manuscripts. Harry Boucouvalas, one of my companions, spoke a little English and struggled to interpret for me. He concentrated fiercely, gripping his head and pursing his lips, trying to remember words. After each explanation poor Harry heaved a heartrending sigh and mopped his brow. I urged him to relax but he was determined that I should understand everything.

We borrowed a mule to carry our packs and followed a trail paved with rough stones exactly like a Roman road. The wooded hills were quiet and peaceful. In the monastic capital of Kariaí we stayed at Coutloumous, a grim fortress-like monastery. Two monks showed us their prized relics, the skull of a saint and the leg bone of St. Ann, both encased in silver. By the flickering light of a single candle the bearded men in patched robes, uncut hair hanging to their shoulders, reverently performed their sacred ritual. The scene reminded me of prehistoric priests enacting some weird pagan ceremony.

St. Andrei is one of two Russian monasteries on Mount Athos. The handful of surviving monks have received no new recruits since the Russian revolution. We watched these feeble, white-bearded ancients celebrating Mass. Most were propped up in little compartments and looked barely alive. One surprisingly active old fellow was making vodka in a shed. He cackled happily when we praised his fiery brew. Walking through empty halls, I noticed a wall calendar for the year 1914.

"Frankly, I wish I were back in Chicago," a monk who had lived for years in America told me. "Nothing ever happens here."

After three fascinating days on Athos we sailed up the west coast past more monasteries, each a great jumble of walls, towers and spires painted in cheerfully clashing colors. Looking back we could see the Holy Mountain rising in solitary splendor at the tip of the peninsula. Returning to Salonika our bus stopped to take aboard a giant wild boar killed by hunters. I said good-by to hard-working Harry and my other friends and headed east into the country of Alexander the Great. Beside a police station where I slept sat a massive stone lion erected, the policemen said, by Alexander's father. King Philip was the man who united Greece, developed the Macedonian phalanx and set the stage for his famous son's military genius.

Two free bus rides carried me through the bare, reddish hills to Alexandroupolis. The Turkish inhabitants of Thrace still wear the fez which has been outlawed in their homeland. I rode with an Armenian merchant over a rutted dirt road running parallel to the Turkish border. The peasant

families traveling to market seemed to bring all their live-
stock with them for safekeeping.

At nightfall I walked through a silent no man's land into
Turkey. The heavily armed soldiers on both sides of the
border reflected the tension between the two countries.

CHAPTER NINE

TURKEY

THE PUBLIC SCRIBES in Istanbul line the sidewalks outside the Yeni Mosque following their age-old profession. But today they use typewriters. The *muezzins* call the Faithful to prayer as they have done for thirteen centuries, their voices now amplified by loud-speakers. Porters still work as human pack animals, walking bent forward balancing their loads on padded saddles—carrying electric motors and automobile parts on their backs.

This contrast between old and new, the clash of Western ideas with Eastern tradition, characterizes present-day Turkey. Under the leadership of Kemal Ataturk the Turks tore themselves out of the Middle Ages and jumped boldly into the twentieth century. Few backward nations have had the good fortune to produce such a remarkable man. Ataturk may have been an atheistic drunkard in his personal life, but he had only one ambition—to modernize Turkey.

He inspired his countrymen so well that their desire for progress has created serious problems. The present government is involved so deeply in long-range development projects—construction of roads and railroads, dams for power and irrigation, new industries—that the nation faces bankruptcy. The Turks are simply moving too fast. Improved communications, food processing plants and land reclamation will benefit even the primitive, debt-ridden peasants whose lives so far have been little changed by the reforms. The feudal landlords who own most of the land and pay no taxes are a major obstacle to progress. But their iron grip is being loosened as Turkey plans for a better future.

I came to Istanbul in a newspaper delivery truck whose driver seemed to be suffering from a case of chronic hiccups. We passed through a string of dusty villages, each with its mosque crowned by a slender minaret, and entered the city through a gate in the Byzantine walls. At the *Yeni Sabah* newspaper office I was interviewed and photographed for a front-page story and treated like a conquering hero. A quirk of Turkish hospitality makes the visitor feel that he is a celebrity.

Istanbul is spread over the hills on both sides of the Bosporus, the only city astride two continents. Split by the fabled Golden Horn, its skyline dominated by domes and minarets, Istanbul is truly exotic, a fitting gateway to Asia. The blend of hills and water reminded me nostalgically of San Francisco.

I stayed at the Y.M.C.A., which may not compare in grandeur with the plush glass-and-chrome Istanbul Hilton but has the most convenient location in town. Across the street stands St. Sophia, the architectural masterpiece of early Christianity, with its profusion of sculptured marble columns encircling a massive unsupported dome. Facing St. Sophia is the Mosque of Sultan Ahmet, called the Blue Mosque because of its colored tiles. I took off my shoes, walked on the thick carpets and watched men saying their prayers. They stood with heads bowed, speaking in hushed tones, knelt for a moment, then bent forward touching their foreheads to the floor. This procedure was repeated several times. Small boys, restless as small boys always are, dutifully recited their lessons from the Koran. One man sat by himself in a corner, rocking back and forth as he sang a high-pitched chant.

The Ottoman Sultans ruled for four hundred years from Seraglio Palace overlooking the Bosporus. This meandering collection of buildings has been transformed into a museum containing everything from Turkish weapons to Chinese porcelain and Swiss clocks. A young Armenian with the improbable name of Sam Bradley guided me through the labyrinth of the Grand Bazaar. Masses of bartering, haggling humanity jammed the covered passageways and peddlers piled their wares in the middle of the streets, adding to the congestion.

"This bazaar was destroyed by fire a year ago," said Sam. "But within a few weeks everyone was back in business."

I wondered whether the Turks had fire sales and if so, how they could possibly improve on the frenzied everyday activity.

Suleiman Mosque, largest in Istanbul and perfectly proportioned, was built by Suleiman the Magnificent at the height of the Ottoman Empire. Seen from Galata Bridge its rising tiers of domes and columns seem poised on the very edge of the Golden Horn. In silhouette against a darkening sky Suleiman Mosque is an unforgettable sight, a gem of Islamic splendor.

I took a ferryboat up the Bosporus to the fishing village of Buyukdere at the mouth of the Black Sea. The Turks claim that this strait separating Europe and Asia is the most beautiful spot on earth. There are palaces on both shores, brightly painted hillside towns and the towers of Rumelihisar fortress, constructed by Mehmet the Conqueror before he captured Constantinople in 1453 and ended a thousand years of the Byzantine Empire.

Istanbul harbor bustled with wooden barges and lighters, sailing craft, ocean-going freighters and ferries belching clouds of smoke from their tall stacks. Fishermen sold their catch from rowboats direct to dockside customers. With a student who insisted on accompanying me to show me the way, I crossed the Bosporus and set foot in Asia. We hopped a freight train to Kartal and drank coffee in an outdoor café while three hunters stood in the street firing their rifles at low-flying birds. They missed every shot but seemed to be having fun. I took another ferry across the Sea of Marmara and continued on to Bursa in a truck. The next morning I discovered that the driver had paid for my hotel room. This kind of gesture happened frequently in Turkey. Since I had bought Turkish lire in Switzerland (8 to a dollar compared to the official rate of 2.8 to a dollar), traveling became ridiculously cheap.

In Bursa a young man from the government tourist department locked up his office so he could show me the sights personally. For the first time I rated the exclusive services of the tourist bureau. Bursa was the early Ottoman capital of Turkey and contains mosques and tombs of numerous sultans. Most outstanding is the richly carved Green Mosque and its companion Green Mausoleum, the latter adorned with brilliant tiles colored by a lost process and never duplicated. The interior of the Great Mosque has superb carpets covering the floor, Arabic inscriptions on the pillars, a huge circular frame of lamps suspended from the ceiling and a fountain in the center where worshipers wash their hands and feet before praying.

Turkish truckers carry on top of their vehicles passengers who pay for their transportation as they would on a bus. But they never asked me for money. The inhabitants of Sindirgi, a small mountain town, seemed overjoyed at having a foreign visitor. I was taken to meet all the local dignitaries, enjoyed a modest feast and drank innumerable cups of strong black coffee. The people were as excited as children finding Santa Claus and competed with each other to welcome me. At the 18¢ hotel I received more personal attention than I would have rated at the Waldorf. My friends arranged for a free bus ride to Izmir and turned out early in the morning to wave good-by.

Izmir is the ancient Greek city of Smyrna, birthplace of Homer, rebuilt in its present location by Alexander the Great. Outlet for the richest cotton and fruit-growing valley in Anatolia, Izmir lies between a wall of blue mountains and a deep bay of the Aegean Sea. From the ramparts of Kadifekale Castle, a fortress constructed by one of Alexander's generals, I gazed at the city and wondered how different it would have looked to a Macedonian soldier. I met high school boys eager to contact American pen pals and a newspaperman who took my picture, which later appeared in papers throughout Turkey.

The U. S. Navy headquarters provided a glimpse of Little America overseas. I ate cheeseburgers, drank root beer and argued with sailors griping about the Turks.

"These *gooks* sure are funny," drawled a Kentucky hillbilly. "You can't do nothing with them without first having a cup of tea."

"Maybe they're just trying to be friendly," I suggested.

"Hell, no. They're after our money."

"They couldn't be after my money. They won't let me spend any of it."

"Well, I don't trust 'em anyway. You can have the *gooks* and their whole damn country."

"Don't you like Istanbul?" I asked.

"Never been there. I ain't been out of Izmir in nine months. There's plenty of women and whisky right here."

What an ambassador of good will this one is! I thought to myself, picturing him back in Dogpatch telling the folks all about the miserable Turks.

When a pompous lieutenant began quoting regulations on civilians' sleeping at naval installations, one of the sailors offered the seat of his car as a bed.

The ruined city of Ephesus, today inhabited by an occasional shepherd, was in its prime a leading cultural center of the ancient world. I explored the remains with a chubby law professor from Ankara. He wore knickers and a floppy cap and beamed at my interest in Turkish history.

"You see that hole," he said pointing to a gaping pit. "The temple of the goddess Diana, one of the Seven Wonders of the World, stood there. A group of English archaeologists searched unsuccessfully for some trace of the temple. So we call it the English Hole."

As we clambered over walls and peered into tunnels he told me, "It is a curious thing that Turkey, a country which is 98 per cent Moslem, has more remnants of the earliest Christian Church than anywhere else. Here in Ephesus St. Paul preached, St. John wrote his Gospel and one of the first church councils was held in the fifth century. Up in the hills there is a tomb where some say the Virgin Mary is buried. I am very interested in the history of your religion."

An oddly assorted pair of road foremen, one a Yugoslav refugee, the other a burly Ethiopian, gave me a lift to Denizli. The highway (I use the term loosely) was under construction and in terrible condition. At one point we waited while workmen blasted clear a path for our truck. Upon arrival we joined other foremen in an impromtu three-hour feast at the best restaurant.

Denizli is a dusty provincial town of horse-drawn carriages, women carrying their babies piggyback and men in tight leggings and cloth caps. Loungers sit on benches outside the cafés drinking tea and puffing water pipes. These hubbly-bubblies are passed from man to man like an Indian peace pipe and the smoke is cooler than that of any filter cigarette. The Turks, like their Greek and Arab neighbors, play with strings of prayer beads while they talk or meditate.

I traveled by tractor to a remote village where peasants were collecting their sugar beets to be hauled away for processing. There was no sign of life on the road so I joined the villagers who were placidly sitting around doing nothing. They fed me an unappetizing but edible meal—thin sheets of rubbery bread, goat cheese, mush, a thick dark liquid like molasses and raw onions. Then we went to the café where the entire male population turned out to look at me. I don't believe a traveler had ever stopped in Karahuyuk before. I felt like a monkey at the zoo and kept thinking I should perform a song and dance to warrant their enraptured attention. They produced one young man who spoke perhaps ten words of English and, mostly in sign language, I told my story. My explanation degenerated into a game of charades with this poor befuddled fellow trying to understand and translate what I was acting. When I showed signs of exhaustion they took me to a house where I bedded down on a straw mat. About midnight my friends announced that a truck loaded with sugar beets was going to Burdur. I climbed aboard sleepily, figuring that another vehicle might not appear for a week.

The Taurus Mountains form a jagged shield north and west of Antalya, giving this pretty coastal town a warm, semitropical climate. Clusters of buildings hung above the round, miniature harbor and barges scuttled back and forth unloading cargo from two freighters anchored in deep water. A flowery park on the edge of the sea and a virtually intact Roman lighthouse added to the charm of Antalya. I spent the day with three forestry students who refused to let me pay for anything. This Turkish generosity can become most embarrassing.

I followed the coast to Manavgat and turned north into the mountains. The road was deserted and at nightfall even the usual villages had disappeared. I walked on through the silent forest, looking for some sign of life, feeling really alone for the first time in ten months of traveling. I had eaten nothing since morning and this further depressed me. After resigning myself to spending a hungry night in the woods, I stumbled upon a road gang's cabin. The foreman, a cheerful fellow with a handsome handlebar mustache, gave me bread and olives and a wooden pallet by the fire. Rustic but deeply appreciated.

Early in the morning my friends hailed a lawyer in a jeep station wagon who drove until evening to reach Konya. We passed camel caravans, each animal sporting the same disdainful, complacent, comical expression. Little girls spun wool as they tended flocks of sheep, and women carried loads of brush on their backs. Peasants worked the fields with crude Biblical plows. The mountain Turks are enthusiastic fighters, hunters and horsemen, but they don't seem to care for farming; they let their women handle most of the drudgery.

Konya was the Roman city of Iconium, later capital of the Seljuk Empire and headquarters for the whirling dervishes. The Seljuk Turks were the forerunners of the Ottomans. They built mosques, gates and schools which displayed their stone-cutting artistry. I took a bus across the flat, bleached, bone-dry plains to Karapinar. Although Turkey has outlawed the veil, peasant women in this desert town wrapped their shawls around their faces, effectively covering themselves.

While waiting for a lift I munched raw beets, fresh from the ground, with a group of farmers. I brushed off the coating of dirt, as they did, and mused philosophically about the adaptability of the human stomach.

One flat tire later I arrived in Ulukisla and met two Germans bicycling to Australia for the Olympic Games. We were entertained at a party by the violin-playing village mayor and his cronies. I rode through the Cilician Gates with a truckload of laborers and the local idiot, a deranged wretch who shouted and sang and mumbled to himself. The driver pointed out an inscription cut into the rock by Alexander's soldiers. The Cilician Gates have been the north-south invasion route since time immemorial, the only gap in the Taurus Mountain chain.

A Greek friend had given me the name of Arnie Roe, an American engineer in Adana. He was one of the designers of the Seyhan Barrage, a massive earth-fill power and irrigation dam. The hot shower and fried chicken dinner at Arnie's house were a welcome change from cold water and *shish kebab*. After a tour of the construction area, I left Adana and caught another free bus ride to Iskenderun. We passed two crumbling Crusader castles, each perched atop a rocky spire dominating the surrounding countryside. On the narrow Cilician Plain between the mountains and the sea Alexander won his greatest victory, outmaneuvering and routing the Persian hordes of Darius.

I looked around the palm-fringed seaport of Iskenderun and proceeded to Antioch. Built by Macedonians, capital of ancient Syria, leading Roman city, conquered and reconquered by Byzantines and Arabs, Crusader stronghold for nearly two-hundred years, held by Egyptian Mamelukes and finally Ottoman Turks, Antioch on Orontes has mirrored the history of the Middle East. From Antioch the Apostles spread Christianity throughout the Roman world and here the term *Christian* was first used. The grotto of St. Peter, a cave in the hills, is supposed to be the earliest Christian church.

At the hotel in Antioch I encountered the most unusual traveler I have ever known. He was a one-legged veteran of Rommel's Afrika Corps driving a specially built motorcycle to Australia. When people speak admiringly of my trip I remember this German, a really determined adventurer.

CHAPTER TEN

THE
ARAB WORLD:
SYRIA
AND LEBANON

"I OWN THAT village," the pudgy Turk announced, waving a well-manicured hand at a cluster of mud and stone huts.

"Do you mean the whole village?" I asked in amazement.

"Everything. The land, the houses—and six other villages in Turkey and Syria. My income is two thirds of the crops that my tenants raise."

No wonder these peasants look so poor, I thought to myself.

This fellow who had picked me up near the Syrian border was the twenty-third descendent of Celaledin, the fourteenth-century mystic poet, philosopher and founder of the whirling dervishes. He was neither poet nor philosopher but a wealthy landlord in sunglasses, silk suit and '55 Ford.

The Arab World I was entering is a complex, baffling, paradoxical, intriguing group of lands and peoples. Torn by jealousy, conflicting interests and ambitions, the Arabic nations are united in language, religion and, above all, hatred and fear of Israel. There are many types of Arabs but certain traits are fairly common among them all. The Arabs are as hospitable as any people on earth, generous to the point of acute embarrassment for their guests. They have an intense curiosity, a casual attitude which exasperates many foreigners, strong ties of loyalty to the family, a lack of political realism, fierce national and individual pride and a deep class consciousness which obstructs progress. Their unlimited willingness to be helpful is a great asset to the hitchhiker. Arab cruelty to animals is difficult to understand when so much of their livelihood depends on these animals. The often-heard phrase *"In ch' Allah"* ("God willing") expresses their fatalistic outlook toward life. The Arab woman has few rights and especially in the villages seems to lead a wretched, hopeless existence. Among the tribes a man still buys his wife as he would a good work animal.

Aleppo is the metropolis of northern Syria, larger than Damascus, purely Arabic in mood and character. The typical male clothing consists of a long loose robe and a white kaffiyeh, the flowing headcloth held in place with twin black rings. A hadji who has made the pilgrimage to Mecca is distinguished by a green band around his fez. The prosperous Syrian wears a luxurious camel's-hair robe over his business suit. Tattooed tribal women brighten their black

· 107

gowns with silver jewelry, sequins and gold embroidery.

Aleppo's landmark is the Citadel, a hilltop stronghold dominating the city. The present fortress, built by the Crusaders, stands on a spot which has been a strategic outpost since the days of the Hittites, 1,000 years before Christ. The walls of the main gate are honeycombed with ingeniously designed passages from which the defenders could direct a cross fire at the enemy.

Ironically, in Aleppo I saw a film called *King Richard and the Crusaders*. Around me sat the real-life characters who were being portrayed so ineptly on the screen. Hollywood's version of Syria was utterly ridiculous, yet the audience thoroughly enjoyed it.

I traveled south past egg-shaped mud-brick houses of the "beehive" villages, through a wind-swept land of treeless plains, red soil and torrential rains. I stopped briefly in Hama to see the *noriahs*—giant wooden water wheels which creak and groan as if they suffer from acute indigestion. At the dumpy little hotel in Homs my roommate took off most of his clothes but slept in his kaffiyeh.

After an hour's delay at the border while Syrian customs searched for contraband I crossed into Lebanon and followed the coast to Beirut. The narrow belt between the mountains and the Mediterranean is green and tropical with orange and banana groves, clean stone villages, a well-paved road and the first Christian churches I had seen since Greece.

Beirut is modern and cosmopolitan and its terrible traffic congestion compares favorably with any European city. Policemen's caps, Lebanese coins and flags are all decorated with cedar emblems but the only live cedar tree I saw was planted at the American Embassy. A few country women still dress in colorful old-fashioned national costume but most of the people could pass for New Yorkers. The campus of the excellent American University resembles a California college. Beirut is more prosperous, Westernized and to me less interesting than other Middle Eastern cities.

Bill Fox, the cousin of a friend in San Francisco, was one of the few Foreign Service men I stayed with while traveling. My usual contacts with Embassy personnel were limited to calling for my mail. An easygoing, intelligent and likable fellow, Bill seemed the right type to represent America effectively overseas. I arrived in Beirut the day before Thanksgiving and was invited to a marvelous turkey dinner prepared by three girls from the Embassy. I lost my head at this rare treat and ate myself into a stupor. Bill and I went to see *Blackboard Jungle*, a very good film but certainly misleading to a Lebanese audience.

"What a picture of life in America," Bill commented. "The Commies will have a field day with that one."

The small community of Byblos north of Beirut has been an archaeologists' paradise. Its successive layers of civilization date back to prehistoric times, starting with the remains of a neolithic village. Three thousand years before Christ Byblos was a leading seaport of the Phoenicians and their miniature sheltered harbor can still be seen. Then came Egyptians, Assyrians, Babylonians, Romans and Arabs, each leaving traces of their occupation. The latest and best preserved monuments are a Crusader fortress and a thirteenth-century French church.

I crossed the 10,000 foot Lebanon Range in a U. S. Embassy truck, visited the impressive Roman ruins of Baalbeck with two pretty Pan American stewardesses and was driven to Damascus by a Belgian U.N. representative. That night I slept in a hotel with the grandiose name of Flower of the Arabian Orient. Actually somewhat less than flowery, it was located in the heart of the produce market.

Damascus is my favorite Arab city, a combination of the very old and the very new. Modern avenues are flanked by the most up-to-date Arabic architecture. The teeming Street Called Straight which cuts through the old town is much the same today as when it was mentioned in the Bible. The River Barada flows out of the mountains, splits into seven streams forming an oasis and then disappears into the desert. Damascus has existed as a green island in the wilderness for 6,000 years.

I met so many Syrian students eager to show me their city that I felt the need of a social secretary to keep my appointments straight. After spending a couple of days trying to divide my time between different friends, I began introducing the Syrians to each other and we all went out together. Three brothers, rhythmically named Ghassan, Bassan and Adnan Attar, and two other high school boys, Ayham Omary and Farouk Moufti, were especially nice to me.

The first thing they did was to move me out of the Flower of the Arabian Orient and into Damascus College where I bunked in a classroom. Then we visited the Omayad Mosque with its vast courtyard, handsome rugs and stained glass, pigeons flying inside and a fancy mausoleum, supposedly the resting place of John the Baptist's head; the tomb of Saladin, the military genius who fought the Crusaders; St. Paul's Window where Paul was lowered over the wall in a basket to escape the Roman soldiers; the Syrian Parliament adorned with reproductions of ancient Arabic mosaics and wood carvings; Hamidiye Bazaar where woodworkers use both feet and hands in operating their crude drills and lathes. They took me to the public baths in which bathers scrub and shave themselves, rub their skins with sticks of smooth wood, then sit and socialize in the steam. The baths are for discussion and relaxation, not just cleanliness. Each room is progressively warmer and the hot water runs in channels along the floor.

A city as ancient as Damascus was an appropriate place for celebrating my twenty-sixth birthday. I bought myself an Arab Legion kaffiyeh and had lunch with the three Attar brothers. They introduced me to their mother, which was quite a surprise. In most Syrian homes the only women a guest sees are servants or very small children. The men do all the entertaining. On the streets virtually every woman has a black veil completely covering her face. The pretty girls usually manage to wear veils of thin practically transparent material. A heavy mask means that she isn't worth looking at anyway. It is strange to see a girl, well-dressed in European suit, hat and high heels, with her face hidden.

Four of my friends and I rented bicycles for a thirty-five-kilometer ride to Sednaya. We pedaled through a canyon of golden trees and terraced fields, mostly uphill and hard work for an out-of-practice cyclist like me. Coming back was simple, coasting all the way. Sednaya's claim to fame is a sixth-century fortresslike convent inhabited by nuns of the Syriac Christian Church. It reminded me of a female Mount Athos. The old lady in charge was very interested in my trip and blessed me repeatedly.

Conversations with my Syrian friends inevitably turned to the burning issue of Israel.

"The United States and Great Britain are responsible for all our troubles with Israel," said Ayham bitterly. "The British betrayed the Arabs by letting the Jews return to Palestine after World War I. Your government was the first to recognize Israel in the United Nations and since then American military aid and money have kept the country alive. Why are you willing to lose the friendship of forty million Arabs for the sake of these Zionists?"

"I think that Americans sympathize with Israel because they feel that the Jews who survived Nazi persecution in Europe deserve a place to live. Israel is a refuge for them."

"But they have created this refuge in an Arab country," spoke up Bassan. "Is it right to build a nation on stolen property?"

"Many Jewish people consider Palestine their homeland for religious and historical reasons," I said.

"But this is what you Americans don't understand," replied Ayham. "The Jews conquered Palestine from other tribes thousands of years ago. But after the Romans destroyed Jerusalem, Arabs lived in Palestine for 1,700 years. Until the United Nations interfered, practically all of the land was owned by Arabs. It is our country, not theirs."

"Nine hundred thousand Arabs were driven out of Palestine to make room for a million Jews," said Bassan. "Is this justice? These people have lived in miserable refugee camps since 1948. They think only of revenge and returning to their homes."

"The Jews plan to expand from the Nile to the Euphrates," added Farouk. "We Arabs must unite to destroy them or they will destroy us."

I could not agree with this harsh indictment of Israel but understood the reasons why the Arabs felt this way.

My friends spoke repeatedly of their dreams for Syria's future. "We have been a free country for less than ten years," said Ghassan. "Traditions which have lasted a thousand years die slowly, but they *are* changing. We need time to become a modern nation. But please, Donald, tell the Americans that we are not all nomads living in tents and riding on camels."

CHAPTER ELEVEN

THE
ARAB WORLD:
JORDAN
AND IRAQ

JORDAN, FLOODED with Palestine refugees, is the poorest and most explosive of the Arab States. In a population of less than a million and a half, fully 900,000 are either refugees or residents of Arab-controlled Palestine. The total industry consists of a cement factory, a cigarette factory and a distillery.

After six days in Damascus I had headed south to Deraa, a weather-beaten collection of flat-roofed, orange and black stone houses on the edge of the Jebel Druse country. I crossed into Jordan aboard an oil tanker driven by the chauffeur of the late, assassinated King Abdullah. Recent rains had turned the bare hills soft shades of green. We passed grazing camels, a shepherd boy playing his home-made flute, an Arab Legion police post built like Hollywood's version of a *Beau Geste* fort and the big RAF base at Mafraq.

In the military camp near Zarka I looked up Warrant Officer Danny Kay, an Englishman serving with the Arab Legion. Together we walked through the bazaar filled with Legionnaires in khaki uniforms and red kaffiyehs.

"That bloke is a Camel Corps Bedouin." Danny indicated a hawk-nosed, mustached desert warrior in ankle-length skirt, red sash and tassels, cartridge bandoliers across his shoulders and a jeweled dagger and large black pistol at his belt. "The Arab makes a good soldier if he is trained and given decent equipment," Danny remarked. "The Legion is a first-class outfit."

He went on to speak about John Glubb, the English Commander of the Legion. "The 'Pasha' is a real friend of the Arabs," Danny told me. "He has spent most of his life in the desert and his soldiers idolize him." A few months later the King of Jordan unceremoniously relieved Glubb Pasha of his command and sent him home.

Amman, the capital of Jordan, is the site of ancient Philadelphia. The shell of a Roman amphitheater lies beside the main road. The city was bursting at the seams with its influx of idle embittered refugees. Stanley Kochendorfer, the manager of Air Jordan and a native of Santa Rosa, California, treated me to dinner and a room at the Amman Club. He asked if I would be interested in working for Air Jordan but I said, "No, thanks."

Next day Ahmad Rabah, a motorcycle policeman, stopped a bus and told the driver to take me to Jerusalem free of charge.

"It is my duty to help you," Ahmad explained, "so that you will have happy memories of my country. When you return to Amman, I will be at your service again."

Peasants were plowing vertical fields on the sides of the gorge as we descended into the lowest valley on earth. The River Jordan marks the boundary between Arab Palestine and Trans-Jordan. These two areas form the present Hashemite Kingdom of Jordan. We passed north of the Dead Sea through Jericho and climbed the scorched hills of Judah to Jerusalem. The Arabs hold the Old City with the Christian shrines, the Israelis control most of the modern city, and the dividing line is a deserted no man's land. Heavily armed Legionnaires patrolled the Crusader-built walls, but all was quiet during my visit—except for one incident.

During my first evening in Jerusalem I paused on a corner to study a map which had been given to me by the government tourist office. While searching for a church in which to sleep, I had gotten lost in the labyrinth of alleys and passageways. Across the street stood David's Tower, the former palace of Herod. Unknown to me, this was the Arab Legion headquarters. The sentries took one look at the map, my beard and pack and jumped to the conclusion that I must be a Jewish spy. Waving their rifles and muttering angrily, they hustled me inside the Tower to a small room. In this place where the Wise Men came for information, a sergeant interrogated me politely but skeptically. We made no progress because I could not understand his questions.

"*Salaam,*" I said hopefully, "I am an American, a tourist who is lost."

The sergeant spoke to me in Arabic or Hebrew.

I must have looked convincingly bewildered.

"You are Hebrew spy," he said in halting English.

"No, no. Here is my passport. See—American. American tourist. Look at my map. It is from your own government."

The sergeant remained suspicious. He asked more questions in Arabic.

I tried a different approach. "If the Israelis were going to send a spy, they would use a Yemeni Jew who speaks Arabic and looks like an Arab. Not me. I would be a terrible failure as a spy."

None of the Legionnaires understood. I tried speaking French but their reaction was blank. So we sat in solemn silence until an officer arrived. He glanced at my passport, then said in perfect English, "Please accept my apologies for this unfortunate incident."

I assured him that no harm had been done and commended the vigilance of his men. After smiles and handshakes all around, they produced fruit, cakes and coffee and we had a party.

Finding a church at night in Jerusalem seemed to be risky business, so I went to a hotel. In the morning I located the German Lutherans and the pastor let me stay in their spare room for the next three nights.

No Christian could come to Jerusalem without feeling some emotion. It is true that the city has been commercialized and the holy places have been elaborately adorned and distorted. Just as in Rome, you wonder what has happened to the simplicity of Jesus Christ. But in Jerusalem the vivid association is important, and the insignificant things that men have done afterwards do not matter. When you sit on top of the Mount of Olives looking out over the city, what difference does it make if this is or is not the exact spot where Jesus ascended into heaven? You know that here a man lived and died and by his example changed the world.

The Church of the Holy Sepulcher, erected on the traditional site of Calvary, is a huge gloomy structure, lighted by flickering wax tapers and propped up by a framework of wooden supports. Anyone expecting a noble and majestic church will be sadly disappointed. Built by the Crusaders, it seems in danger of imminent collapse. Outside the city walls is a simple chamber cut into the rock, a quiet spot of flowers and trees. Some people believe this to be the garden of Joseph of Arimathea where Jesus was buried. At the foot of the Mount of Olives lies the Garden of Gethsemane with olive and evergreen trees surrounding an onion-domed Russian Church. The Tomb of the Virgin Mary had been flooded by heavy rains and bearded Orthodox priests, their robes pulled up to their waists, directed Arab workmen cleaning out the mud.

Every Friday afternoon a procession of monks, priests and pilgrims follows the Via Dolorosa from the site of Pilate's Pretorium to the Church of the Holy Sepulcher. There are fourteen stations along this Way of the Cross and the procession stops at each one. The devout kneel to pray while bored onlookers puff water pipes and play dominoes. An Arab flunky armed with a long staff chases away the swarms of curious children.

Jerusalem abounds in religious costumes. There are

bearded Armenian priests in pointed hats, dark-skinned monks of the Ethiopian Coptic Church, Franciscans wearing brown hooded robes and sandals, French nuns with flaring white headdresses, Egyptian Copts in red and blue turbans, black-robed Dominicans in round flat hats, white-robed Jesuit missionaries, Chinese, Indian and Eastern Orthodox clergymen.

The Arabs call Jerusalem *Kuts* (The Holy), for next to Mecca it is the most sacred Moslem city. The blue Dome of the Rock, one of the oldest Islamic shrines, was built in the seventh century on Mount Moriah where the Temple of Solomon stood. From the Rock Mohammed is believed to have ascended into heaven. During centuries of Moslem rule the Jews were allowed to mourn the fate of Israel at the Wailing Wall outside their former Temple.

I rode to Bethlehem with an Arab graduate of Colorado University who said he missed the pretty girls and football games.

Bethlehem was cold and squalid, a rather disappointing town. A big electric star which lights up at night lends a garish touch to the fortress-like Church of the Nativity. The supposed site of the Manger is marked by a silver star and cluttered with lamps and incense burners.

After leaving Jerusalem I spent a day in Jericho. From the Greek monastery perched halfway up the Mount of Temptation I looked over the metallic waters of the Dead Sea, the blue hills of Moab fading into the wilderness, the River Jordan tracing a green life line through the heat-soaked valley and the orange and banana groves encircling Jericho. Water has flowed from Elisha's Fountain since Biblical times. A steady procession of women came from refugee camps to the well, balancing clay jugs or discarded Army jerry cans on their heads. They were not veiled but wore bandannas or shawls like the North African Berbers. Some had strings of gold or silver coins across their foreheads and around their necks. Damascus is usually considered the world's oldest continually inhabited city. But recent excavations indicate that Jericho may be 8,000 years old and the archaeologists are still digging. I went swimming in the Dead Sea, 1,300 feet below sea level. The water is very warm and so salty that you float like a cork.

I stayed overnight with a group of American Mennonite relief workers who were distributing food and clothing to the more than 50,000 refugees in mud hut camps around Jericho.

Carl was a blond Kansas farmer, a conscientious objector doing this work in lieu of military service. I asked him, "Did all these thousands of people fight against the Israelis?"

"No," he said, "most of the refugees are innocent victims. Israel claims that the Arabs who didn't fight were left alone but it just isn't true. Jewish extremists drove them out of their homes in a reign of terror. They said it was a question of survival. Maybe so, but Israel still must be blamed for what they did."

"Will there ever be peace between Arabs and Jews?"

"I don't know," Carl answered slowly, scratching his head. "Both sides will have to back down. If the Arabs will face reality and recognize that Israel is here to stay. If the refugees can be resettled—perhaps in Iraq—and the United States will bring pressure on the Israelis to pay them compensation. *If* the United Nations becomes strong enough so that its decisions can be enforced. Then perhaps there will be peace."

I returned to Amman in a banana truck. At the RAF base the Corporal of the Guard fixed me a mattress on the floor and sent for tea and sandwiches. The airmen on duty were very young, very British and very homesick.

My journey to Petra began on the morning train to Ma'an. This Hejaz railroad carried pilgrims to Mecca until Arab guerrillas tore up the tracks during World War I. The rickety coaches compared favorably with those on Spanish or Yugoslav trains. Just before departure a muezzin came aboard to announce time for prayers. Eyeing me as if he thought I needed to pray, he appealed lustily to the Faithful. No one seemed to respond and we departed in a cloud of smoke and confusion. The southern Jordan desert was as bleak and desolate as anything I had seen since Sahara. I engaged in a sign language conversation with a Bedouin Legionnaire whose wife looked like Elizabeth Taylor's double. Or perhaps it had been some time since I had seen a pretty girl.

After eight monotonous hours we reached Ma'an. The Police Sergeant, a fat fellow in a spiked helmet, welcomed me effusively. He showed me his medals and said wistfully that he would like to marry a nice American girl. We ate tiny roast birds and eggs fried in sheep's fat and I slept in the police station. An ex-Colonel in the Scots Guards and personal friend of Glubb Pasha was going by Arab Legion Land Rover to Wadi Musa. I had arrived at just the right time to accompany the Colonel. Wadi Musa is the Valley of Moses on the route of the exodus from Egypt. Horses were waiting for us at the police fort and we rode into Petra.

I had seen ancient and ruined cities before but Petra was unique. "The rose-red city, half as old as time" is carved from the living rock, its massive temples and tombs blending into the sandstone cliffs. Hidden in the purple mountains, Petra is guarded by towering bastions of rock. The only entrance, a narrow chasm called the Siq, winds for almost a mile between sheer walls. In some places there is barely room for a horse to squeeze through. A couple of men could defend the Siq against an army. We emerged without warning from under the overhanging cliffs and directly in front of us stood the Treasury. I couldn't appreciate the size of this pink colossus until I climbed to a ledge on the opposite wall and gazed down at the tiny figure of the Colonel standing between giant pillars.

The entrances to some of the tombs, eroded by wind and sand, look as if they have been splashed with multi-colored, liquid rock. Most impressive of Petra's monuments is the Deir which seems to dwarf the mountainside from which it was cut. Isolated at the head of a ravine, the Deir probably served as a kind of monastery.

Petra was the capital of the Nabateans, an Arab tribe which flourished at the time of Christ. The Arabian-Syrian caravan route passed through Wadi Musa, and from their impregnable stronghold the Nabateans levied a toll on every loaded camel. With this wealth they built their remarkable city. The Colonel and I explored Petra for two days, after which the Land Rover brought us back to Ma'an.

Before leaving southern Jordan I had the good fortune to

be invited to a Bedouin feast. The occasion was a meeting whose purpose remained a mystery to me. With several local dignitaries I went to the nomads' encampment, a cluster of goat-hair tents outside town. We sat cross-legged on rugs in the sheik's tent which was sparsely furnished with metal chests, a nickel-plated samovar, a large wooden crate and a couple of incongruous pin-up girl pictures. Our host was the perfect desert hawk—lean, dark-skinned, with close-cropped beard, piercing black eyes and the smooth, graceful movements of a panther. The main course of the feast consisted of a whole roast sheep with rice, unleavened bread, fruit and glasses of tea. We ate using only the fingers of our right hands. Rolling the rice into balls and popping them into my mouth was the hardest trick to learn. The sheik offered me a fork but I preferred trying it his way, and managed quite well without making too much of a mess.

I joined a truck convoy heading north from the Gulf of Aqaba to Amman. There was no road; we simply followed a rutted track across the desert. That evening we stopped at a mud brick general store, restaurant, hotel and social club in the wilderness. The drivers congregated here to eat, play cards and shave. Most of the boys curled up on the floor but being a guest, I was given one of the two beds. At 5:00 A.M. our convoy rolled out and soon a heavy rainstorm began. This proved to be disastrous, transforming the track into a treacherous morass. We struggled through several mud traps but eventually bogged down completely. Most of a wet and discouraging day was spent trying to extract our truck from the quagmire. Late that afternoon a truck arrived from Amman, and deciding the route looked impassable, turned back. I hated to abandon my friends but they insisted that I should go to Amman while there was a chance. I wonder how and when they managed to get out of the mud.

It had been an exhausting day and I was soaking wet, cold and hungry. The Air Jordan clerk let me dry my clothes and sleep in their warm, cozy office. If Air Jordan treats paying customers as well as they do hitchhikers, their service must be unexcelled.

In the morning I found my friend Ahmad the policeman.

"Where are you going this time?" he asked.

"To Bagdad."

"Ha, that is easy. Come with me."

At the garage of the Iraq Transport Company he introduced me to Gadon Naber.

"This is my friend," said Ahmad, "who brings stone to Bagdad for the King's new palace. He is a very good man."

Gadon *was* a good man, a laughing, carefree companion for the next forty-eight hours. We drove to Mafraq and turned east into the desert. The road to Ramadi in Iraq crosses a 750-kilometer expanse of flat, parched rock and dirt. Surprisingly it is asphalt-paved, courtesy of the British Army. We followed the pipeline of the Iraq Petroleum Company which runs from the Kirkuk oilfields to the Mediterranean. The pumping stations are little islands of modern buildings, storage tanks and green trees in an otherwise uninhabited wilderness. At H4 station a searchlight, sweeping the night sky as a beacon for lost travelers, is visible for almost forty miles. After the blazing crimson sunset the desert grew very cold and I wrapped my kaffiyeh around my head, Bedouin style, for warmth. We passed through the squalid settlement of Rutba whose prison must provide the Iraqi equivalent of exile to Siberia. During this journey we slept twice; once curled up in the truck and again on benches in a rustic teahouse built of sun-baked mud and flattened oil drums.

From Ramadi to Bagdad our route crossed the Tigris-Euphrates Valley. This is the land of the Garden of Eden, the Sumerians and man's earliest civilization. The complex irrigation system which supported twenty million people in ancient times was destroyed during the terrible thirteenth-century Mongol invasion. Iraq has never really recovered from this calamity. Today most of the former granary is wasteland and the population of the entire country barely five million. The government is using oil revenue in an effort to restore the old network of dams and canals.

In the days of Harun al-Rashid, the Caliph of the *Arabian Nights*, Bagdad was a truly fabulous city. Spread along both sides of the muddy Tigris, it has been sacked and rebuilt so many times since then that little of the ancient grandeur remains. Rashid Street, the narrow main thoroughfare with its covered sidewalks and cluttered shops, is as congested as midtown Manhattan. The *souks* of Bagdad are the scene of never-diminishing activity. Most colorfully costumed among the crowds are Kurdish tribesmen in bright red or green pantaloons, short jackets and fat, fringed turbans. Iraqi women wear black cloaks called *abahs* which cover them from head to feet but do not conceal their faces. Traffic police look like old-fashioned firemen in their big bucket helmets.

While wandering along Rashid Street, I met William Willa, a young Assyrian. He took me to the back-alley

Mosul Hotel where I shared a room with him and a diminutive Frenchman named Max. The Assyrians are a Westernized, Christian minority in northern Iraq and western Iran. Extremely pro-British in their sentiments, living apart from the Arabs, they are skilled artisans and office workers. I met a number of Assyrians and every one spoke English. Willie was passionately fond of America and questioned me incessantly, particularly about Hollywood. He was the most avid movie fan I have ever known. Dressed in leather jacket and blue jeans, Willie looked just like a high school boy at home. I told him so and made him radiantly happy. Rooming with a real, live American was apparently a thrilling experience for Willie.

Max, my other roommate, owned a motorcycle, and when he wasn't teaching French we cruised around Bagdad. Only a five-minute drive from the center of the city there is a vast shantytown of mud huts, naked children, wallowing water buffalo and dung cakes drying for fuel. Not on the tourist itinerary, visitors and even foreign residents don't know it exists. Max took me up the Tigris to Kadhimain, a shrine of the Shiah Moslems. The Iraqis are Sunni Moslems but the Iranians are the more orthodox Shiah. Some time ago an Iranian pilgrim to Mecca, seized with a fit of religious ecstasy, was sick on the sacred Kaaba stone. For this blasphemy he was beheaded on the spot. Since this unfortunate incident most Iranians have made their pilgrimages to the shrines of Karbala, Najaf and Kadhimain, all in Iraq. These places are closer to home and less dangerous. The streets around the Kadhimain mosque are crowded with mullahs and pilgrims and the atmosphere is distinctly Persian. The mosque itself has a gold dome, covered with pigeons, golden minarets and exquisitely tiled gateways. Non-Moslems are not allowed inside.

I spent Christmas in Bagdad and went to a couple of parties given by Embassy people. Singing carols, decorating a tree, and the Christmas Eve church service brought memories of home and family. I enjoyed being with other Americans and joined briefly in the holiday festivities. I also received a welcome stack of cards and mail.

The day after Christmas Max and I started out for Basra on the Persian Gulf, supposedly a two-day trip. Four days later we both arrived, although not together, after an unbelievable journey. It had rained Christmas night and the dirt roads were muddy and slippery as ice for a motorcycle. We fell down—first in the mud, later in the sand—a total of nine times, collided with a donkey, ran out of gas, were lost in the desert, and had frequent mechanical difficulties. Max's motorcycle, a small Austrian Puch, had come overland from France and suffered from assorted disabilities. Even in her prime carrying two people through such rough country would have been a strain.

We stopped to see what little remains of Babylon where Nebuchadnezzar's Hanging Gardens are piles of rubble. In Najaf, another Shiah shrine, we were guests at the jail. The police put us into a little room next to the well-populated cells. The prisoners' wives brought them food early in the morning.

We navigated across the desert following the tracks of other vehicles and came to the Euphrates, which flows over a low, flat plain of tall grass, crisscrossed by waterways. Having crossed the river on a flimsy bridge, we bogged down in the muddy oasis of Sukhair. Our poor engine suc-

cumbed from exhaustion and Max spent an hour tinkering
while I looked on helplessly: I know as much about mechanics as an Iraqi camel herder. We stopped for lunch at a
canal village where the people lived in huts of woven reed
mats. The local sheik pried open our can of sardines with
his knife and gave us bread and drinking water.

Diwaniyah is undistinguished except for a ludicrous traffic circle, bordered with flowers and sitting proudly in the
middle of perhaps ten yards of paved street. We bounced
on to Hamza, drank tea with the schoolmaster and admired
more beautifully designed traffic circles. We seemed to be
the only traffic making use of them. Hamza is a typical
Iraqi village set in groves of date palms. The mud-brick
houses are roofed with a framework of palm logs covered
by sticks and a thick layer of mud. The women wear a gold
or jeweled ring piercing one side of the nose.

We spent the night at another police station where an
officer told us cheerfully about travelers dying in the desert. The third day our engine was wheezing pitifully and
the rear frame of the cycle was beginning to break from
the constant jolting. Temporary repairs were made in
Samawa. As Max negotiated a slippery path through shift-
ing sand, a foolish donkey trotted in front of us. We
couldn't stop, careened off his rump and sprawled on the
ground. The donkey didn't bat an eye and we suffered
no damage except to our peace of mind.

That afternoon there was no place to buy gas and we
waited patiently with our empty tank until a jitney bus
came along and gave us half a gallon. Beyond the mounds
marking the ruins of Ur, the great Chaldean city, the country is utterly desolate. It is anybody's guess which of the

meandering desert trails leads to Basra. We followed the railroad tracks and about nine o'clock stumbled onto the tiny station of Jaliba. My legs were so sore from the steady bouncing, I could hardly walk. The stationmaster was sympathetic and provided us with food and soft beds. In the morning we discovered that the cycle frame had broken completely and my weight was pressing on the rear tire. So Max went on alone and I rode the last sixty miles in the caboose of a freight train. The brakeman seemed to have a girl friend at every station and these young ladies gave us hard-boiled eggs and bread.

Basra is the Persian Gulf seaport at the mouth of the Tigris and Euphrates, export harbor for dates and oil, one of the hottest cities on earth, home of Sinbad the Sailor. Jets of burning gas from the oil fields light the sky at night. The Iraqis call Basra the "Venice of the East" but it is an optimistic comparison. There are a few canals but the atmosphere is purely Arabic. Among the various types of Arab sailing craft, most interesting is the dhow. A crude vessel of rough unpainted wood, the dhow has a billowing, lateen-rigged sail and a long curving hull, pointed fore and aft. Its unusual features include a massive wooden rudder, painted symbols on the bow and a mud oven for baking bread in the stern. The Persian Gulf ports are the last refuge of these graceful old ships which once dominated the trade routes to Africa and Asia.

Basra is not a large city but Max and I tried unsuccessfully for three days to locate each other. We had planned to meet at the railway station and I slept there, courtesy of the plump and rumpled Assyrian stationmaster. But when Max came to look for me the station clerks did not understand and told him that I had left.

On New Year's Eve I decided to live riotously. I moved to a small hotel and treated myself to a can of tuna fish, a can of corned beef and a bottle of Iraqi wine. After an elegant dinner I read the latest copy of *Time* magazine until midnight. At exactly twelve o'clock I rushed out into the deserted streets, shouting "Happy New Year." The citizens of Basra slumbered peacefully, ignoring this outburst, so I went to bed.

The following evening when I returned to the railroad station, there was Max. We had both decided to take the night train back to Bagdad. Some of our fellow passengers were quite ingenious. They brought blankets and climbed up onto the baggage racks to sleep. The women curled up under the seats. In the morning we unloaded the rejuvenated cycle and drove triumphantly back to the Mosul Hotel.

After a farewell party with Max and Willie, I set out for Iran. An English construction foreman, a truckload of homeward-bound pilgrims and a splendidly dressed Kurdish sheik in a jeep carried me to Khanaqin. At the customs post I was informed that an exit visa was necessary to leave Iraq. One of the inspectors, a helpful fellow named Faik, arranged this with a minimum of red tape and then took me home for dinner. Faik was a Kurd, as are most of the people in Khanaqin. The Kurdish tribes inhabit southeastern Turkey and the mountainous frontier of Iraq and Iran. The majority are nomads moving with their flocks, superb horsemen, born fighters, proud and independent like the Bedouin.

CHAPTER TWELVE

IRAN

"HAVE SOME MORE chicken," offered the sergeant, puffing on his cigar. "You look pretty hungry."

"Thanks, I am. And I never knew how good G. I. chow could taste."

I ate and the sergeant talked.

"It's a funny thing about these Kurdish tribesmen," he said. "Every once in a while they get restless and raid a village or put up a roadblock and rob a few trucks. Then the Iranian gendarmes chase them all over the hills. But the Kurds are clever and the gendarmes usually lose about half their men and all their weapons. The Kurds would make damn fine soldiers," he added laughing, "but the government is afraid to give them more guns than they already have."

A second G.I. spoke up. "When we go out hunting our ammo is rationed and we're responsible for every round. If we don't bring back the brass the Kurds find it and reload the empty shells."

"The Kurdish tribes in Iraq seem peaceful enough," I said.

"Well, maybe they don't go on the warpath over there."

I had traveled by truck from the desert foothills across the Zagros Mountain barrier onto the cold Iranian plateau. The change in climate was like flying from Florida to New York in January. Snow was falling in Kermanshah where I discovered to my surprise a dozen American soldiers living in a comfortable apartment house. They were part of a military mission training the Iranian Army.

After a guided tour of Kermanshah, I was put aboard a bus for Hamadan. Persian buses are painted in brilliantly clashing colors and are ponderously overloaded. Every passenger brings along bulky sacks and bundles which are piled on the roof and stuffed into the aisle. Climbing in and out of the vehicle requires patience and agility. The travelers pass the time by singing greetings to Mohammed. One man starts the chant and everyone joins in the chorus. The first line of this refrain sounds as if they cry, "Hello, Mohammed." Like a community sing, it goes on and on.

The landscape is split into arid plateaus by mountain ranges bare of vegetation. Only along the streams and around the villages are there trees and brush. We stopped at Kangavar while the driver bargained for a chicken and then chased his escaped purchase all over the fields. Crossing a high pass, we barely managed to churn through the deep snow.

Hamadan is the oldest city in Iran but no trace of its antiquity remains except a badly mauled stone lion. The bazaar, a maze of covered alleys lined with stalls, is typically Persian. There are carpet weavers at work on their wooden looms, coppersmiths pounding trays and bowls, donkeys loaded with sheepskins and coils of freshly dyed yarn hanging from the roofs to dry. Men squat around charcoal braziers drinking tea and smoking fat long-stem wooden pipes. Women wear cloaks called chadars, blue in color to ward off the evil eye. A large statue of the Shah on horseback stands in the center of town.

I stayed at the Presbyterian hospital with a family of medical missionaries. Dr. Rice told me about the founder of present-day Iran.

"Old Shah Reza, the father of the present Shah, was an illiterate army sergeant when he took over from the Sultan. They say he couldn't even write his own name. But he had the same ambition to modernize his country that Ataturk had. He built Teheran from a provincial town into a westernized capital. He outlawed the veil and his soldiers used to tear the veils off women in the streets. Shah Reza had a tougher job than Ataturk because Iran was, and still is, more backward than Turkey."

En route to Teheran I was picked up by a convoy of Assyrians. Each driver wanted to talk with me so I rode alternately in three trucks and felt quite important. We had lunch and, as usual, I could pay for nothing. Along the road they pointed out abandoned caravan shelters, giant mud kilns for baking bricks or pottery and *ganats*, underground canals which bring irrigation water from the mountains. Every Iranian property owner builds a high mud wall around his house and garden. I wondered whether this was for protection or from an acute desire for privacy.

In the cafés where we halted frequently for tea there were no chairs or tables, just low platforms covered with Persian rugs. Here the customers sat cross-legged or could lie down for a little nap. Potbellied iron stoves and earthenware jugs completed the furnishings.

I went to the NCO Club in Teheran and was again the guest of the United States Army. Sergeants Novak, Moran and Green invited me to their elegant suburban house in the foothills.

"Make yourself at home," they said—and I did. Staying with them was a refreshing interlude of American food, long-playing records, iced drinks and central heating. I also visited Mr. Madjd, an engineer with the Point Four program. We spent an evening around the *korsi*, a practical device for Iranian homes in the winter. The *korsi* is a charcoal heater placed under a low table which is covered with quilts. Propped up on pillows, you are bundled snug and warm while eating. It is so comfortable the family often sleeps at the *korsi*.

Mr. Madjd took me to an American movie. Instead of adding translation titles as the film proceeds, the Persians interrupt each scene to flash written dialogue on the screen. Literate members of the audience then read loudly to their less fortunate companions. This method is distracting, to say the least, particularly in a musical.

The Shah has several palaces set among gardens and guarded by stern soldiers with bayoneted rifles. One plush building was pointed out as being exclusively for his bedrooms. The carriage horses of Teheran are decked out in bells, tassels and beaded fringed harnesses. Teheran is the largest city in the world without an underground water system. Talk of building one has gone on for years. As in other Iranian towns, the water flows in open ditches along the sides of the streets. These *jubes* furnish everyone with a supply for drinking, washing, cooking and watering the animals. Most of the citizens seem to survive this dubious arrangement. The United States Embassy helpfully boils water for American residents.

I rode in a Point Four station wagon to Resht on the Caspian Sea coast. The road winds across the Elburz Mountains, the legendary stronghold of the "Old Man of the Mountains" and his professional killers, the "Assassins." In this country of rocky buttresses and thick forests the peasants earn their living cutting firewood and making charcoal. Resht is more Balkan than Iranian in appearance with its blue and yellow wooden buildings, hanging balconies and iron grillwork, aging brick and tile. The streets in the old quarter are so narrow that even a jeep has trouble rounding the corners.

Pahlevi is the Caspian seaport for trade with Russia. A Soviet steamer was loading caviar, which the Russians buy in large quantities and export as their own. Along the shore fishermen in yellow slickers spread their nets and haul their catch onto the beach. I was taken on a tour of the caviar factory where the roe is prepared and packed in barrels, and sturgeon and elephant fish are frozen for shipment.

I traveled along the coast with a disillusioned young teacher.

"I feel very sad for my country," he said mournfully. "Everywhere there is bribery and corruption. Nothing can be done without paying baksheesh. Students who fail their examinations bribe their teachers to pass them. Even the postman must be paid baksheesh to deliver the mail."

"That is terrible," I said. "Can't people like you do something to change this?"

"What can we do? The government is run by wealthy landowners. They are very greedy, the most corrupt of all. An honest man has no chance in the government. The Shah favors reforms but he is powerless."

The Caspian plain lies a hundred feet below sea level, isolated from the interior by the Elburz Mountains which rise to an elevation of 18,500 feet. It is an area of heavy rainfall, rice paddies, orange groves and tea gardens. The houses look distinctly Oriental with their tall, pointed thatched roofs. This semitropical coast differs completely from the rest of Iran.

From Shahsawar I began a memorable fourteen-hour journey back to Teheran. Intermittent rain turned to snow as our bus climbed into the mountains. Outside a tunnel at the top of the pass a snowslide blocked the road. We waited for two frozen hours while workmen shoveled a path. I learned later that our bus was among the last vehicles through the tunnel before it closed for the rest of the winter. After a painfully slow descent to within five kilometers of a town, the driver announced cheerfully that we were out of gas. This is ridiculous, I thought; buses don't run out of gas. But there we sat for another hour while I brooded about what a fathead our driver was. Cold and disgusted, I marveled at the unconcern of the Iranian passengers. Their patience set a good example for me. We finally borrowed some gas from a truck and limped into Teheran.

Another side trip took me south to Isfahan. I stopped in Qum, a Moslem religious center swarming with robed and turbaned mullahs. This strictly orthodox town has no movie theater and I was told even radios are not allowed. The golden-domed mosque is absolutely off limits to infidels. Two police lieutenants arranged for me to sleep in the manager's room at the hotel. One spoke English, the other's French was worse than mine. His linguistic efforts, of which he was quite proud, baffled me completely. For all that I understood, he could have been speaking Outer Mongolian.

At 6:30 A.M. my friends arrived with a special treat for breakfast. This Iranian delicacy proved to be boiled head, feet and entrails of a sheep. Few sights could be more of a shock to a person waking up. I would have preferred coffee and doughnuts, especially at this early hour, but tried hard to be gracious. I ate most of it and silently gave thanks for a strong stomach. Fortunately I have forgotten how this meal tasted.

The lieutenants spoke to bus company officials and I was given a free ride to Isfahan. The trip was slow because of the usual terrible roads and lengthy stops. Fortified villages were enclosed by high mud walls with round towers at each corner and low wooden gates. Bedraggled peasants with rolls of cloth bound around their legs looked like pictures of serfs in medieval Europe. Surrounding each village and scattered along the road were crumbling walls and skeletons of deserted buildings. There seemed to be more ruins than places currently inhabited.

Isfahan has retained the old Persian atmosphere better than other cities. During the golden days of Shah Abbas in the seventeenth century it was a cultural and trade center of the Middle East. The great square, originally a parade ground and polo field, is encircled by a double arcade lined with shops. At one end is the mighty Imperial Mosque, opposite are the bazaar entrances. On one side stands the only remnant of Shah Abbas' palace, a gateway in a state of near collapse. The rectangular courtyard of the Juma Masjid (Friday Mosque) once could accommodate the entire male population of Isfahan. Four open vaults lead into the prayer sanctuaries. The enameled tilework of these vaults represents the finest Persian artistry. Flower patterns are interwoven with intricate designs and inscriptions from the Koran. Shades of blue, green, yellow and brown predominate.

The pungent smells of the bazaar are often rather startling to an antiseptic Western nose. But to me the fascination of an Eastern market is derived from a blend of sight, sound and smell. The odors may not be charming but they add to the charm of the scene. Camel caravans bring feed and firewood from the countryside. Peddlers hawk their wares from baskets and pushcarts and carry piles of used clothing balanced on their heads. Deep in the maze of the bazaar is a grain mill where blindfolded camels walk in circles supplying power for the grinding stones. Pajamas worn during the daytime are high fashion in Isfahan.

Tom Scotes, the American Vice Consul with whom I stayed, was a year younger than I. Genuinely interested in the Iranians, learning their language and studying their culture, Tom was an energetic and able young diplomat. The Foreign Service needs more men like him.

I returned to Teheran courtesy of four Iranian Army generals. Their station wagon was filled with baggage, so instead of giving me a ride, they presented me with a bus ticket. In Qum we were delayed by the inevitable difficulties. The passengers, bus company agents and a number of bystanders became involved in a violent argument with two peasants who tried to bring several large sacks aboard without paying extra fare. Much shouting and arm-waving later, the police settled the dispute by arresting the troublemakers. Then our driver suddenly became ill and we waited until his assistant took charge for the rest of the trip. Toward nightfall a large gray wolf loped nonchalantly across the road.

After a farewell party with my U. S. Army friends, I left Teheran in a slow truck. The driver, a taciturn unshaven fellow, stopped at a teahouse for evening prayers and removed his pants before praying. Next day my fellow bus passengers were heavily armed gendarmes escorting a band of chained prisoners. These convicts acted as carefree and unconcerned as if they were bound for a Sunday school picnic. It was a strange attitude but admirable under the circumstances.

As we approached Meshed the clothing of the people began to show Afghan influences. They wore loose, knee-length white shirts. Turbans replaced the felt skullcaps seen throughout the rest of Iran. Peasants cultivating their landlords' fields used the simplest type of plow imaginable, a long pole attached at one end to a yoke and at the other end to a pointed piece of wood for scraping shallow furrows in the ground. Laborers were making a halfhearted effort to repair the road by shoveling dirt into the gaping potholes.

Meshed is the principal city of eastern Iran, a holy shrine for Shiah Moslems, some twenty-five miles from the Russian border. This was as close to the U.S.S.R. as any place I visited. The American Consul in Meshed invited me to lunch and supplied a little welcome information about Afghanistan. He was the first person I found who knew anything definite about this mysterious land.

A tough old American sergeant training Iranian cavalry drove me to Turbat-i-Shaikh Jam, a village near the Afghan frontier. With this good luck I expected to reach Herat the following day, but five days passed before I arrived. During that time not a single vehicle crossed the border. I began to appreciate the extent of Afghanistan's isolation.

The sights of Turbat-i-Shaikh Jam are extremely limited. Three men butchering a cow on the main street provided the sole activity. One shopkeeper who spoke French was the only person in town I could talk to. I slept on a wooden platform in a mud-plastered room behind the teahouse and waited patiently. After twenty-four hours in Turbat-i-Shaikh Jam an Army truck gave me a ride to the last village in Iran. The next morning the garrison commander sent me on to the frontier and I walked into Afghanistan.

CHAPTER THIRTEEN

AFGHANISTAN

AT FIRST I SAW no sign of life, just bare hills. Suddenly three animals that looked like wolves charged out of a ravine, barking furiously. A ragged shepherd materialized from the ground and drove off his wild sheep dogs with stones and curses. We solemnly shook hands and sat down in the middle of the road. He produced a slab of dry bread from his robe and gave it to me: Welcome to Afghanistan!

I trudged on to a mud fort and ate more bread and drank unsweetened tea with the garrison. I had seen tattered soldiers before but never such a motley crew as these Afghans. Their uniforms, of a coarse brown cloth like homespun, were torn and patched. Everyone was barefoot since their boots were only used on duty. The corporal in charge, a small, spare man with a neatly trimmed mustache, wore a striped robe over his uniform. I conversed with him in sign language. He wondered about my religion and I tried to explain by drawing crosses on the floor and repeating "Christian" in every language I knew. But neither he nor his men had ever heard of Christianity. This is plausible because Afghanistan is the only country in the world which has always barred missionaries.

The corporal sent one of his soldiers with me to carry my pack. We walked three or four miles to Islam Kala, a frontier station consisting of customs office, police post, hotel and nothing else. The hotel manager was extremely proud of his overstuffed Victorian furniture and shiny plumbing fixtures. The latter could be admired but not used because there was no running water. An occasional herd of cattle or string of camels crossing the road, a cavalry patrol departing for the hills, a band of horsemen galloping in the distance, the ruins of an abandoned village— this was Islam Kala.

After two and a half days of solitude, the Afghan mail arrived from Herat. There were three Aussies on board bound for Europe and I was overjoyed to be able to talk again. The mail bus crossed the border and then returned to Islam Kala. The afternoon was spent loading freight. The customs officials sat in a semicircle while bundles of rugs and clothing were opened for their disdainful inspection. As soon as everyone had lined up in a row and said their prayers, we left for Herat.

Since riding the Afghan mail I feel that I qualify as a bona fide traveler. All other means of transportation pale into insignificance compared to this remarkable institution. The Afghans put an oversized wooden body on an International Truck chassis, jam several benches behind the driver for distinguished passengers, load the roof and back with sacks and crates and stuff assorted tribesmen, their animals and possessions on top of the baggage. There are continual delays and breakdowns but the amazing thing is that the contraption runs at all. With heart-rending creaking and wheezing sounds, as if we were about to fall apart, our bus struggled over the worst road I had ever seen.

We reached Herat after five torturous hours. An Arab from Jerusalem and I searched the deserted, unlighted streets for almost an hour until a stray policeman directed us to the hotel. Like everything else of any value in Afghanistan, the hotels are operated by the government. Each town has one hotel. If travelers are dissatisfied it is too bad because there is no other place to stay.

Visas had never been a problem before I came to Afghanistan. But appropriately for this fantastic country the Afghan Embassy in Bagdad had issued a visa which expired two weeks before I arrived. For nine days the Herat police, the hotel manager and the provincial governor tried to obtain permission from Kabul to renew my visa. Because of the apathy of everyone concerned, it took this long to send a telegram to the capital and receive an answer. There was nothing I could do to influence the ponderous pace of bureaucracy so I adopted the philosophy of the East. I sipped glasses of tea and forgot about time, meanwhile sending daily messages of encouragement to the governor and police. As a semipermanent guest at the Park Hotel, I was given a special rate. My room and most of the meals for these nine days cost me $3.50.

During the first two days of my sojourn, a couple of Americans were staying at the Park Hotel on a visit from Kabul. They gave me some Army rations to vary my diet of rice, lamb, potatoes and eggs. Canned hamburgers tasted like filet mignon to me. After they left the only other guests were two Russian wool buyers. I tried to talk with them but aside from a smile and "Salaam," they erected their own little iron curtain. But I think I met every local citizen who spoke more than three words of English. There was Mr. Amanullah, the polite, nervous hotel manager, who fluttered about like a bird trying to please his guests. He played the piano with one finger by the hour and cried when he read the romantic Persian poets. A newspaperman invited me to his home for tea. He published the only paper in western Afghanistan—which boasted a circulation of six hundred copies.

The post and telegraph manager, a courtly gentleman who wore tweed knickers and a karakul skin hat, told me about the fruit raised in the summer.

"The melons are the finest grown outside of paradise. And the grapes are so sweet that they hurt your teeth."

"Where do you sell this fruit?" I asked.

"Only here in Herat," he shrugged. "There is no way to ship it to foreign markets. What we cannot eat rots in the fields."

Herat is the second city of Afghanistan but it has been seen by few Westerners. The rare visitor stays for two or three days at the most. I think I can claim, without being seriously challenged, to know Herat better than any other American, living or dead. Admittedly this is not much of a distinction. Since I was stranded indefinitely, I decided to explore the city thoroughly, examining every alley, peering into every shop. Crowds collected to stare at me wherever I went. The Afghans are childlike in their curiosity and I must have been a strange sight drifting through the bazaars day after day. Because of my beard the people could never quite figure out who I was. Some thought a pilgrim, others decided a peculiar variety of mullah (Moslem holy man).

In its prime Herat was one of the strategic cities of Asia situated on the East-West caravan routes. But after Genghis Khan's warriors slaughtered the entire population, Herat never regained its former importance. The new town built outside the mud walls was carefully designed by a European planner but remains unfinished. The streets are wide and straight and lined with neat rows of pines but they have not been paved. In fact Afghanistan's only paved streets are in Kabul, a job done by the Russians in a clever propaganda maneuver. At each Herat intersection stands an impressive concrete police box equipped with traffic lights which do not work. From these boxes policemen solemnly direct the camels, donkeys and horse-drawn taxis which comprise the traffic. They sit in the shade until carts or animals approach, then leap to attention and execute a series of snappy hand signals. Camel herders and mule skinners seem indifferent to this grand performance.

A mud brick castle squats on a commanding hilltop and is used as a garrison for the bedraggled soldiers of the king. Under the walls stand rows of rusty cannon which look at least seventy-five years old and are still in active service. Every afternoon an incredible military band paraded through town with drums beating and trumpets blaring. I had heard out-of-tune marching music before but never anything like this. I listened carefully and am certain that no two men ever played the same tune. They sounded like a Bavarian brass band gone mad. Their ill-fitting uniforms and battered horns added to the air of comic opera. The Afghans love music but they should confine themselves to their native instruments.

Outside town are several giant minarets, all that remain of a great religious school built in the days of Tamerlane. The climb up the ruined steps inside a minaret is perilous but the view of Herat valley is worth the effort. I found a group of students having a party inside the empty shell of a mausoleum. They had spread a blanket on the floor and were brewing tea and singing. One fellow played a mandolin-like instrument, another beat a small drum and a third tinkled little bells. Their simple music was happy and rhythmic.

The people of western Afghanistan speak the Persian Farsi language. The majority are of mixed Iranian-Semitic ancestry. The men are strikingly handsome in appearance with finely chiseled features and a proud bearing. Except for an occasional old United States Army jacket or faded suit coat, the clothing of Herat is purely Asian. The typical costume consists of a long turban wrapped around an embroidered skullcap with one end hanging down the back, a loose shirt reaching almost to the knees, an open vest, baggy pantaloons and slippers with pointed, curled-back toes. Since the weather was cold in February some men wore quilted or striped robes. Others had coats of white felt with embroidered sleeves which practically touched the ground. I was told that they sleep with their feet tucked into these long sleeves. I learned the difference between Hazara and Turkmen, both of whom resemble the Chinese. *Hazar* means "thousand" and the Hazara are descendents of the Mongol conquerors left in strategic cities in thousand-man garrisons. The Turkmen are refugees from Russian Turkestan, persecuted by the Soviets because of their Moslem religion. They can be identified by their Cossack-type boots and huge shaggy hats of karakul wool.

The treatment of women is the most damning indictment of Moslem society. And nowhere are women so utterly subjugated as in Afghanistan. The observance of purdah is supposed to protect them from evil influences. Afghan women are covered from head to foot by a pleated shroud with a heavy mesh over the face. This shroud is a symbol of their tragic servility. Women squat on the ground in front of the shops because they are not allowed inside. They cannot enter restaurants, teahouses or other public places. The movie theater has special morning shows for women. If they buy bread and *kebab* on the streets, the food is eaten underneath their shroud. When visiting an Afghan home you never see a woman. They do not even answer the door. Although most Moslem countries are beginning to emancipate their women, conditions in Afghanistan remain unchanged.

The tiny shops of Herat contained the industry of a primitive economy. Bakers shaped balls of dough into flat, circular slabs and baked the bread in underground oven holes. Pairs of woodcutters sat on the ground sawing thick logs into boards by hand. Looms clacked and thread spun in the weavers' shops. Craftsmen of the copper bazaar fashioned bowls and jugs while puffing placidly on their hookahs (water pipes). Small boys pumped the goatskin bellows. Six men standing in a circle beat in perfect rhythm a piece of red-hot metal from the forge. If anyone swung his hammer out of turn, there would be one less worker. Tribesmen with battered muskets on their shoulders clustered around the gun shops bartering for ammunition and watching spare parts being made by hand.

The cloth shops, piled to the ceilings with bolts of bright material, were favorite spots for social gatherings. A dozen men and boys could squeeze into a space little bigger than a closet. The general-merchandise cubicles sold a staggering variety of goods. There were sacks and wicker baskets of wheat, rice, raisins, sugar, beans and nuts, coarse tobacco, piles of onions and tiny potatoes, white and purple turnips, Russian wooden matches, hard candies, boxes of tea, eggs and pomegranates, strings of red peppers, rope and cord, cotton seeds, charcoal, pumice stone, assorted skins and furs, wool, straw and stacks of firewood. On market days nomads and villagers spread their products over the ground and there seemed to be more camels than humans in Herat.

The government finally renewed my visa and I triumphantly set forth on the afternoon mail for Kandahar. Our bus had a windshield but no windows. I sat on the front bench beside the driver, a character who looked like a dissipated Burt Lancaster. The bus made several stops before we had even left Herat. First we filled the tank with Russian gasoline, which performs well enough but has a nauseating smell. Then we halted at a stream to add water, another place for oil and again to load more people and baggage. Finally Burt let the passengers out to say their evening prayers. All finished quickly except for one particularly fervent fellow who prayed on and on. At last he rolled up his rug and we roared away.

The rocky spires which rise from the plain turned rose-red and sparkling gold in the rays of the setting sun, then faded to midnight blue. We forded one river without difficulty and stopped in Sabzawar for dinner. After urging us to finish our mutton and bread quickly, Burt proceeded fifty yards down the road where we spent an hour in a teahouse. This was standard procedure for the Afghan mail.

Later that night, true to form and all predictions, we broke down. At first I thought we had simply stopped for tea at a roadside shelter. But when the passengers curled up in their sheepskin cloaks I realized that this wretched mud hut was to be our hotel. The only warmth came from a brushwood fire in the middle of the floor. The roof had no smoke hole and if you stood up, the smoke enveloped your head. My feet by the fire were hot, the rest of my body was cold. I can't remember spending a more uncomfortable night.

At dawn Burt and his assistants set to work to repair our wounded bus. The Afghans are wonderfully ingenious mechanics. They tore the vehicle's rear end apart, built a crude forge and succeeded in mending the broken springs. Meanwhile I inspected a roadside shrine decorated with flags and mountain sheep horns and took a nap in the middle of the road. There was no traffic to disturb me. I also engaged in a lengthy sign language discussion with a wandering hunter who wanted to trade his rifle for my boots or watch.

Repairs were finished about noon and we soon reached the Farah River. This is a wide stream and must be forded with caution. At each river crossing in Afghanistan there is a washed-out bridge. Some have been down for many years. The government plans imminent rebuilding of these bridges but nothing is ever done. During high water people and freight are ferried by boat or camelback. We crossed slowly with no trouble and then foolish Burt roared through a shallow side creek and flooded the engine. This blunder caused such a delay that we went no farther than the town of Farah that night. Farah is a dusty, uninspiring place but I was happy to relax at the hotel and eat a hot meal.

In the morning various people tinkered with our engine for a couple of hours. Then we drove all day across bleak hills and plains rimmed by gaunt mountains, mile after mile of empty rock and dirt. The terrain of Afghanistan looks like the valleys of the moon. The infrequent villages are clusters of domed mud huts, so low that they are hidden by slight folds in the hills. Occasionally you see a shepherd boy with his flock of goats. In this country even camels are scarce. After dark, packs of jackals roam along the road. For some reason we began stopping at every crossroad to deliver mail. Each delivery led to a long discussion and time out for tea. Then we became involved with the police who erect roadblocks to check all travelers. Usually the mail bus is not delayed but this time a terrific argument ensued. Burt kept bellowing the Farsi equivalent of "Make way for the Afghan mail!" and the policemen stubbornly refused. The passengers joined the fray and I expected a riot. But suddenly the dispute was settled and we proceeded. After sleeping at another teahouse, we set out in the bitterly cold predawn and reached Kandahar at seven o'clock. What a trip!

The American construction company of Morrison and Knutsen has been working in southern Afghanistan since

1946. At their compound outside Kandahar I consumed a gigantic breakfast. My only meal the day before had been a concoction called *rogan*, eggs cooked in two inches of sheep fat and the whole mess dipped up in pieces of bread. I looked, and probably smelled, like a wild man but George Gavin and his charming Pakistani wife befriended me. Mr. Gavin was M. and K.'s chief engineer, a mild mannered veteran dam builder.

"We are doing a job here," he said, "that could change this country's feudal economy. The Helmand River valley is being irrigated with a system of dams and canals, sort of an Afghan TVA. Men from the University of Wyoming are teaching the farmers how to use the water."

I mentioned my surprise at finding a modern village rather than a rough construction camp.

"This place was built to be self-sufficient. We have a swimming pool, club, movies, our own electricity and water supply. American food is shipped in through Karachi. You know, there are wives living here who have never been outside this compound."

"That's pretty funny. What do they do all day?"

"Play cards and gossip," said Mrs. Gavin.

Kandahar is the market center for the Pushtu tribes of eastern Afghanistan. Sullen camels and splendidly plumed horses thronged the bazaar. A handful of trucks sparkled like art exhibits with their painted murals and dazzling designs. Nomad women were unveiled in haughty contempt of purdah. Fierce-looking tribesmen wore incongruous red or green ladies' topcoats. Children played in the ditches which carry the city water supply. Belligerent fighting cocks were exercised by their owners in brief skirmishes. Two pet vultures hopped around the market place. Pottery makers spun their wheels with foot power and fashioned bowls from lumps of clay. Bearded patriarchs sat on the ground weaving wicker baskets.

I had heard rumors about conflict between Afghanistan and Pakistan, so I asked Mr. Gavin what the trouble was.

"There are several million Pushtu tribesmen," he explained, "living on both sides of the border. In Pakistan they are called Pathans. The Afghan government is agitating for a separate state of Pushtunistan. But the catch is that they want independence only for the Pathans. They don't talk about their own Pushtus. And since everyone in Pakistan has more freedom than anyone in Afghanistan, the whole business is foolish."

I caught a ride to Kabul with an official of the ICA (International Co-operation Administration). His jeep station wagon was pure luxury compared to the Afghan mail. We passed through Ghazni, the stronghold of one King Mahmud who crossed the Khyber Pass and invaded India no less than seventeen times. He must have been a determined fellow.

I looked up Dick Vites, one of the Americans who had been in Herat, and bunked on the floor of his room at the ICA Staff House.

"This may sound hard to believe," Dick said, "but Kabul has a booming social life. There is absolutely nothing else to do so the diplomatic corps throws parties all the time."

"Is that bad?" I asked.

"Well, I get pretty tired of going round and round with the same people. Especially since there aren't any unmarried women under forty."

Kabul shows a slight awareness of the twentieth century, partially due to the influence of foreign diplomats and technicians. There are a number of modern buildings, a radio station and a fleet of new Russian buses. A few foreign-made products are available in the shops. The Soviets have built some oil storage tanks and have promised to construct a hospital.

Afghanistan is as totally regimented a police state as any nation outside the Iron Curtain. There are no political parties, no free press and no freedom of speech. Loud-speakers, conveniently supplied by the Russians, have been placed at main intersections for government announcements. All non-Moslem religious activities are strictly prohibited. The King and his family maintain a tight political and economic control. In spite of the regimentation everything is so disorganized that the country appears to be in a state of semi-anarchy. The government imports machinery, establishes a woodworking factory and then finds that there is no wood supply. They buy equipment for a sugar mill and leave it crated in the warehouse for fifteen years. Afghanistan is unique in having no railroads. And the roads are little better today than when Marco Polo traveled on them.

Even the simplest task becomes a major production. Buying stamps at the post office, for instance, can be virtually impossible. Stamps may not be available on that particular day or the clerk, for some reason, may refuse to sell more than two or three to a customer. Afghanistan belongs to the International Postal Union but does not deserve the honor. The only safe way for me to send mail out of the country was through the diplomatic pouch of the U. S.

Embassy. Letters sent to me did not arrive. Postcards are such a rarity that they must be mailed in envelopes; otherwise the pretty pictures will never reach their destination.

Kabul was filled with soldiers—smartly dressed officers and enlisted men in the familiar homespun. Everyone in the army and police salutes everyone else; even privates salute each other. Busy arms go up and down in a continual, ludicrous performance. Restaurants in the bazaar served a heaping plate of rice, mutton and potatoes with bread for five Afghanis (ten cents). The government stone-cutting factory with its modern German machinery was the only place I saw in Afghanistan which seemed to be fairly well organized.

Forty Russians delivered a convoy of Soviet trucks while I was in Kabul. The drivers all looked alike with their cloth caps and round faces. They spent their time buying capitalist products in the bazaar. I amused myself greeting them in different languages; they would nod and smile but never speak. At the Russian Embassy I inquired about a rumor that tourists would be allowed to visit Samarkand. The suave secretary was very polite and gave me a cup of tea and a cookie.

"Unfortunately these things cannot be decided immediately," he explained. "Your request for a visa will be forwarded to Moscow and perhaps after two months . . ."

"Thanks anyway," I said and thought to myself, it was worth a try but there had to be a catch somewhere.

I left Kabul aboard another dilapidated chariot of the Afghan mail. The weather had been cold and clear but this day snow was falling. As we climbed into the Hindu Kush a genuine blizzard developed. Our bus was blazing its own trail through the drifts and making such slow progress that a man on camelback passed us. Eventually we turned back, in the process spending half an hour stuck in the ditch. Then the driver changed his mind and turned around again. Complete confusion prevailed. We managed to reach an army hut but could go no farther and spent the night snow-bound. Two dozen passengers jammed themselves into a ten-by-twenty-foot room. Although there was not enough space to lie down, my close-packed companions kept me warm. They sang and passed around the hookah and I soon forgot my morbid thoughts about the Black Hole of Calcutta. Except for being cramped and hungry, I really could not complain. I munched dry bread and felt grateful to be out of the storm.

Fortunately a snow-plow tractor was parked at the hut. In the morning the snow had stopped and we followed the tractor across the pass, moving literally at a snail's pace. A caravan overtook us and I was offered a camel ride. I climbed aboard and clung to the rugs piled over his hump. The camel rose from his knees, rump first, and I almost pitched forward over his head. But I hung on and was soon accustomed to the rolling, jolting motion. To ride a camel had been one of my minor ambitions and I lurched along happily for an hour or so. Near the top of the pass we came upon a man lying frozen in the road. The camel herders said a prayer and stroked their beards, the Moslem equivalent of crossing oneself. When the bus caught up with the caravan I reluctantly left my camel.

That afternoon in Sorobi we ate our first real meal since the morning before. We emerged from the Hindu Kush onto a warm plain in the shadow of snow-clad mountains.

Jalalabad is a pretty town set among groves of semitropical trees and encircled by fields of green wheat and sugar cane. The bus driver and I had become great pals and he let me sleep at the garage. I was exhausted.

We continued along a dry, stony valley where gangs of soldiers in slouch hats and ragged overcoats were repairing the road with no visible effect. They resembled an Asian W.P.A. and were a sad-looking excuse for Afghanistan's first line of defense. At the frontier station a group of passengers became involved in a loud dispute with the guards. Someone's papers were not in order. After a small bribe was passed openly to the corporal in charge, he allowed us to cross into West Pakistan.

CHAPTER FOURTEEN

PAKISTAN

ABOVE ME LOOMED the Khyber Pass, the historic gateway to India. Every conqueror since Alexander the Great had come this way. As a little boy playing with toy soldiers I had dreamed of seeing the Khyber. The slowest vehicle would be moving too fast for me, so I started walking.

The road twisted like a snake up the western slope and at first glance the hills seemed empty. Upon closer inspection I could distinguish the maze of fortifications. Concealed bunkers and pillboxes were sunk into the rock, gun positions leered from high in the cliffs and tank traps straddled the road. An armored lookout tower perched on every hill and imposing steel-and-concrete forts guarded the summit. Regimental plaques of the troops who had been stationed here were carved in the rock. I could imagine bearded Sikhs and moon-faced Gurkhas, proud Hussars and kilted Highlanders parading past me. "Gunga Din" came to life before my eyes.

The present guardians of the Pass are soldiers of the Khyber Rifles, sharp and businesslike in marked contrast to the Afghans. In the summit village of Landikotal they escorted me to Abdul Hameed Khan, the tribal *tahsildar* (government agent). Abdul was a husky college-educated Pathan who looked like a football player. He gave me my first taste of the justifiably famous Pathan hospitality. After an excellent dinner we talked of his turbulent domain.

"The Pathans in this area belong to the Afridi tribe," said Abdul. "They are fighters—proud, independent men who resent being told what to do. The British Army never really conquered the Afridis. There was more or less continuous guerrilla warfare on the frontier for generations."

"Do they fight the Pakistani Army now?"

"There has been no real trouble in recent years. Since we have become a free country they confine their activities to family feuds, mostly over land or women."

"I was warned to be very careful around the Khyber Pass," I said. "People in Kabul told me that the tribesmen were likely to slit my throat for my boots."

"It is not true," Abdul said emphatically. "The Afridis have a very strict code of honor and a stranger like yourself is in no danger. Even the wildest tribesmen respect the roads as safe territory, a kind of neutral zone, for any man. If two blood enemies meet on the road, there is never violence. The feuding goes on only in the hills and crimes are settled according to tribal law."

Bright and early in the morning I started walking again. Beyond Landikotal railhead and a couple of military camps the Pass widened. The fortified villages of the Afridis began to appear. Each was a miniature stronghold of thick mud walls pierced along the top with rifle loopholes. There were square blockhouses on the corners and tall watch towers in the center. Heavy wooden doors guarded the single gates. They looked like American pioneer stockades made of mud brick instead of logs.

Abdul had failed to warn me of the one serious difficulty that I encountered in the Khyber. At every village the men invited me inside to eat boiled eggs and drink *chi* (tea). They became quite upset when I explained that I could not stay. The villages were close together and if I had accepted all the invitations I might still be in the Pass. One particularly ferocious-looking group of tribesmen presented me with a razor-sharp, bone-handled, engraved Pathan dagger.

"Take this with you to America," said their leader, "and do not forget your brothers in Pakistan."

Most of my friends carried rifles or pistols, cartridge bandoliers and daggers in their belts. Their weapons were modern, not like the antique guns of the Afghans. They wore either a stiff cap and starched turban or a brown hat similar to a beret, white shirt and vest, pantaloons and sandals, a blanket wrapped around the shoulders. A handlebar mustache often added the finishing touch to this costume.

I passed several Kuchi caravans on their spring migration into the high country of Afghanistan. These nomads with their unveiled women and herds of camels cross borders freely, scornful of passports and travel formalities. Late in the afternoon a jeep brought me down the eastern slope of the Pass to Peshawar, green and flowering as California in the spring. Peshawar is divided into two parts, the cantonment and the old city. The cantonment was built as a military area during colonial days and here the British lived in splendid isolation. It is a sedate district of parks, gardens and neat white bungalows inhabited now by wealthy Pakistanis. The city by contrast is a teeming, roaring conglomeration of sights and smells, color and squalor. Along crooked alleys are shops of the Pathan craftsmen, fruit stalls piled high with oranges, dates and pomegranates, open cafés with bubbling kettles of meat and vegetables. Through the bazaars surge masses of humanity like the relentless waves of the sea. The clamor and congestion, haggling and shouting, arguing and begging is an overpowering spectacle. I spent hours looking and listening.

The Peshawar Fort, built of brick with double walls and three gates, has been held successively by Moguls, Afghans, Sikhs and British. It was besieged as recently as 1931 by my old friends, the Afridis. The commanding Brigadier himself escorted me around the Fort. He and his men were Pathans so of course I was treated like royalty.

One morning I rode out to the village of Darra in the Kohat Pass. This is the center of a remarkable industry, the tribal gun factories. Pathan craftsmen, using simple hand tools, manufacture rifles and pistols from raw steel. They cut and file the pieces of the firing mechanism, bore the barrels with crude wheel-operated drills, painstakingly rifle the barrels guided by their sense of touch, carve the wooden stocks and even load their own cartridges. The finished product is an exact copy of the British Enfield complete with serial numbers. It is a good serviceable rifle; during the war these factories supplied thousands of guns to the Indian Army. The pistols are copied from German and Czech models.

The single street of Darra could be a scene from Kipling. Crowds of Pathans, armed to the teeth, drink tea and gossip in front of the gun shops. Tribesmen bargain and test the rifles for hours, sometimes days, before buying them. The sound of firing echoes from the hills. I watched a shooting match between three skeptical British engineers and a local sharpshooter. Although the Pathan won the contest, the Britishers convinced themselves that the rifles really were accurate. Returning to Peshawar I passed the men of one village, all heavily armed and marching along the road like a small army.

Next day a Pakistan Air Force pilot drove me to Rawalpindi. His jeep covered the hundred miles in three hours, unbelievably fast considering the procession of bullock carts and peasants which clogged the road. We crossed the Indus River at Attock where a yellow Mogul fort sprawls on the black cliffs. The mighty Indus is swift and narrow this far north.

In Peshawar I had met S. A. Raschid, a traveling salesman, who invited me to stay at his home when I reached Rawalpindi. Raschid lived in the heart of the old city next door to a houseful of eunuchs. His unusual neighbors were singers and dancers who entertained in the streets. He took me to a public bath, where I scrubbed off several layers of dirt, and on a tour of the city.

The architecture of Rawalpindi is a hodgepodge of Indian, Victorian and semi-modern styles. Building materials are a mixture of concrete, stone, red brick and tile, carved wood, white and yellow plaster, corrugated iron, mud brick and scrap lumber. Like the architecture, the speech of educated Pakistanis is an intriguing blend of Urdu and

English. Many English words have been incorporated into the Urdu language. When I listened to my friends talking to each other I often could follow parts of their conversation.

Raschid found me a truck going to Lahore. The first half of the trip is through dry eroded hills. Beyond Jhelum the country changes abruptly into the flat fertile plains of the West Punjab. *Punjab* means five rivers, and this well-watered region, divided between Pakistan and India, is a vast granary. Endless fields of green wheat, sprinkled with farm villages, roll away in every direction. In addition to multitudes of people and animals the countryside is over-populated with birds. Great swarms of crows and kites fill the air. Flocks of filthy vultures perch silently in the trees.

The peppers and seasoning used in curries make a Mexican dinner, which I formerly considered "hot," seem like strained baby food. While I was eating a dish of this stomach-scorching curry in a Lahore restaurant, a student introduced himself. His name was Aktar, he said, and if I had no other plans, would I consider staying with his family? He was eager to improve his English, which was already excellent. I assured him that I had no plans whatsoever and accepted gratefully.

I lived at Aktar's house for the next six days. During this time I never saw his mother, his aunt or his brothers' wives. Like most Pakistanis, the family observed strict purdah. Whenever I arrived there was a scramble as the ladies dived for cover. I wandered all over the house but they managed to remain hidden. The only female who appeared openly was a baby sister. Aktar's mother sent our meals to his room and washed and mended my clothes.

When I left he told me, "My mother says that she has been honored to have you as a guest in her house. She hopes that you will return someday. If you bring your wife or your mother, she will enjoy entertaining them."

Before partition, Lahore was the hub of the Punjab and it is still an important historical and commercial center. Intensely proud of his city, Aktar was eager to serve as my guide. The Badshahi Mosque, largest in Asia, is a structure of symmetrical and majestic simplicity. Three white marble domes, each topped by a golden spire, rise above an open vault of red sandstone inlaid with marble design. On the corners of the wings flanking this vault stand four minarets. Around an enormous courtyard are four more lofty minarets. Opposite the Mosque is the Yellow Fort. Its ramparts enclose gardens and buildings including a palace with walls and ceilings of glass mosaic. Nearby is the temple and mausoleum of Ranjit Singh, the Sikh King of the Punjab. Outside the city are the famous Shalimar Gardens, laid out by Shah Jahan, the Mogul Emperor who built the Taj Mahal.

The rooftops of Lahore were the scene of continual activity. From Aktar's house I watched women working in unveiled privacy, boys flying kites (a popular pastime) and whole families eating and sleeping. On the night of a religious holiday candles were lighted on every rooftop and the city sparkled like a Christmas tree. Devout Moslems sang praises to Mohammed until dawn. Of numerous government agencies in Lahore the most intriguing was an "Office for the Recovery of Abducted Women." Such brave and noble deeds this title brought to mind!

The streets of Lahore bustled with *tongas*, overloaded

carts, water buffalo, half-naked fakirs, women in purdah, beggars, swarms of urchins and idle loungers who had nothing better to do than stare at me. I saw a wedding procession led by the bridegroom dressed in a glittering spangled shroud and riding a gaily festooned white horse. Behind him marched a dozen musicians in faded red and white uniforms. This motley group resembled a New Orleans parade band but their music was far removed from jazz. The bride, carried in a covered litter, followed at the rear of the procession. Her role in the marriage, as throughout her life, was definitely secondary.

Aktar told me of the turmoil and bloodshed at the time of partition. "Those were very bad days in the Punjab. I was just a small boy, but I remember the mobs running through the streets, burning the shops. There was too much killing. I saw one man cut to pieces with knives in the Anarkali bazaar."

"It's terrible when such crimes are committed in the name of religion," I said.

"And too many people suffer," he said, shaking his head. "Millions of Moslems were driven out of India and the same thing happened to Hindus and Sikhs in Pakistan. It is difficult for people in both countries to forget."

I regretfully bid farewell to my good companion Aktar, and crossed the border into India. I had spent only fifteen days in West Pakistan but felt a deep affection for this young and struggling nation. The Pakistanis expressed, as well as any people, the warm-hearted friendliness and hospitality characteristic of the Islamic world.

CHAPTER FIFTEEN

NORTH INDIA

To SEE INDIA has been my ambition for as long as I could remember. On March 15—after more than a year of traveling—I arrived there. For the next five months I crisscrossed the country—north, south, east and west. Poor transportation, heat and illness made traveling slow and difficult. But my experiences more than compensated for discomfort and inconvenience. The variety of color and custom, the extremes of beauty and ugliness, wealth and poverty, exist nowhere else. India is a land of fascinating contrasts.

The fringes of the subcontinent were most interesting to me: the Punjab country of the Sikhs, the former princely states of Rajasthan, the fabled Malabar Coast where the Portuguese came in search of spices, the emerald island of Ceylon, Nepal's unspoiled Katmandu valley, the snow peaks of the Himalayas, Darjeeling's polyglot mixture of peoples, and the disputed land of Kashmir.

You are never alone in India. Travel through desolate empty desert during the heat of the day, stop for any reason and peasants will appear as if by magic. The average married woman has a baby every year and the population grows at the rate of five million annually. *Five million more people each year!* This tragic fact threatens to destroy all of India's hopeful plans for the future. A highly industrialized country might be able to absorb the increase. But in India the benefits of limited progress have been offset by this flood of people. Important social reforms have been adopted since independence. There is a strong feeling of national pride and a spirit of optimism, particularly among the upper classes. I am convinced that the key to India's future lies in educating the villagers (80 per cent of the population) in a simple and drastic method of birth control. If the population could ever be controlled, some degree of prosperity would spread to the poverty-stricken masses. And no people on earth are more in need of a little prosperity.

Amritsar, my first stop in India, is the Holy City of the Sikhs and the site of their Golden Temple. Sikhism is a religious outgrowth of Hinduism, the main difference being that Sikhs believe in one God and do not worship idols. As symbols of his religion, the Sikh wears a turban and a beard, a bracelet on one wrist, and may carry a dagger. He does not cut his hair but coils it into a knot held in place with a wooden comb on top of his head. He carefully trims and curls his beard, often keeping it well groomed with a hair net tied around his chin. This fussing with their beards might indicate that the Sikhs are effeminate. On the contrary, they rank with Pathans and Gurkhas as the famed fighting men of India. A clever and industrious people, they have spread throughout the country from their homeland in the Punjab.

The Golden Temple is a gilded building set in a body of water called the Tank of Immortality. Sikhs bathe and pray around the Tank. My guide was an Irish convert and he explained the complicated procedure for entering the Temple.

"Take off your shoes and cover your head with this kerchief. Do you smoke? We don't believe in smoking so you must leave cigarettes and matches outside. Now kiss the doorsill and step over it. Be careful not to touch it with your feet."

Inside the richly adorned Temple musicians played and chanted. A white-bearded ancient read aloud from the Sikh scriptures.

"They sing continuous hymns of praise to God," said my guide. "Groups of musicians alternate and the music goes on from four o'clock in the morning until midnight."

Fascinated by this turbaned Irishman, I inquired how he had become converted to Sikhism.

"It is quite simple," he laughed. "During the war I was stationed here in India. I met a Sikh girl who is now my wife and she interested me in her religion."

I slept in the rambling guest house which provides free food and lodging for pilgrims of all religions. Wherever the Sikhs have a temple there is a community kitchen for feeding the poor. Women prepare *chapatis*, the bread staple of north India, and a special candy given to everyone in the Temple.

The bazaars of Amritsar were even more crowded, if

this was possible, than those in the Middle East. I wondered how so many merchants could earn a living when a dozen shops in one short block sold the same products. I encountered a new traffic hazard in the form of bicycle rickshas careening along cramped alleys and around blind corners. If one can survive on the streets of India, he will be safe anywhere.

Walking out of Amritsar I passed a funeral procession with four men carrying a bed on which the deceased lay. A dignified patriarch on horseback trotted by, a shield in one hand, a long lance in the other. Where could he possibly be going? Among the Sikh villagers on the road several had swords hanging from their belts.

Two Sikhs on bicycles came along and invited me to visit their villages. An opportunity to see the real life of Mother India could not be turned down. Fauja Singh was a bearlike man with a bristling black beard whose soft-spoken manner belied his appearance. His friend, Umrao Singh, was chubby and jolly. In spite of his beard, he resembled a pixie. Both had served in the Burma Army and were leading citizens of their respective villages.

With me on the handlebars of one bicycle and my pack tied to the other, we pedaled almost twenty-five miles. In Sathiala I was introduced to every village dignitary, including the temple guardian and the midwife. The local people were building a rural college of which they were rightfully proud. Without any government assistance these peasants, many of them illiterate, had constructed one wing of a planned quadrangle. While work continued, classes met in the completed section. Villagers helping themselves are an encouraging omen for India's future.

Most of Sathiala's houses were low boxes of mud brick. Fauja Singh lived in a more substantial two-story building of kiln-baked brick, a pucca house in Indian terminology. Animals were quartered downstairs, family upstairs. The simple furniture consisted of a large table, several chairs and *charpoys*, the wooden-framed woven rope or canvas beds. Cooking was done on an outside porch. The fuel supply was dung, made into round cakes and plastered on walls to dry in the sun. Toilet facilities were nonexistent; the great outdoors served as the rest room. Strings of buckets on revolving chains called Persian wheels drew water from the wells. Women carried the water in two or three copper bowls balanced on their heads. The village streets were rutted mud tracks where cattle and buffalo disputed the right of way. Transportation was by bullock carts—creaking wooden-wheeled contraptions. The drivers often slept soundly as their teams plodded along. Wild peacocks ran through the wheat fields and bright green parrots flew in and out of the houses. Most village women were shy and silent with strangers.

I saw a strange spectacle which was like a flashback to the days of Ranjit Singh. A band of Sikh warriors mounted on bucking horses came galloping through the countryside. With drums beating and banners streaming, they brandished swords and lances and shouted war cries.

"They are riding to the hills to celebrate an old battle victory against the Dogras," explained my friends.

After a day in Sathiala we pedaled to the neighboring village of Jodhe. At Umrao Singh's house a feast of chicken curry was prepared. His father, an Army pensioner who practiced medicine on the side, called in his cronies and quite a party developed. We drank Punjabi moonshine, a home brew with the kick of Tennessee "white lightning." I listened to stories of the Northwest Frontier, East Africa and Shanghai. The village Sikhs all seemed to be retired soldiers or policemen.

I traveled to Delhi in a wealthy businessman's Plymouth. The fast, comfortable ride was an unaccustomed luxury. As an unpleasant aftermath of my visit to the Punjabi villages, I suffered an attack of dysentery. Fortunately this happened while I was staying at the Quaker Center, a sort of international house in Delhi. Donald and Olive Lawrence, the kindly English couple in charge, treated me like their own son. I spent three days in bed and consoled myself with the thought that this was the first time that I had been sick in fourteen months of travel.

Delhi has long been the historic guardian of north India. Seven different cities have stood on this strategic spot. The Red Fort was the palace of Mogul emperors and contained the fabulous gold and jeweled Peacock Throne worth some $30,000,000. The 750-year-old Kutab Minar is a flawlessly designed tower in five contrasting levels. The Jami Masjid (Great Mosque) is not as impressive, in my opinion, as the Badshahi Mosque in Lahore. The Chandni Chowk, bazaar of the silversmiths, was once reputedly the richest street in the world. A simple flower-strewn square of concrete stands as a memorial to Mahatma Gandhi.

New Delhi radiates from the hub of Connought Circle along wide avenues flanked with modern buildings. Its expansive area reminded me of Los Angeles. The headquarters of the Indian Communist Party and the Delhi Stock Exchange are side by side. I attended a session of Parliament and heard a long-winded debate, in English, on freedom of the press.

Traffic conditions in New Delhi make Rome or Paris seem like Sleepy Hollow. The serene and courteous Indian undergoes a startling transformation behind the wheel of an automobile. He drives with an air of desperate bravado, blowing his horn like a man possessed. He neither signals nor attempts to stay on one side of the street. Other drivers are hopeless idiots, he tells you bitterly, and pedestrians are beneath contempt. Compounding the confusion are supremely indifferent sacred cows, hordes of bicyclists, *tongas* and motorcycle rickshas, slow-moving bullock carts which never stop at intersections and imperturbable Sikh taxi drivers. But somehow there are few accidents.

India is filled with sadhus, the holy men who meditate, practice yoga and live by begging. Many are sincere ascetics, others are parasites on society, too lazy to work. Most genuine sadhus are off in the mountains withdrawn from the world. The ones in the cities are often imposters. A sadhu wears a white or orange robe or perhaps simply a loin cloth. His uncut hair hangs in long greasy locks. Charms and beads are strung around his neck and painted stripes on his forehead denote his sect. He may smear his body with ashes and carry a small ax or a trident. His scanty possessions usually include a ragged blanket and a water pot.

While I was sick Delhi celebrated the riotous festival of Holi. "It is the beginning of summer," explained an Indian friend. "For two days people splash each other with colored water. Some start throwing paint and dyes. Even the city buses stop running during Holi."

I decided that I was lucky to be in bed.

En route to Agra I progressed slowly, spending as much time drinking tea as traveling. April and May are the hottest months in India. Before the monsoon comes in June, the north is an oven. After Holi the wheat harvest begins. Early in the mornings carts loaded with singing women rumble into the fields. Peasants cut the grain by hand and drive their bullocks round and round on the threshing floors.

The Japanese Consul in Bombay, his wife and son brought me to Agra and I accompanied them around the city. We drove out to Fatehpur Sikri, a Mogul ghost town. The Emperor Akbar had erected a splendid red sandstone palace with council chambers and harem quarters, a mosque distinguished by its massive gateway, a jewel-encrusted room for his favorite wife, stables for some hundred and fifty horses and even a memorial to his favorite elephant. Outside the palace walls a city flourished. Akbar overlooked only one detail: there was very little water available. Fatehpur Sikri had to be abandoned soon after Akbar's death.

We visited Akbar's tomb and the Red Fort of Agra and saved the best until last. The Taj Mahal was as gleaming and perfect as I had imagined it to be. I was surprised only by its size. Having pictured the Taj as small and jewellike, I was unprepared for such an imposing structure. Built of pure white marble, it is crowned by a great dome in the center flanked by four lesser domes and a minaret at each corner. Shah Jahan erected the Taj Mahal as a memorial to his favorite wife and in doing so, virtually bankrupted his empire. He and his princess are buried inside the mausoleum. Particularly as seen by moonlight, ghostly and unreal, the Taj is surely the finest achievement of Moslem architecture.

I slept in the back room of a curio shop with several tourist chauffeurs. One of them was driving two Americans, husky female hockey players, to Jaipur. The girls had stopped en route to the international hockey tournament in Australia. So I embarked on a second luxurious tour. We crossed the hot and dusty country of eastern Rajasthan to Jaipur. During colonial days this area was known as Rajputana, a number of small states ruled by wealthy maharajahs. Today the hereditary succession of these rulers has been abolished and their political power will die with the present generation. Although they have lost some of their lands, none of the ex-maharajas are candidates for the poor house. The Maharaja of Jaipur owns three lavish palaces, a few elephants and other odds and ends.

Jaipur is a city of pink sandstone lying in the shadow of hilltop forts. Its houses are gaily painted with murals of warriors and elephants. The Hawa Mahal (Palace of the Winds) is built in row upon row of bulging layers like a giant wedding cake. The pink coloring gives all the architecture a frosted fairy-tale appearance. The Rajputs have a military tradition like that of the Sikhs. They fought long and hard against the Moguls and the Rajputana Rifles are still the pride of the Indian Army. Rajput men wear fat bright red or orange turbans, long white shirts and jodhpurs (our word comes from the city of Jodhpur in Rajasthan). Their women dress in lengths of vivid red cloth splashed with sunbursts of orange, short-sleeve jackets with bare midriffs and quantities of jewelry. Armfuls of bracelets and heavy silver anklets jingle when they walk. They are barefoot, their faces and arms tattooed, their hands smeared with henna.

The American girls hired an elephant to climb up to an old fortress outside Jaipur, and I hitched a ride with them. Beggars and itinerant musicians followed us, clamoring for baksheesh. Souvenir vendors descended upon us selling assorted trash. The elephant mahout complained that his tip was too small. I felt lucky not to be a rich tourist.

At the Caltex service station I met a sales representative. Seth could have been mistaken for a New Yorker except for the caste tattoo on the back of his hand. He was delighted to discover that I was a former colleague in Standard Oil.

"There is an extra bed at the hotel where I live," Seth offered. "You can have a bath and the *dhobi* will wash your clothes."

We saw two white-robed Jain holy men, the most strict believers in nonviolence.

"Why do they wear gauze masks over their mouths?" I asked.

"The masks are to protect bacteria in the air," explained Seth. "And those soft mops that they carry are for sweeping insects out of the way before they sit down."

These are the people who literally would not hurt a fly.

The night train to Udaipur was my first experience with the chaos of third-class Indian rail travel. The coaches were so jammed that I could not even force my way through the doors. Eventually I found crouching space and spent a long uncomfortable night wedged between fellow passengers. I talked with a pessimistic young sadhu who could see no hope for India's future. His whole attitude was negative and depressing.

"I want to go to America," he informed me, "to study racial prejudice."

Udaipur is built around a lake with one palace on an island and two more along the shore. There certainly is no shortage of palaces in the Rajput states. The late Maharaja had expired only a few months before and his wives, one Hindu and one Moslem, were languishing in one of the homesteads. The others were open to anyone who could pay the two anna (3¢) admission fee. They looked forlorn and decrepit with seedy Victorian furniture, ugly paintings, peeling plaster and a single bored elephant. I saw a sweating water carrier in loin cloth and turban who could have been Gunga Din.

The local Hindu temple was a stone tower completely covered with carved figures of gods and goddesses. Inside were garish pictures, bells, relics, incense burners, oil lamps and idols smeared with ocher and decked with flowers. I inquired at the newly-organized Udaipur Tourist Bureau and the officials became quite excited. I must have been their first customer. They provided a guide, lunch at their office and a private room in the government hostel, all free of charge.

From Indore I journeyed south with a chunky Sikh in a polka-dot turban. His car, a prewar Austin, looked sturdy and reliable.

"This will be a fast trip," I told myself, blissfully unaware that it would take eleven hours to cover the next 150 miles. Our first flat tire was changed with no trouble. But the second blowout left us without a spare and service stations are rare in the countryside. Our driver set out to search for a patch and we took refuge in a roadside shrine. A sadhu who meditated there fed us vegetable curry, mangoes and paw paws. It was blisteringly hot.

"We must accept fate," announced my friend and promptly went to sleep. Having no better plan, I did the same. Three hours later the driver returned triumphantly and within another hour we were under way. After a further delay caused by mechanical difficulty we reached Dhulia.

I had ordered a restaurant meal of rice and curry when Dr. Panwar, the local health officer, introduced himself.

"Do not eat this food," he warned. "It will surely make you ill." The proprietor who spoke no English stood by, beaming and nodding agreement. "Come with me, Mr. Donald."

From the terrace of Dr. Panwar's room we watched a wedding procession on the street below. First came the men of the family doing a shuffling dance in unison and beating drums. Musicians followed making a great racket with reed pipes and brass horns. The bride and groom rode in a *tonga*, the groom wearing an incredible headdress of colored paper and flowers. The women trailed behind singing and carrying their babies.

Dr. Panwar and his friends were so congenial that I spent an extra day in Dhulia. I was invited to lunch by a doctor named Shah. He and his family were Jains, therefore strict vegetarians, who ate only fruits and vegetables.

"We have prepared eggs especially for you," said Dr. Shah.

That evening at the Jain temple a man was chanting and

waving an incense pot. Dr. Shah smiled as he explained, "The priest is putting the god to bed for the night. At dawn he will come to wake the god."

From Dhulia I continued to the Ajanta caves. These Buddhist meeting halls are carved into the cliffs and adorned with painted frescoes. Scenes from the life and reincarnations of the Buddha show a high degree of artistic skill. The animals in particular are as lifelike as those painted today. And some of these frescoes date from the third century B.C. Each cave has at least one stone figure of the Buddha in the cross-legged pose of meditation.

I arrived in Bombay aboard a so-called express train. Bombay is the pride of India, the modern industrial city, the place that Indians mention when they speak of progress and the future. There are sleek office buildings, broad avenues and imposing residential districts. The Marine Drive sweeps around the bay, lined with a chain of pastel apartment houses. Mahatma Gandhi Road is as busy and purposeful as Fifth Avenue in spite of the heat. Red double-decker buses and solid Victorian architecture remind one of London. The Gateway to India arch and the Taj Mahal Hotel stand together. Both are symbols of the British *Raj* and times gone by. Within a few blocks of the business center are some of the most festering slums in the country.

I had not seen a seaport since leaving Basra so I indulged my passion for inspecting waterfronts. The docks buzzed with activity, as mobs of half-naked coolies handled the cargo. Bombay's modern steel and concrete buildings were being constructed by extremely primitive methods. Workmen swarmed over rickety wooden frameworks erected around the shells of new buildings. Human chains passed pans of cement up the ladders from head to head. Women and children sat on the ground breaking rocks with small hammers.

Bombay had been the scene of bloody rioting shortly before my visit. The clash between working class Mahrattas and Gujerati merchants backed by the Delhi government concerned the city's future status. The violence accompanying a nationwide reorganization of states has illustrated an unhappy fact to Indian leaders. They have been forced to adopt the same police methods for which the British rulers were so heartily condemned. It has been embarrassing but necessary for the government to maintain law and order among its own people. Today there are no foreigners to blame for cracked skulls and jailed rioters.

The Mantzouranis family in Athens had given me the address of their uncle in Bombay. Costas Mantzouranis was a gruff balding cigarette manufacturer, typical of the shrewd Greek businessmen who settle in so many parts of the world. In spite of his brusque manner, he displayed the hospitable nature which must be inborn among the Greeks. Mrs. Mantzouranis, a jolly German woman, took me shopping with her to the Crawford Market.

"This is one of the few places in India," she said, "where you can buy beef. The butchers are Moslems and Hindu coolies won't even go into the beef market."

The idea of sacred cattle seems quite ridiculous to Westerners until the reason is understood. The bullock is to the Indian farmer what the camel is to the Bedouin Arab. It pulls the cart, plows the field, threshes the grain, draws the water and provides dung for fuel. The cow supplies milk.

Because his simple life is so utterly dependent on cattle, the Hindu peasant worships the animals. He paints their horns, bathes them in the rivers and feeds them even when he is hungry. Under no circumstances will he slaughter bullocks. The result is that India is literally overrun with scrawny hump-back cattle, the largest and least productive bovine population on earth.

The water buffalo, on the other hand, is a slapstick comedy character whose appearance counts heavily against him. He is not very bright but could not possibly be as dumb as he looks. When a buffalo thrusts his head forward and stares blankly into space, the most charitable description which comes to mind is "benign." A buffalo lumbering along at an awkward gallop runs like a fat old maid frightened by a burglar. But in spite of his defects this foolish animal is as important to the farmer as the bullock.

CHAPTER SIXTEEN

SOUTH INDIA
AND CEYLON

THE BEARDED Spanish priest kicked his motorcycle into action. With his white cassock flapping in the wind, we roared into Poona. A full-sized parade band was practicing in the courtyard of a house. Early Sunday morning hardly seemed the time for such a deafening performance.

"It doesn't matter to the Indians," said the Spaniard. "Anyone who sleeps after five A.M. is considered hopelessly lazy. And Sunday is no different from other days."

Heading south from Bombay, I had stopped at De Nobili College, a Jesuit training school outside Poona. Father Fonseca advised me that five American priests were vacationing in the hills nearby. So I detoured to the hill station with the unpronounceable name of Mahabaleshwar. There I found the Jesuit retreat in a house formerly owned by the Aga Khan. Mahabaleshwar is located on the crest of a mountain whose wooded ridges extend in all directions like the tentacles of an octopus. After dutifully attending early mass with my friends, we pedaled bicycles to a tiny canyon-side village. Here stood a 2,000-year-old temple of Hanuman, the Monkey God.

"This village is sacred to Hanuman," said Father Richards. "The monkeys you see around here destroy crops and steal anything that isn't nailed down. Sometimes they even bite children. But the villagers wouldn't think of harming them or trying to drive them away."

I continued toward Bangalore in a succession of trucks. Along a river lines of sweating coolies unloaded wooden sailing vessels, balancing baskets of sand on their heads. An elephant chained beside the road contentedly pulled up bunches of grass for his lunch, biting off the green stalks and discarding the roots. Peasants cut sugar cane and picked cotton in the sweltering fields.

The deadening aura of poverty permeates the land. This is a poverty so stark and bitter as to be incomprehensible to a Westerner. It is reflected in the weak cry of emaciated babies, the hungry eyes of potbellied children, the men whose legs are as thin as my wrist. Families live in wretched grass huts, laborers earn twenty cents daily, the lifetime diet consists of two meals of bread or rice a day. This is the tragedy of overpopulation.

Bangalore is probably the cleanest city in India. Its parks and gardens, white public buildings and comfortable homes invariably appeal to visitors. The Flame of the Forest, full-grown trees dripping with scarlet flowers, were in bloom, adding to the city's beauty. I had hoped to find Rahman Rao, an old friend from Stanford, in Bangalore.

"Rahman has returned to San Francisco," his father informed me, "but you are welcome in his home."

Before ill health forced him to retire, Mr. Rao had been a director of Hindustan Aircraft and finance minister of Hyderabad State. His wife was a gracious lady who wore the lovely silk saris which express so well the character and personality of Indian women. Suspecting that I was not wildly enthusiastic about vegetarian food, they sent me with different members of the family to an excellent Western-style restaurant.

After a couple of thoroughly enjoyable days in Bangalore, Mr. Rao arranged transportation to Mysore. I settled down in the guest room of the Mission Hospital and went sightseeing with a group of Indian teachers. We saw the Maharaja himself, one of the fattest men I have ever had the pleasure of staring at. His palace is an elephantine pile of granite with pillars, towers and a gilded center dome, surrounded by gardens and temples. Here the Maharaja does Puja (paying homage to the animals, carriages, automobiles, etc. that he uses) during the annual Dessera festival. The Mysore zoo is one of the Maharaja's few contributions to the public. The confinement of the animals is so informal that the elephants are merely tied to stakes and I could reach over the railing to pet the blasé hippo.

Ootacamund, known locally as Ooty, is the Queen of South Indian hill stations in the cool Nilgiri Mountains. A carload of wealthy Parsees from Bombay, a long walk and a gallant old truck brought me to Gudalur, a jungle village at the foot of the Nilgiris. Here I met one of those truly dedicated men whose lives are devoted to the unfortunate. Dr. Bachrach was an Anglican medical missionary operating dispensaries for the jungle villagers. Born a Russian Jew, he had begun his present work after surviving a Nazi concentration camp. He reminded me of Albert Schweitzer.

On the lower slopes of the Nilgiris coffee is grown. As you go higher there are tea estates and chinchona trees from whose bark quinine is made. The rolling fields on the very crest of the hills produce potatoes. After the exotic crops below this seems anticlimactic, but most of India is too hot and dry for raising the lowly spud.

Dr. Bachrach had given me a note of introduction to Paul Rimmer, the Anglican padre of Ooty. Rev. Rimmer was a young exuberant Englishman, as unlike a conventional churchman as I could imagine. His wife Joan was an equally delightful person. With their two children we squeezed into Rimmer's miniature Morris convertible and drove up Dodabetta Mountain for a picnic. At least we drove until the car gasped and died on the steep trail and we walked to the top. Dodabetta is the highest peak in the Nilgiris. A panorama of tea estates and jungle hills stretches away to the distant heat-soaked plains. In these mountains the unfortunate Tippu Sultan, last independent ruler of Mysore, was defeated and killed by the British.

I visited a settlement of Todas, aboriginal tribesmen, in Ooty. The origin of these people is obscure but to me the tall full-bearded men with their finely chiseled features resembled the ancient Greeks. I wondered if perhaps there was some remote link between the Todas and Alexander's Macedonians. Several Toda women squatted in a circle, chewing betel nut and singing monotonous off-key tunes. For this miserable performance they expected baksheesh. Their houses were long and rounded with sloping thatched roofs which almost touched the ground. They looked like

Quonset huts.

The Rimmers let me borrow their car to drive across the hills and see a tea estate. Dennis Jarvis, the estate manager, was a giant ex-rugby player and his wife a beautiful blonde. They seemed an unlikely pair to be leading the isolated lives of tea planters.

"The coolies pick a bud with a leaf on each side," explained Jarvis, breaking a shoot off one of the tea bushes. "The trees are planted along the rows for shade."

Later in the tea factory he said, "The green tea is spread on these racks to dry. This is called withering and is the secret of making good tea. The picking goes on the year round but the proper withering time depends on the season. The machines dry it more, sift the tea into different grades and finally pack it in crates." Handing me a cup of tea, he grinned, "We're trying to educate you Americans to drink less bloody coffee."

"It's the foolish tea bags we use," I said. "If Americans brewed tea like this, you would sell a lot more to us."

The green tropical rain-soaked Malabar Coast, west of the Nilgiris, was my destination after leaving Ooty. In Calicut I was the guest of the magnificently titled English and Scottish Joint Co-operative Wholesale Trading Company, Limited. I had a large house, modestly called a bungalow, and two servants all to myself, plus a company car and driver. I was treated, somewhat to my embarrassment, like a pucka sahib.

Calicut is one of the oldest centers of the spice trade which lured Europeans to India. The local rulers were vigorous opponents of the early Portuguese captains. The town is situated at the jungle-edge along a crescent of sandy beach on the Arabian Sea. Because there is no harbor, dhows from the Persian Gulf and coastal steamers anchor offshore. Narrow wooden boats propelled by men with round paddles ride the breakers bringing in the cargo. Coolies dive into the surf, chanting lustily as they drag the boats onto the beach. The street scene is quite different from other parts of India. Here the bullock carts are high and narrow with woven canopies and wheels as tall as a man. Peasants in giant palm fiber hats carry fruit in baskets slung on poles across their shoulders. The rickshas are pulled by trotting men rather than cyclists. Policemen wear pointed turbans, shorts and no shoes. In fact almost everyone, rich or poor, on the Malabar Coast is barefoot. An umbrella for rain or sun, a cotton shirt and the *dhoti*, a flowing white garment like a cross between sarong and pantaloons, are the standard costume.

I caught a very slow, very crowded train to Trichur. The coaches were stuffed with red-shirted young Communists bound for a May Day jamboree. They brought forcefully to mind the strange paradox of Travancore-Cochin, the state we were entering. Here are found more Christians and more Communists than anywhere else in India. With both the highest literacy rate and the greatest population density, Travancore-Cochin's problem of educated young men unable to find jobs is unusually acute. In their disillusionment the unemployed intelligentsia turn to Communism. This is the only place where the Communist Party has ever won a free state election.

Rev. Francis, pastor of the Syrian Church in Trichur, was the brother of a friend in Delhi. "We are the original Christians of India," he told me. "Our church was founded by

· 185

the Disciple St. Thomas in the first century. You have come here at the right time. Tomorrow is Palm Sunday and we are dedicating a new church."

In the morning a colorful procession wound through the streets. Solemn dignitaries marched under red, silver-fringed umbrellas, singing crowds carried palms and banners and a band blared the usual dissonant music. I was introduced to the white-bearded metropolitan, resplendent in his costly robes, before he officiated at the four-hour ceremony. I wandered through the back alleys where people earn their living making wooden matchboxes by hand. Above a Hindu temple a hammer and sickle flapped among the prayer flags. Peasants and buffalo were plowing the flooded paddy fields.

The jungle between the mountains and the sea is laced with a network of streams and bays, a natural inland waterway. Many families live in boats covered from stem to stern with round canopies of palm leaf matting. The jungle itself is a luxuriant tangle of paw paw, jack fruit, mango and pepper trees, slender coconut palms, giant ferns, clumps of green bamboo and tall thin betel palms. The *pan* so widely chewed in India consists of betel nut wrapped in a lime-smeared betel leaf. In my opinion it tastes as bad as it sounds.

The whitewashed or pastel village houses look solid and well built. Their roofs of red tile or palm thatch curve upwards at both ends like the hulls of sailing ships. There are wooden bars at every window. The coconut is an important crop along the Malabar Coast. Split coconuts are spread in the sun to dry into copra. Cottage industries make bowls from the shells and twist the fiber into rope. Rural women stretch their ear lobes with heavy gold rings or solid discs

186 ·

larger than silver dollars. Some peasant women wear nothing but a sarong wrapped around the waist. Unfortunately this interesting practice is usually confined to those middle aged or older. Most young ladies are modestly covered. However, the rare opportunity to admire a village belle keeps the traveler continually alert.

At a school in Cochin run by Indian Carmelite priests we ate from palm leaves instead of plates, a common custom in the South. The rice and curry are mixed with the fingers of the right hand. Using both hands constitutes a serious social blunder. The mixture is then popped, more or less accurately in my case, into the mouth.

Cochin is the most famous of all the Malabar spice ports, stronghold of the Portuguese and later the Dutch. But the Portuguese were comparative newcomers. Long before them trade flourished with Arabs and Chinese. Cochin is still a busy port with cargo boats scuttling back and forth between the docks and freighters anchored in the bay. The blue-and-yellow-painted houses with thick walls and shuttered windows show the Portuguese influence. The Dutch left a stone church, sturdy as a fortress, and a crumbling graveyard. The architecture appears more European than Asian.

"Who are those people with light hair and blue eyes?" I asked an English acquaintance. "They don't look like Indians."

"They are Jewish descendants of refugees from the Spanish Inquisition. There is a colony of them here."

I walked south along a narrow peninsula, crossed an inlet on a raft and drifted downstream aboard a barge. The only traffic was on the water. I eventually reached Alleppey, a little Venice of canals, fishing boats and battered steam launches. At a sawmill I watched an elephant carrying logs with his trunk. In Quilon, another coconut and canal town, I stayed at a Franciscan monastery, then took the train east to Madura. As we chugged across the mountains the lush jungle disappeared and once more the land was brown and dry.

The Madura temple is an outstanding Hindu monument. It is actually a temple complex with nine *gopuras*, pyramid-like towers, each a mass of carved figures, surrounding a tank of holy water. Inside the shrines devotees prostrated themselves in prayer and beat gongs and drums. Bathers splashed and prayed in the tank, sadhus sat around meditating and looking holy. One yogi performed his morning ritual standing on his head. Some of the more orthodox worshipers wore their hair shoulder-length or had the fronts of their heads shaven. A popular hair style left the head close-cropped except for a single long lock in back, often tied in a cute little knot.

The streets of Madura were festooned with red flags remaining from May Day. I saw a monstrous wooden cart used to transport idols in religious processions. The local *tongas* were small brightly painted boxlike affairs with no seats. Passengers huddled on the floor or hung out the back.

After spending the night at a mission school, I proceeded to the Ceylonese quarantine camp. The atmosphere was like that of a prison. With a mob of Indian laborers I went through an involved routine of questions, forms and a medical examination for cholera and typhoid. The Ceylonese authorities are afraid of both epidemics and illegal immigration from India. After convincing one and all that I was healthy and harmless, I was released. From the fishing village of Dhanushkodi a dumpy little steamer carried me across the twenty-mile strait to Ceylon.

The police sergeant at Talaimannar greeted me expansively, an appropriate introduction to a charming country. Ceylon is clean and shining, surely one of the world's prettiest islands. Compared to India the living standard is high, the people are better fed, dressed and educated, there is far less disease and squalor. Ceylon is Westernized and prosperous mainly because it is not yet overpopulated. But the population is growing at an alarming rate.

In addition to its other virtues, Ceylon is an excellent place for hitchhiking. Distances are short and traffic is plentiful. I rode across the flat jungle plains of the north to Anuradhapura, the ancient capital of the Sinhalese kings. Remains of palaces and monasteries, statues of Buddha and artificial lakes are scattered through the jungle. A holy shrine for Buddhist pilgrims is the Bo tree, supposedly a branch of the original tree under which the Buddha attained enlightenment 2,500 years ago. Of several ruined stupas (Buddhist temples) in Anuradhapura, one has been restored. A stupa is a solid hemisphere of brick, topped by an umbrellalike spire, in which sacred relics are buried. Devotees bring offerings of flowers and money to shrines around the outside of the towering white structure. They sit with hands held together reciting their prayers, and bending forward, touch their foreheads to the ground. Oil lamps burn and the air is heavy with the aroma of incense. Saffron-robed monks, their heads as bald as eggs, wander about or meditate serenely. At sunset two drummers and a horn player bring the day to a close with a spirited musical performance.

While eating in a hotel I struck up a conversation with Bonney Kanagathungan, a Shell Oil salesman. Awe-inspiring names like Kanagathungan are common in Ceylon. Bonney brought me to his home for a second dinner and a party with his friends. The next day being Sunday, he drove his family and me to the rock of Sigiriya. Rising out of the plain like a land-locked Gibraltar, Sigiriya was the fortress of a fifth-century king. This enterprising fellow built his palace right on top of the rock. Under an overhanging shelf are preserved paintings of ladies which closely resemble the frescoes of Ajanta. The hornets which inhabit Sigiriya are particularly unfriendly and easily disturbed, so the authorities have thoughtfully provided a wire cage into which the climber can flee if he is being attacked.

On the road again, along came a delivery truck driven by a Tamil Indian with the improbable name of Francis P. Ryan. The majority of Ceylon's people are the native Sinhalese but there is a large Indian minority. Ryan was short and very dark with an infectious grin. He wore a dapper outfit of bright plaid sarong, wide leather belt, cream-colored shirt and blue scarf knotted at his throat. Ryan spoke a fractured brand of English but we understood each other perfectly. In fact he was such a cheerful and accommodating fellow that mere language became almost unnecessary.

We climbed from the plains past rubber and cocoa plantations to Kandy. This was my first glimpse of Ceylon's storybook hill country where jungle flowers bloom in wild profusion and the shades of green are so brilliant that they look artificial. Thatched cottages are tucked among coconut palms on the edge of terraced rice fields. Ceylonese girls are slender and pretty, with skin the color of milk chocolate and flowers in their braided hair. They bathe in the streams or at the village wells, preserving their modesty by clever manipulation of their sarongs. A girl washes herself under the garment, slips a dry sarong over her head and wiggles out of the wet one. This convenient custom allows both men and women to bathe in public, even on the main street.

In Kandy I moved into Ryan's room. After dinner at a Chinese restaurant, he took me to the Temple of the Tooth. One of the Buddha's molars is enshrined here, making this an extremely holy spot. The Temple contains exotic wood carvings, painted murals and gold-plated statues of the Buddha. The stalls of flower sellers fill the air with perfume and grave monks stand silently on guard. We were allowed to pass through the sanctuary, a dazzling display of silver and jewels. The tooth is unveiled only on special occasions.

Kandy was the best place I found for observing elephants. You see them ambling along the roads early in the morning, bathing in the river during the afternoon and homeward bound in the evening, clutching bundles of greenery for dinner with their trunks. The elephants lie down in the river with their heads under water and use their trunks to breathe like submarine snorkels. The mahouts give them a brisk rubdown with coconut shells and then take a bath themselves. The elephants spend hours happily loafing and blowing water.

"They are very wise animals," said a Ceylonese on-looker. "They refuse to work more than half a day. So each afternoon the mahouts bring them here to play."

From Kandy I traveled upcountry to Nuwara Eliya. This is the tropical heart of the island with a panoramic vista in every direction. River banks drip with jungle and women wade in the flooded paddy, transplanting the green rice shoots. Aluminum tea factories sparkle like diamonds on the emerald hills and planters' bungalows are doll houses across the valleys. The tea pickers with big baskets on their backs gather the wealth of Ceylon. I rode with a plump, idle-rich landowner, a member of the Westernized upper class.

Nuwara Eliya is an Anglicized hill station of sturdy wood and corrugated iron houses on top of the mountains. The rolling moors are reminiscent of the Scottish High-lands. I visited Rev. Arden Constant, an older but no less entertaining version of Rev. Rimmer in Ooty. These padres were a far cry from the pompous, stereotype Anglican clergyman with his gaiters and glass of port who is so "aw-fully British" he can hardly talk. Rev. Constant told me an interesting fact about Ceylon.

"This is a country," he said, "where people of different religions live together peacefully. Most of the Sinhalese are Buddhists, the Tamils are Christian or Hindu and there are quite a number of Moslems. Between these four there has never been discrimination or violence. Ceylon can be proud of its unique religious tolerance."

Leaving Nuwara Eliya, the road twisted off the high plateau past tea gardens and silver waterfalls on distant cliffs. During one slightly nerve-racking ride the poker-faced young man behind the wheel hurtled down canyons like a frustrated jet pilot. In Nawalapitiya who should come running with a big grin and loud greeting but good old Francis P. Ryan? We hopped into his delivery truck and returned to Kandy, stopping in Peradeniya for a look at the botanical gardens and the new campus of Ceylon University.

That night Ryan took me to a Tamil language movie, *Ali Baba and the Forty Thieves*. The plot was easy to follow, but Indian films are difficult for a Westerner to appreciate. They are usually as long as *Gone with the Wind* so that the audience feels it has gotten its money's worth. The flagrant overacting and exaggerated emotions are in the best tradition of nineteenth-century melodrama. Without the slightest provocation the cast breaks into song and dance. An Indian film, regardless of the story, includes at least half a dozen musical numbers. The hero of *Ali Baba* was fat and awkward and seemed exhausted by his strenuous part. I dozed, squirmed and felt sorry for myself for three and a half hours. Ryan enjoyed the show very much.

En route to Colombo a race horse owner picked me up and pointed out the rocky crag where Ceylon's Robin Hood had hidden from the British.

"He was betrayed by his wife," my friend said ominously. Evidently he attached considerable significance to this female treachery.

On the outskirts of Colombo we passed the headquarters of the St. Paul's Communist Youth League. Having had such good luck with the Anglicans, I went to their church in Colombo. The padre let me stay in their meeting hall. I slept on a table and ate one huge pineapple for two days.

I swam in the Indian Ocean surf and watched the Moslem community celebrating the end of Ramadan, the month-long sunrise-to-sunset fast. Crowds promenaded along the seawall in their holiday best and even the sheltered Moslem women joined in the festivities.

I caught the night train back to Talaimannar and had an entire wooden bench to myself. This would be unheard of on the Indian railroads. Aboard the steamer returning to India I met a French couple with two small children. They were driving to Europe, all four on one motor scooter. The man had built a covered compartment over the rear end of the scooter and they had already crossed the 3,000-mile length of Australia.

Madras is the metropolis of South India. The city sweltered in the premonsoon heat, cluttered and littered and pulsing with raw humanity. Early in the mornings the sidewalks swarm with women cooking, men bathing and naked children scurrying about. Some of these families have no other home. They sleep on the streets and the piles of ragged mats, bundles and blackened pots are their sole possessions. Heavily loaded carts are pulled by two coolies while two or three more push with their heads. Labor is cheap and men eat less than animals.

I traveled up the flat, dry Coromandel Coast and inland to Hyderabad. The miserly old Nizam, one of the world's richest men, formerly ruled Hyderabad state. The atmosphere of the city is Moslem, more like Pakistan than India. White minarets and domes of innumerable mosques rise over the flat roofs. The rickshas have tops and purdah curtains to prevent lecherous males from gazing at virtuous females. But sometimes the ladies cheat by peeking through the curtains. I saw a touring car with its side windows carefully screened and the women passengers peering out the open back window. Numerous beards, hookahs, karakul hats and Pathan turbans are signs of a predominantly Moslem society.

In the river women washed clothes and boys scrubbed water buffalos. These animals have such tender skin that they must be allowed to soak or wallow every day. Otherwise they will suffer badly from sunburn.

The symbol of Hyderabad is the Char Minar, a lofty structure which once served as a gateway in the city walls. *Char* means "four" and its name comes from a tower on each corner. Many citizens enjoy their afternoon nap in its shade.

My quarters in Hyderabad were the first-class waiting room of the railway station. When the jam-packed Delhi express arrived, the stationmaster slipped me into a compartment reserved for employees. A tough Sikh blocked the door and kept everyone else out. The Indian railroads are probably the cheapest and most congested on earth. They are like the New York subway handling rush-hour crowds on a twenty-four-hour-a-day basis. Travelers bring their own bedrolls and families set up light housekeeping on the platforms. Night and day people are camped beside the tracks, usually sleeping while they wait. The arrival of a train sends a howling mob converging on already loaded coaches. Quarter is neither asked nor given, this being the wrong place to observe the peaceful nonviolent Indian temperament.

The trains progress spasmodically, stopping for never

less than ten minutes and often for half or three quarters of an hour. Passengers are harassed by peddlers who clamber from car to car, in and out of the windows while the train is moving. Then there are beggars, some of whom sing to the captive audience. They usually hold a hand over one ear while entertaining. This may or may not indicate disapproval of their own voices. Traveling is rarely comfortable but never dull.

Inevitably, for me there were political and racial discussions with intense young men.

"Why does America arm our enemy, Pakistan?"

"To protect her against Communist aggression."

"But Pakistan will use these weapons against India."

"If she commits aggression we will support you."

Or, "How can America be democratic with a color bar?"

"Race prejudice is our biggest problem. It is similar in some ways to your caste problem."

"But caste has been abolished by law in India."

"So has school segregation in our Southern states. But it takes time to change men's thinking. The Harijans (untouchables) have the same rights as anyone else but can they use Brahmin temples or village wells?"

"They are happy to use their own temples and water supply."

"That is what prejudiced people in America say about the Negroes."

During the marriage season entire clans go by train from one village to another. Peasants who have no money seem to be continually traveling. The women sport rings on their toes and an array of bracelets, anklets, beads and earrings. Small children wear short shirts with no pants or nothing except a G-string around their waists. Heavy eye shadow is used to beautify the babies.

Before reaching Delhi I stopped in Gwalior to see the Mogul fort and paid a second visit to the Taj Mahal. With my Japanese friends time had been too short, and I went back to enjoy the Taj at my leisure. The longer I looked, the more convinced I became that it is unsurpassed in beauty.

CHAPTER SEVENTEEN

NEPAL

I CLIMBED UP into the baggage rack and wiggled forward on my stomach. The space between the rack and ceiling was so narrow that, in trying to roll over, I became wedged on my side and could not move. Two fellow passengers extracted me by pulling on my feet. I tried again and managed to squirm into the rack on my back. As long as I did not shift my position or breathe too deeply, I could sleep fairly well.

The night train to Lucknow was the first stage of my journey to Nepal. Lucknow, the capital of Uttar Pradesh state, seemed even hotter than Delhi. I saw decaying tombs, cool gardens and flocks of ghoulish vultures on mud banks along the river. The Residency is a group of shell-scarred, burned-out buildings where British soldiers, civilians and loyal sepoys were beseiged during the Indian Mutiny. For three blistering summer months the garrison fought against heavy odds. When a relief column appeared, to everyone's embarrassment they found themselves trapped with the original defenders. Several weeks passed before relief reached the relievers and the siege of Lucknow was finally lifted. Today the ruined Residency is a peaceful park.

The following day I arrived in Raxaul, a sleepy town on the Nepali border. An English doctor and his family operated the Mission Hospital. They were religious fundamentalists dispensing a mixture of evangelism and badly needed medicine.

Until 1951 Nepal was probably the most isolated country in the world, less known even than Tibet. The all-powerful Rana family controlled the government and the king was a mere puppet. Wary of disturbing outside influences, the Ranas excluded everyone except neighboring Indians and Tibetans. The lone Western resident of Nepal was a British representative in Katmandu, the capital. His handful of yearly visitors were virtually the only foreigners to enter the country. Some years ago a revolt curbed the power of the Ranas and transformed the king into the actual ruler. Since then a few missionaries, doctors and teachers have been admitted, but Nepal remains basically unaffected by modern civilization. Much of the interior is still unexplored. Outgoing letters must be sent with Indian stamps since Nepal does not belong to the International Postal Union. A road to Katmandu has been partially completed by the Indian Army but it is jeepable at best and becomes impassable during the rains. Travelers to the capital have a choice of flying or walking.

The narrow-gauge Nepali State Railway runs from the Indian border through the Terai, a malarial jungle belt between the plains and the Himalayan foothills. This toy railroad, chugging twenty-nine miles in four hours, may very well be the world's slowest train. Amlekhganj, a collection of wooden shacks and teahouses, is the end of the line.

The arrival of our train touched off a scene of frenzied confusion. For no apparent reason everyone was shouting at the top of his lungs. Porters rushed about aimlessly, officials bellowed and waved their arms frantically, engines sputtered and roared, children screamed and one Gurkha woman was hysterical. An air raid could not have induced more panic. The only calm onlookers were two Indian Army engineers and I. I don't know about them—but I was awed into stunned silence.

After an hour of deafening clamor, four bedraggled buses were loaded and we headed north into the hills. Progress was slow, since the engine of our bus died on the slightest incline. We paused at a roadside shrine and the passengers threw offerings of coins to the idol. From Bhempedi village a twenty-mile trail leads into Katmandu valley. There is also a rope-way across the mountains but a large amount of freight is transported on the backs of porters. These wiry little brown men use a pack board with a strap across the forehead to carry enormous loads. They wear shorts, open vests and round black caps with either straw sandals or bare feet. Some have a single string of fat red beads around their neck and a gold ring in one ear. The female porters are as rugged as the men, carry almost as much weight and sing while they hike. Their voices echo melodiously across the wild jungle gorges.

The Nepalis are a pleasure-loving people who gamble

incessantly and drink great quantities of *chang* (homemade beer). Men, women and small boys smoke like chimneys. They live on hard bread or rice and never seem to sleep. Yet their stamina is unaffected by this strenuous routine. They scramble over the steep trails like mountain goats.

I climbed straight up from Bhempedi and reached Chisapani Gara before dark. There is a free resthouse in this mountainside hamlet. An old man agreed to cook my dinner and after four hours, produced a plate of rice and potatoes. If he had taken much longer I could have eaten the food for breakfast. At five A.M. I was routed out of bed to begin the big trek. From the top of the pass mountains thrust and tumble and the river is a shining thread far below. The trail drops down to cross and recross the foaming stream on swaying suspension bridges. Along the narrow gorge, fields are planted in corn and houses are scattered on the river bank. As the valley widens, terraced paddies and more villages appear. The Nepali farmhouse is a solid, two-story structure of wood and brick, brown and orange in color. Oddly enough, it has no chimney. Smoke from cooking fires billows out the windows or seeps from under the roof.

The trail is as busy as a highway with lines of porters, Gurkha soldiers on leave, herdsmen driving buffalos, well-to-do women being carried in four-man sedan chairs and entire families walking to Katmandu. Public-spirited citizens have built resting places beside the trail. These stone seats are designed for a porter to prop his load against and relax. The Nepalis never miss this opportunity and I joined them quite often. The villagers had seen few Westerners and I was the object of much pointing and giggling. People stopped dead in their tracks or rushed out of their houses to stare at the funny man. A traveler in Nepal will surely lose any feeling of self-consciousness.

After a steep climb at the far end of the valley, I stood looking toward Katmandu, the Jewel in the Lotus, a city of temples. The snow peaks of the High Himalayas rose above low-lying clouds, blazing gold in the rays of the setting sun. I cannot remember a more overwhelming sight.

The following nine days were a glimpse into the distant past. In spite of a few cars and jeeps, paved streets and an erratic electrical system, Katmandu is a primitive city. Harvesting and threshing wheat is done by hand. Women beat the stalks with wooden clubs and toss the grain into the air to let the chaff blow away. Men carry the sheaves over poles across their shoulders. They trot in from the fields, their hips wiggling like burlesque dancers. Because the valley is so extensively cultivated, there is little pasturage for domestic animals. This prevents the use of cattle or buffalos on threshing floors. The lack of transportation animals also explains the great number of porters. "Human taxicabs" carry people in baskets on their backs. Coolies trudge out of the hills with great stacks of firewood. The king's elephants are ridden through the streets and Army officers gallop along on little Tibetan ponies.

Girls use simple footpower to crush grain into flour. By stepping on and off seesaws, they pound the grain in hollow logs. Spinning is done by hand and color patterns are printed on cloth with design blocks pressed on dye pads and stamped on the material. In the paddy the peasants work bent over from the waist, digging with short-handled hoes. This would seem to make the back-breaking cultivation even more difficult than necessary.

I stayed at St. Xavier School in Patan, the twin city of Katmandu. Father Moran, a Jesuit from Chicago, is probably the most widely known Westerner in Nepal. He has been there since 1951.

"I had a boys' school in Patna, India," said Father Moran, "where the sons of leading Nepali families were educated. Just before the palace revolution the government invited me to Katmandu. They gave me permission to open the first foreign school in Nepal. Now we have five Jesuits— three American and two Indian—and two schools."

The temple square of Patan is said to be the finest in Asia. There are several brick temples built with one sloping roof above another in Chinese pagoda style. The Nepalis claim that this architecture originated here and was copied by the Chinese. The square contains statues of lions and elephants, a giant bronze bell, a cylindrical Indian-type temple and shrines cluttered with colored streamers, candles and oil lamps. Decorating doors and windows are intricate examples of the Newar wood carving art. The Newars were the ruling tribe before the present Gurkhas. The unusual, often startling, feature of Nepali temples is the brightly painted figures which adorn them. These carvings of sexual activity and phallic symbols represent fertility. They appear amusing or pornographic only to Western visitors. The Nepalis consider the temple art to be perfectly natural expressions of religious symbolism.

The center of Katmandu is called Hanuman Dhoka in honor of the monkey god. Here are more temples, the old palace and the statue of a bloodthirsty, many-armed Hindu deity holding weapons and decapitated heads. A huge drum is pounded early every morning to wake anyone who might be oversleeping. The street scene is like a continual pageant. You see Indian sadhus, red-robed Tibetan monks and wild mountaineers with uncut hair, homespun capes and razor-sharp kukris (Gurkha knives). Pigtailed Tibetans on pilgrimage to Buddhist shrines are properly awed by the sights of the big city. Nepali women dress in long skirts with wide sashes wrapped round and round their waists. They wear beads, charms, strings of silver coins and either a jeweled ring in the nose or a small ornament in each nostril. Upper-class gentlemen are dapper in white jodhpurs, tweed jackets and little caps with lopsided peaks.

In a courtyard I watched a wedding ceremony with everyone marching around to the accompaniment of a young man playing a nasal horn. The only discordant note was provided by a cow which lay dying nearby. None of the spectators knew what to do with the poor animal.

"Are you a doctor?" they inquired hopefully. They found it hard to believe that an American was not automatically a medical expert. Slaughtering a cow is no longer a crime punishable by death but the Nepalis are still extremely solicitous of their sacred cattle's welfare.

On a side street I discovered a monstrous wooden-wheeled cart topped by a towering mast of brush and banners. A milling crowd gave offerings to an idol squatting inside the cart. At some later date this contraption would be pulled through the city to celebrate the harvest festival.

One morning the Army paraded in review for the new commander-in-chief. The Gurkha soldiers carried kukris at their belts and wore British-style uniforms with wide-brim felt hats. The Gurkhas are legendary fighters, unexcelled in jungle and mountain warfare. Some of these men had served in North Africa and Burma with the British Army. One sergeant sported five medals for valor. After the parade the king drove away at the wheel of his fire-engine-red sports car.

Throughout Katmandu are heroic statues of various members of the Rana family on horseback. These life-size, bronze reproductions were carried into the valley by gangs of coolies. Before the road was opened statues, automobiles, anything too heavy for the ropeway, were brought in over the trail. Stripped of its wheels, a car was placed on a platform and transported laboriously by upwards of fifty men. After walking the largely vertical track, I can imagine what a job this must have been.

When the weather is clear, particularly in early morning or late afternoon, most of the Nepali Himalayas are visible from Katmandu. Closest of the famed snow peaks are Manaslu, Gori Sankar and Himalchuli, the vividly named "Snow Oven." Far to the west I saw the cone of Annapurna, and Mount Everest was an insignificant bump on the eastern horizon. One evening word came that the Swiss team had not only climbed Everest twice but had conquered Lhotse, its twin giant.

Of some 2,500 shrines around Katmandu, two are especially venerated spots for Buddhist pilgrimage. In searching for one of these shrines, I got lost and found myself in a village on the crest of a steep ridge. This place was distinguished by its packs of howling dogs. They followed me about, causing an ear-splitting commotion. The local temple had the usual collection of idols and metal statues of fierce lions plus an assortment of rusty swords, shields and spears hanging on the walls.

The next day I tried again, this time with Mac Douglas, an Australian newspaperman who was writing a history of Nepal for Father Moran. Mac was a quiet lanky Tasmanian, the possessor of a really remarkable handle-bar mustache. It thrust out from his face like a pair of wings. We climbed to a hilltop stupa whose spire is crowned by a golden umbrella fringed with tinkling bells. Below the spire a large pair of eyes is painted on each of the four sides. Between these eyes are elongated question marks somewhat like noses.

"Big Brother is watching you," said Mac dryly.

Prayer wheels encircle the base of the stupa. Inside each of these round containers are thousands of prayers written on scrolls. As the pilgrims walk by spinning the wheels, countless prayers are set in motion.

"What do you think, Mac? Maybe it's not such a bad idea."

"Righto, we can't lose."

So we marched solemnly around and spun the wheels.

At altars containing small statues of the Buddha, devotees place offerings of flowers. The monkeys who live around the temple follow right behind the worshipers and eat the flowers. Sometimes the offerings survive only a few seconds but no one would think of harming the monkeys. Beside the large stupa stands a gilded Hindu temple. Nepal has a unique system of religious co-existence. Often Buddhists and Hindus worship at the same temples with both groups believing that the idols represent their own gods. This can be considered either extreme religious tolerance or plain ignorance. For the shy, uncomplicated Nepalis, I prefer the former.

I also had trouble finding the second Buddhist shrine and wandered for hours through fields and villages, fording streams and drinking tea with peasant families. This stupa is located in a village inhabited largely by Tibetans. The brooding eyes look down on the houses, watching every move of the people. In addition to prayer wheels, there are long white flags covered with written prayers which fly from the stupa.

Obtaining a Nepali visa had been surprisingly easy but securing permission to re-enter India was a complicated procedure. The amount of red tape seemed ridiculous since the only other place I could go from Nepal would be into Tibet. The Indian authorities admitted that this was highly impractical.

I said goodby to Father Moran and his bright-eyed little boys and started back over the trail. Rain fell intermittently, warning of the approaching monsoon. I walked with five Gurkha soldiers on leave from Malaya. We stopped at a ramshackle trailside hotel where the atmosphere was quite informal. The guests cooked their own meals in the corridors and one gentleman brought his goats in with him. We slept on straw mats and set out again about 4:30 A.M. In Bhempedi my Gurkha friends presented a kukri to me as a souvenir of Nepal. I had known them for less than twenty-four hours but, as happened so often, a close bond had developed between us. Our brief friendship transcended the barrier of language so that words were really unnecessary.

I departed for Amlekhganj aboard a spastic truck. We wheezed slowly southward, had engine trouble only once, and made connection with the Raxaul train. I had been invited to return to the Mission Hospital and there enjoyed a much-needed bath. Heading east across the plains of North Bihar, I saw peasants riding buffalos and wearing bamboo hats as big around as car wheels. Fields are irrigated by two men scooping water from one ditch into another with a basket slung on ropes between them. Instead of sitting down, a laborer rests balanced on one leg like a stork.

In the railway station at Siliguri a neighborly Indian family staked out a claim on the floor of the third-class waiting room. We spread our bedrolls in a cozy cluster. I talked to a group of Sherpas led by Antharky, the veteran "Tiger" (high altitude porter), who is second only to Tensing in fame.

"We are going to Kashmir," he said, "to climb with an Indian team."

The Sherpas are short and stocky like Nepalis with the pronounced Mongoloid features of Tibetans. Their stamina in carrying heavy loads at high altitudes is legendary. Because of their crucial role in every mountain expedition, the Sherpas have become an elite clan, far above the ordinary porters. Antharky's men were equipped like Alpine guides in excellent boots and parkas.

Early in the morning I boarded the miniature train for Darjeeling. Within fifty miles it climbs from Siliguri, just above sea level, to an altitude over 7,000 feet. The train resorts to some peculiar railroad tricks such as making a corkscrew circle to cross its tracks at a higher point. It also uses an ingenious system of going forward to a dead end, throwing a switch and backing to another stop, then moving forward again on a third line. The movement resembles that of a clock's pendulum, with each swing raising the train to a higher level. The tiny engine labored mightily, bouncing up and down and shaking itself vigorously like a dog coming out of the water. At times its exertions became so strenuous that I feared it would throw us bodily off the track. We moved so slowly that ticketless passengers were able to hop on and off in a game of hide-and-seek with the conductor.

Darjeeling spreads in an arc below the crest of a ridge. The most famous of Indian hill stations, its gabled wooden houses resemble those of an Alpine village. Across deep valleys looms the icy mass of Kanchanjanga, the world's third-highest mountain. So close that it seems to overshadow the town, Kanchanjanga dominates a vast range of snow peaks stretching off into Tibet. At this season the best time to see Kanchanjanga is soon after sunrise before the monsoon clouds roll in.

My first night in Darjeeling I set up light housekeeping in an alcove of a Hindu temple. The sadhus were polite but aloof since I was a casteless person. But they allowed me to watch the priests performing the nightly ritual with drums and chanting and burning torches. On Sunday I met a group of evangelists and moved into an annex behind their house. They were holding a revival meeting featuring a quartet of three Indians and a New Zealand girl who sang Negro spirituals beautifully.

"Well, you can hitchhike around the world," said my American host, "but you can't hitchhike to heaven."

"That's true," I admitted, "but it's a good way to learn the meaning of Christianity as practiced by others. And many of them are not Christians."

Darjeeling's bazaar contains the most varied assortment of people in India. There are Sikhs, Anglo-Indians, English boys in school uniforms, Gurkha soldiers, Afghan traders, European missionaries, American tourists, Jesuit priests and West Bengal police in shorts and pillbox hats. Husky, black-mustached Baluchis wear flowing turbans and vests over loose shirts. Tibetan men have in one ear large gold rings set with jade. Anglicized Bengalis from Calcutta speak to each other in perfect English. Some of the Chinese merchants dress in silk robes, the women in silk or cotton jackets and trousers.

Nepalis and Bhutias comprise the majority of the area's population. *Bhutia* means "people of the borders," such as Sherpas, Sikkimese, Bhutanese and Lepchas. The Tibetan and Sherpa women look alike in long dark dresses, jade jewelry, braided hair and brightly colored, striped aprons. The main difference seems to be that Sherpanis wear two aprons, front and back, and Tibetans only one. Rickshas are operated by four men, two pulling and two pushing, because of the steep hills. The Maharaja of Sikkim, a frail little fellow in an orange silk robe and felt hat, drove by in his Buick Roadmaster. And in the park the bagpipe band of the Rajputana Rifles wailed lustily.

One morning I walked across town to the home of Tensing, Darjeeling's favorite son. I had met virtually no celebrities but he was one person I admired and was determined to see. Tensing is soft-spoken and modest, seemingly unaffected by his sudden fame. A chunky, black-haired man with a gentle, mischievous face, he is the director of the Indian government's mountaineering school.

"Most of the students are Army officers and others sent

by the government, but we have a few Europeans," he explained in precise English. "The instructors are Sherpas, all 'Tigers' who have climbed above 25,000 feet."

"Will you ever climb again?" I asked.

"No, I have been to the top of Everest and I am satisfied."

"Mountains are for young men," he added with a flashing grin. "Now I am too old."

On the hillside below Darjeeling I visited the Tibetan monastery of Bhutia Busti. Inside the prayer room sat a serene gilded Buddha flanked by lesser deities in tall pointed felt hats. Around the Buddha oil lamps flickered and little bowls contained offerings of rice and coins. The walls were lined with musty prayer books and scrolls, bizarre tapestries and Chinese-looking, painted wooden dragons. There were gongs, cymbals, a big drum and fat copper horns, about four feet long, which the monks blow in the mornings. A single paper prayer wheel revolved slowly. A sleepy monk acted as my guide and banged loudly on the collection box as a pointed reminder.

From Bhutia Busti the trail dropped down through tea gardens to the woods along the river, a descent of 6,000 feet. I watched tea pickers and hiked for a while with a platoon of soldiers. Across the stream lay Sikkim, a semi-autonomous state under the protection of India. I had never come so close to a country without actually entering it. I reached the main road and caught a ride with a Scottish tea planter to Kalimpong.

This hilltop town is the terminus of the caravan route from Tibet. The Tibetans come across the high passes driving herds of ponies loaded with skins, felt, yak wool and musk. They exchange these goods for the products of civilization and head back into the wilderness. The Chinese Communists have made no effort to restrict this trade because to do so would be far more trouble than it would be worth. So the trail to Kalimpong is one of the few holes in the Bamboo Curtain.

There are so many Tibetans in Kalimpong that they have an association and a newspaper. Of all the unusual peoples I have seen, the Tibetans are the most colorful. Their resemblance to American Indians is startling, even to the tall felt hats like those worn by Sioux and Blackfeet. They have the same powerful physique, broad flat face, high cheekbones and copper complexion. The men braid their hair in a long pigtail tied with red string which they wrap around their heads. They wear embroidered felt boots, leather pouches at the waist, charms around the neck and often a bright silk shirt purchased in the bazaar. Every man and boy carries a sword-length knife in a metal sheath. In hot weather some Tibetans simply pull their heavy coats off their shoulders and tie them across their stomachs. The heat evidently does not bother men in fur hats with ear flaps.

Early in the morning a misty rain fell at the big caravan sheds where women were brewing tea flavored with rancid butter. A grinning buccaneer offered me a mug of the sirupy liquid and I sipped it gingerly. I consoled myself with the thought that drinking sour tea with Tibetans was an experience to remember. Men were loading crates and bundles on ponies and mules for the long trip home. Each pack animal had a brass bell and some sported a red felt emblem on the forehead. The drivers sent them straggling up the trail, then swung onto their wooden-saddled, blanket-draped ponies and followed.

George McCabe, the brother of a missionary friend, operated the farm at Doctor Graham's Homes, a school for Anglo-Indian orphans. He and his wife were a dedicated couple, the kind of people who are a pleasure to know. George told me that Prince Peter of Greece is an anthropologist living in Kalimpong.

"The Prince has a clever method for collecting information on the Tibetans. The police notify him when the caravan men report for routine questioning. He measures their heads and examines them carefully and the Tibetans think that this is part of the police interrogation. So the Prince is the only anthropologist today who can study native Tibetans."

CHAPTER EIGHTEEN

KASHMIR

"WE BELONG TO Andhra state," announced a spokesman for the three hundred Hindu farmers. "We have come on a pilgrimage to the holy places."

I met this group at Buddh Gaya, the spot where Gautama meditated under the Bo tree and gained enlightenment to become the Lord Buddha. Outside monastaries inhabited by monks from China, Tibet, Ceylon and Burma, these Telugu-speaking southerners were conversing in English with their north Indian countrymen. Turning to me, the spokesman asked, "Will you accompany us to the temple of Vishnu?"

We piled into chartered buses and drove to a pile of black rock topped by a golden flag. Some of the farmers had been here since dawn engaged in an all-day purification ceremony of prayer and meditation. A heated argument developed between the temple priests and my friends as to the amount of offering they should leave. The priests behaved like gangsters and if it had been up to me, we would have given nothing. Later at the Gandhi Memorial everyone sat on the floor while a tall gaunt man led a hand-clapping chant.

"We are singing Gandhiji's favorite hymn of peace and brotherhood," explained one of my companions.

Using football tactics, a couple of Indians and I fought our way onto the train for Benares. There I ran into a German friend I had known in Ceylon. Horst took me cruising on his motorcycle. Benares is the most sacred city in India, the center of pilgrimage to Mother Ganges. Along the river banks are countless temples, some partially collapsed from the 1952 flood, and the bathing ghats, scene of a truly fantastic spectacle. Early every morning a torrent of worshipers pours down the stone steps and splashes into the Ganges. They stand in the murky water praying, washing themselves and their clothes, cleaning their teeth. The procession is endless—chattering peasant women, old widows with shaven heads, *dhoti*-clad men, shouting children, wealthy women carried in sedan chairs. I wondered how they kept from being trampled or drowned.

The steps are lined with wretched beggars and sadhus reading aloud from the holy books. Pilgrims coming out of the river distribute rice and coins to them. Merchants squatting under shade umbrellas or hawking their wares do a brisk business on the ghats. Clothes are spread to dry in the sun. Cows and goats mingle complacently with the masses. Horst and I hired a boat for eight annas (10¢) and were rowed along the banks seeing these sights at every ghat. Did this scene capture the heart and pulse, the faith and despair of India better than any other?

We stood outside the Golden Temple, which we could not enter, watching worshipers and cows pour in and out. The sacred cattle are in their glory in Benares. Benefactors have bales of grass brought to the ghats for them to eat. The cows become adept at snatching greens from irate vegetable sellers. The peddlers chase them away and even go so far as to give them a healthy boot in the rump. A more violent outburst against the cattle would be unthinkable for a Hindu.

The wooden Nepali temple, a special attraction for shocking tourists, is unimpressive compared to so many in Katmandu. At the burning ghats the dead are cremated and their ashes thrown into the holy river. The bodies are wrapped in red or white cloth and laid on the logs, more wood is piled over them and the pyre goes up in flames. Especially at night with mourners chanting and ghostly shrouded figures lying in the light of the fires, it is an eerie sight.

In the bazaar where Benares silks and saris are sold, I met two San Diego schoolteachers on a flying world tour. They were really flying, rushed from place to place so fast that all they could think about was getting some sleep. How lucky I was to have enough time!

I took to the road again and traveled along the Ganges with a highway engineer to Kanpur. We passed four-wheeled carts pulled by camels and *tongas* with tiny fringed tops. These horse taxis are always overloaded with passengers clinging to the sides since no villager would think of hiring one for only himself. He brings the family and the neighbors when going to town.

Kanpur is a hot and smoky industrial city. I inquired

at a shipping office and was told that trucks were leaving for Delhi that night. We started about 11:00 P.M. and the 250-mile journey took seventeen hours. The drivers believed in frequent breaks. We stopped to eat *chapatis* and *dal*, drink tea or hot buffalo milk, take baths and let one of the boys have a haircut. The mud-hut roadside cafés serve the best *chapatis* in India. They are made with a sprinkling of onion and fried in *ghee* (clarified butter). We were further delayed by two checkpoints at every town, on entering to pay a toll and on leaving to prove that we had paid. It was like traveling in the Middle Ages when each baron collected tolls on his private roads.

In Delhi I returned to the Quaker Center, my home away from home, and obtained a permit to visit Kashmir. My friend Seth from Jaipur was in town and we went to a Western-style restaurant for hamburgers and milk shakes.

"I'm surprised that they use beef," I said.

"These hamburgers are made of ground lamb," laughed Seth. "Anyone who sold beef in Delhi would be arrested."

From Pathankot, the gateway to Kashmir, I hitched a free lift on a bus to Jammu. The road runs close to the Pakistani border and is patrolled by Indian troops. Machine gun emplacements guard every bridge in this disputed territory. Jammu is a temple city of the Dogras who inhabit the Himalayan foothills. Next morning the same bus brought me to Banihal. From here the road twists upward to a tunnel at 9,000 feet elevation, the only entrance into the Vale of Kashmir. This tunnel had collapsed during the previous winter and was closed every afternoon for further repairs. So we waited in Banihal and that evening saw a government-sponsored education program. Films on irrigation and village projects were shown in the square, using a blank wall as a screen and a portable generator for power.

Kashmir is India's Achilles heel, a lovely, mountain-ringed land of political dispute. The Indians are trying with money and propaganda to win the loyalty of the Kashmiris. But as we Americans have learned, you cannot buy friend-ship. Unfortunately for India, most Kashmiris happen to be conservative and orthodox Moslems. I believe that no amount of economic aid will alter the determination of the majority to be united with Pakistan. Although their future would probably be more prosperous under Indian rule, emotion is stronger than logic.

A young lawyer summarized the general feeling when he said, "We live under military occupation. The Indian gov-ernment has promised a United Nations plebiscite but they know that the people would vote against them. So they re-fuse to hold the plebiscite. No one can travel in or out of Kashmir without a permit. The police control is very strict and anyone who speaks against the government is impris-oned. We are victims of Indian imperialism."

This situation weakens and embarrasses India in her roles of mediator between East and West and champion of self-determination. The lack of freedom in Kashmir is in sharp contrast to the democracy throughout the rest of the coun-try. The miniature war between Pakistan and India in 1947 and subsequent unrest have curtailed the tourist trade on which so many Kashmiris depend. The British who used to come for two or three months are no longer available and postwar travelers, particularly free-spending Ameri-cans, have been scared away by the political difficulties.

Srinagar, the capital of Kashmir, is called the City of the

Sun. Because of cold and snowy winters the steep-roofed, wooden architecture has a European rather than Indian aspect. The central mosque is a round, timbered building with a tower, quite different from others I had seen. But the crowds are purely Eastern. Bearded Kashmiris wear skullcaps, pantaloons and Persian sandals with pointed, curling toes. Unveiled Moslem women dress in long blue bandannas and billowing red robes which give them a bloated, dumpling appearance. The loose-sleeve green gowns and white headdresses of Hindu ladies are like costumes of medieval Europe. Holy men dye their beards with henna.

Ahmad Khan lived on a houseboat moored beside a park of massive *chenar* trees. Srinagar is a city built on canals and the winding Jhelum River and many families have floating homes. Ahmad's father rented houseboats to tourists. Since business was slow, he offered me the use of an empty boat. The canal was an ideal place to live. Women washed clothes along the banks and picnicked under the trees, gossiping and drinking tea brewed in big brass samovars. Children splashed and shouted in the water. Peasants paddled to market, squatting on their heels in the bows of their narrow canoes. Long, low houseboats drifted past, usually poled by hard-working women. There was occasional commotion when a family chicken fell overboard.

The *shikaras* (water taxis) of Srinagar are small craft with striped canopies and soft seats. While reclining in a *shikara*, it is easy to imagine oneself a splendid Oriental potentate. The boatmen are loud and persistent in their efforts to lure passengers and cannot comprehend why anyone would want to walk. Ahmad took me for a ride through the backwaters, past shops on stilts and floating gardens, to a hidden village. In a mud-brick house aged craftsmen were painting exquisite floral patterns on papier-mâché bowls and vases.

As I puttered around my houseboat, enterprising salesmen would paddle alongside and burst through the open windows with bundles of handicrafts. In spite of my protests that I had no money for souvenirs, they spread out their wares on the floor. When I did not buy, they offered to trade for my wristwatch or even my pants. For aggressive salesmanship no one equals the Kashmiris. Their sudden invasions were startling but always amusing.

Late one afternoon I wandered far beside the Jhelum River, a sheet of glass reflecting the *chenars* and poplars on its banks. The rays of the setting sun threw a canopy of crimson across the sky and touched the snow peaks with fire. Boats glided silently past, barely rippling the water. The only sound in the still air was the cry of a shepherd boy and the tinkle of goats' bells.

Ahmad and I set out on bicycles to visit the Mogul gardens on the shores of Dal Lake. At Nishat Gardens, a dozen terraces glowing with red flowers, we conversed with an elderly Englishwoman. Turning to Ahmad, she said, "And you are looking after the sahib."

I interrupted in embarrassment, "Ahmad is my friend and I'm no sahib."

"What a stupid thing for her to say!" I exclaimed later.

"Never mind. She is old and cannot understand our being together unless I am your servant."

We bought delicious Kashmiri fruit, fat cherries and apricots sweet as sugar, and continued to Shalimar. The fountains were not playing and this most famous garden seemed drab compared to Nishat.

A bus ride across the valley was uneventful except for a brawl between our driver and two motorcyclists. For some reason the cyclists were trying to cut us off, so the driver leaped out of the bus and punched one of them. This fellow beat a hasty retreat until his friend charged to the rescue. Then, his courage restored, he began chasing the driver around the bus. When passengers intervened the cyclist shouted that his honor was at stake and demanded revenge. I thought that they might engage in a duel but after many heated words, peace was restored, apparently to everyone's satisfaction. The only person who seemed upset by this Keystone Kops episode was an old lady whose servant, happily embroiled in the dispute, ignored her pleas for neutrality.

Gulmarg is a fading resort of British days located in fir and pine forests and accessible only by trail. If the weather is very clear, which it was not, you can see Nanga Parbat, the killer mountain which has taken more climbers' lives than any other Himalayan peak. I was a guest of the local tax collector. Gulmarg's elevation is 9,500 feet and the night was cold. We huddled around a charcoal brazier, smoked the hookah and drank Kashmiri salt tea, a reddish liquid as unappetizing as it sounds. I discovered that the women slip baskets of coals under their shapeless robes to keep warm. I wondered if they ever set themselves on fire.

A rocky path leads upward to an open meadow at the foot of snow-streaked cliffs. From here the Vale of Kashmir with its sparkling lakes and mountain bastions lies far below. Several tea and cake vendors had erected tents on the field and one fellow in particular worked frantically to lure customers. Tall and awkward, he rushed about, stumbling over the rocks, like a man possessed with devils. Flapping his arms and bellowing at his befuddled assistant, he seemed on the verge of a nervous collapse. Awed by his efforts, I bought my two-and-a-half-cent cup of tea from him.

On the trail again I joined a party of prosperous Kashmiris who were riding ponies and singing American pop tunes and Urdu folk songs. One of this group, obviously a man of importance, was extremely arrogant in his treatment of porters and other social inferiors—an attitude which unfortunately is found among many upper-class Indians. This pompous oaf was the brother of the prime minister of Kashmir. I disliked him, but nevertheless accepted a lift to Srinagar in one of his two cars. Hitchhikers must not be too particular.

I departed for the Lolab Valley, a remote area to the north, on the Fourth of July. I did not see another American, or European for that matter, much less celebrate the holiday. Anyone wanting to visit Lolab must walk an eighteen-mile circular route, but it is well worth the effort. The valley is an unspoiled little wonderland enclosed by pine-clad hills. The villages are tucked among walnut and apple trees at the foot of the slopes and the valley floor is splashed with paddies and meadows in every shade of green. Houses are tall and solid, built of logs or rough planks, with thatch roofs and what look like escape hatches on top. These trap doors are actually outlets for smoke. The upper floors are open and serve as storage space for firewood, hay, sacks of food and clay pottery. The men sit and meditate on the second-floor porches. Fences around the houses are made of sticks and brush woven together.

Peasant women wear silver jewelry, strings of coins across their foreheads and clusters of rings piercing their ears. The hair style is peculiar, with many little braids looped on both sides of their heads. The men carry heavy, hand-woven wool blankets over their shoulders even during the heat of the day. They wrap themselves in these blankets at night and wear them as cloaks in cold weather.

At a forest rest house the caretaker greeted me as if I were Nehru, and with great ceremony produced a plate of rice and potatoes for dinner. The following day while hiking I could find nothing to eat. Each village has one tiny shop selling tobacco, cloth, odds and ends, but no food. The peasants eat only what they raise so I could not even buy bread. That night I stayed at Lalpur with the district police chief, a jovial bearlike fellow. Realizing that I was starved, my friend provided a whole roast chicken, rice and various curries.

After a final sojourn on my houseboat, I reluctantly said farewell to Ahmad and his excellent family. Along the road I stopped at a Hindu shrine built around a spring full of fish. For a fee the priests here will give anyone a certificate which guarantees entrance into heaven. I declined this tempting offer and proceeded up the Lidar Valley. Gradually paddies and orchards disappear as the fertile farmland narrows into a rock-ribbed canyon. In this mountain fastness lies the village of Pahalgam, a favorite camping spot for Indian families. These city dwellers rent large tents, beds, chairs and tables and bring along their servants so that they can rough it in style and comfort. Two rug dealers invited me to spread my sleeping bag on the well-carpeted floor of their shop.

I retraced my steps out of Kashmir since there is only one route. The manager of the government truck park at Kazigund dispatched vehicles across Banihal Pass. He was another of these individuals who simply could not do enough for me. After dinner with the drivers, he fixed a comfortable bed in the back of one of the trucks. Next morning I was put aboard the convoy going through the tunnel. From Banihal a policeman arranged further bus transportation. In the quaintly named village of Kud astride the high ridges guarding Kashmir, I shared a room in a dumpy hotel with other passengers. During the night I awoke scratching furiously and discovered that small guests had invaded my sleeping bag. This was my only encounter with bugs other than mosquitoes. I felt no regrets on leaving Kud. At the Jammu rest house everyone had lunch except the driver. That gentleman decided Jammu prices were too high so we waited while he ate in a café outside town. Sort of a foolish arrangement, I thought, but as a non-paying passenger I felt it was none of my business.

My final visit to Delhi lasted longer than I had planned. A merchant named Kapoor had previously invited me to his home so I took this opportunity to stay in the heart of Old Delhi. Most visitors thread their way down the Chandni Chowk, look at the shops and return to the wide-open spaces of New Delhi. But to appreciate the infinite color, the appalling congestion, you must explore the alleys leading off the Chowk and actually live there. Kapoor and an uncountable number of others resided in a musty building on one of these alleys. Kapoor himself was a strange host. After a brief greeting, he ignored me and I hardly saw him for three days. I slept in a downstairs office and never met his family or set foot inside their top-floor apartment. The fact that I was a casteless person, unworthy of being entertained by an orthodox Hindu, may have caused his odd behavior. If so, I wondered why he had bothered to invite me. Perhaps he was simply being polite and was dismayed when I accepted his invitation.

I intended to spend a day at the Quaker Center and leave immediately for Calcutta. But while sipping lemonade with my friends, I suddenly began feeling very dizzy. Before I realized what was happening, I had keeled over onto the floor. With this dramatic exit, I retired from the quiet tea party to shiver and sweat through the chills and fever of malaria. Combined with a second attack of dysentery, the malaria kept me in bed for a week. Fortunately both of my illnesses occurred while I was at the Quaker Center. Donald and Olive Lawrence took the best possible care of me.

"I couldn't have picked a better place to be sick," I told them gratefully.

The Janita, a third-class express, makes the 900-mile trip to Calcutta in two nights and one day. A ticket costs less than five dollars and every passenger has a reserved bench. This is pure luxury for the Indian railroads.

Calcutta is said to be the dirtiest, most overcrowded, disease-infested city in India. It is the only area which suffers from a more or less continual cholera epidemic. The staggering problems of health and housing have been further aggravated by the flood of refugees from East Pakistan. The industrial slums which skirt the city are wretched even by Indian standards. Lower-class Bengalis seem more helpless in their poverty, more apathetic in their servility than other Indians. Pitiful lepers, crippled and diseased beggars, emaciated people like walking skeletons, women picking lice from each others' hair—these sights which shock one in spite of their familiarity are seen more frequently in Calcutta than elsewhere.

Soon after my arrival, I suffered a relapse of malaria. A kindly Jewish refugee doctor gave me medicine and food, let me rest in his home and would not accept any money. He took me to the Salvation Army hostel where I recuperated again. Recurring malaria could become a terrible nuisance but luckily this was my last attack. Next door to the hostel stood a temple from which a great racket of chanting, bells and drums arose every evening promptly at dinnertime. It sounded like a crowd banging tin cans and was distressing to the digestion of elderly missionary ladies.

Chowringhee, the main street of Calcutta, is lined on one side with hotels, theaters and stores. Opposite stretches the Maidan, a vast park containing football fields, tree-lined drives and the racetrack. Here are found statues of British kings and generals, the Victoria Memorial, a bulbous copy of the Taj Mahal, and a tall pillar where demonstrations and riots often begin. One afternoon a procession of workers marched through the streets, waving flags and banners, and gathered around this pillar to hear fiery speeches. It was frightening to watch how a few energetic leaders manipulated the mob of simple, ignorant men. They were driven like animals, pushing forward in long, docile columns, obediently shouting slogans. The scene resembled a football rally with students following the commands of their cheerleaders. I remembered that the bloody partition riots started in Calcutta.

At the Temple of Kali animals are sacrificed to the goddess of destruction. I watched two bleating goats held on the forked block and beheaded with a stroke of the executioner's sword. Priests pounded drums and devotees dipped their fingers into the blood and marked their foreheads. The meat is cooked and distributed to the poor. Most of the unlucky animals are goats, but on special occasions water buffalos are sacrificed.

CHAPTER NINETEEN

BURMA

"How WAS THE trip?" asked Tom.

"Very dull, but cheap. I was hungry most of the time for three days. There were three Germans on board who had pedaled their bicycles from Stuttgart to Calcutta. They are also heading for the Olympics. We traveled deck class together and brought our own food but not enough of it."

I had sailed across the Bay of Bengal to Rangoon on the British India ship *Santhia*. During the monsoon the overland route from India into Burma was impassable so I had no choice. Tom Manton was an American student, son of the Methodist pastor in Rangoon. We had met two months before in an Indian railroad station and he invited me to stay with his family. In honor of Tom's birthday I had a haircut and the first trim on my whiskers in eleven months. I must admit that the beard looked better. One of Tom's Burmese friends prepared a typical meal of chicken, fried rice and meat balls for us. You find genuine Burmese food only in private homes, since restaurants like most other businesses are operated by industrious Indians and Chinese.

Rangoon is filled with round smiling faces. The Burmans are a pleasure-loving people, easygoing and unsophisticated, the Irish of the East. Their happy-go-lucky temperament combined with a rebellious, independent streak has caused the postwar instability which paralyzes the country. Burma's freedom from British rule was sudden and complete and the government has been fighting armed revolt ever since. Because of internal disorder the Burmese have never been able to recover from the ravages of Japanese occupation and Allied reconquest.

The forces opposing the government are comically diverse. Two separate groups of Communist insurgents, Stalinists and Trotskyites, engage in guerrilla warfare. The Karen tribesmen, missionary-educated Baptists who carry a rifle in one hand and a Bible in the other, fight for an independent state. Then there are dissatisfied Shan rebels whose objectives seem rather vague, and large numbers of plain ordinary bandits. To further complicate the situation, remnants of the Chinese Nationalists have been battling the Burmese army for years. And while I was in Burma Red Chinese troops were moving into the wild northern Kachin and eastern Wa country.

"These areas are so isolated during the monsoon," explained Dr. Manton, "that no one in Rangoon knows how far the invasion has progressed. The Burmese are too weak to protest effectively. Their policy of strict neutralism has left them in a tough spot. The Chinese claim territory on the borders but we can't understand why they would frighten every country in Southeast Asia for a few square miles of jungle."

"What do you think will be the outcome of all this confusion?" I asked.

"The chaos will continue until the Burmese learn respect for law and order. If the people who oppose the government use ballots instead of guns, I think Burma will have a bright future. This country is not yet overpopulated and the land is very rich."

Before the war there were few Burmans in Rangoon. Most of the inhabitants were Indian laborers and merchants, Chinese traders and British civil servants. The city was a clean, orderly monument to colonial rule. During the postwar years a flood of refugees from upcountry plus officials for the new government have almost tripled the population. The capital has become shabby and dirty from neglect. Inefficiency, which admittedly plays a part, is not solely responsible for this decline. Finances are used in fighting rebels and bandits and there is little money available for civic improvements.

The men of Rangoon dress in richly colored sarongs called *longyis*. Some old gentlemen still wear the traditional pink gauze cap, tight on the head and knotted on one side. The woman's costume is also a *longyi* with a transparent nylon blouse and flowers in her hair. She wears a slip but for some reason no brassiere. Little girls have a distinctive hair style. A part runs around the crown of their head—above this line the hair is tied into a pony tail, below it hangs straight down in a fringe. I think that Burmese babies must be the cutest in the world. They are roly-poly and bare-bottomed, with button noses and enormous eyes peering from chubby faces. Miniature military caps or knitted bonnets perch on their shaven heads. I found myself following mothers through the streets to admire their babies.

Bicycle rickshas are called *trishaws* and have little sidecars attached to the bikes in which two passengers sit back to back. The *trishaw* boys, of whom there must be thousands, are quite dapper in pork-pie hats and rakish kerchiefs. None work very steadily but they seem to enjoy life immensely. Burmese women smoke long fat cheroots, while the men prefer smaller cigars. If there is some significance in this, it escapes me.

The pie dogs of Rangoon are the mangiest, scrawniest, most degenerate mongrels imaginable. Running wild, brawling and howling day and night, their behavior in public is disreputable enough to appall the most ardent animal lover. Although pie dogs roam every town and village, they are a particular nuisance in the capital. The only people who take positive action against this canine curse are the Wa tribesmen. The primitive Was, some of whom still do a bit of head-hunting, periodically come out of the jungles, round up the pie dogs and eat them. This admirable solution would not be practical for the rest of the population.

The Shwe Dagon Pagoda, colossus of Burmese Buddhism, is a gold-covered spire rising 370 feet into the sky. Sparkling in the sunlight or etched against a rust-red sunset, seen far across the city or close at hand, it is a memorable sight. The main entrance leads up flights of covered steps lined with shops selling flowers, toys and religious trinkets.

Around the Shwe Dagon itself are gaily painted shrines containing statues of the Buddha, smaller pagodas and pavilions.

I met two Stanford students, Craig Barnes and Dave "Waldo" Buck, who were spending six months at Rangoon University. Craig's father worked as a civil engineer with the Burmese National Planning Board. He was driving to Mandalay on a business-pleasure trip and offered me a lift. Craig, a handsome, soft-spoken Colorado cowboy, and Waldo, a round-faced, witty fellow, were both excellent traveling companions. Ten days with them meant a welcome change from wandering alone.

At 5:30 one morning we left for Upper Burma on the road to Mandalay. The highway was narrow, full of gaping potholes and busy with trucks. Our driver barreled along like a contestant in the Indianapolis 500. The delta north of Rangoon was a waterlogged rice bowl with villages semi-flooded from heavy rains. Houses of woven bamboo strips squatted on wooden piles and ducks paddled in the front yards. Beside the road lay rusty skeletons of Japanese tanks and every railroad siding was clogged with strings of burned-out boxcars and shells of bombed locomotives. The Burmese plan to use this mass of scrap to supply their infant steel industry. We passed numerous rice mills, corrugated iron sheds topped by tall, slender smokestacks. In Pegu, a ramshackle sawmill town, we admired the lofty pagoda.

Burma is the land of pagodas. You see them scattered throughout the countryside, on the hills and in the smallest village. Great merit is attached to building these Buddhist temples but no credit is gained from repairing them. A cluster of pagodas will contain some that are new and gleaming white, their golden umbrellas fringed with tiny bells which jingle in the breeze. Others will be neglected, crumbling mounds of brick. This may seem wasteful but who can judge ancient religious custom?

We stopped to inspect a new sugar refinery set among fields of ripening cane.

"This mill was built and equipped by the Japanese as war reparations," said the manager.

"And paid for with American aid to Japan," added Mr. Barnes with a smile.

We moved into a spacious apartment at the Mandalay Housing Board's headquarters and were greeted by a Burmese friend of the Barnes family. A University of Chicago graduate and inexhaustible source of information, Joe became our expert guide to Mandalay. The former palace grounds, a rectangle enclosed by brick walls and a lily-filled moat, now houses the army garrison. On the banks of the mighty, rain-swollen Irrawaddy cargo is loaded aboard river steamers. The Arakan Pagoda, rising in golden tiers, resembles a Chinese temple. At the entrance stand fierce concrete Chinthes, the mythical Burmese lions. Fruit and flowers offerings are blended together into strikingly beautiful arrangements. The pagoda nuns, toothless old hags with heads as bare as cue balls, look more like men than women.

The streets of Mandalay are thronged with wildly careening *trishaws*, crawling bullock carts and pretty girls on bicycles. Deafening music emanates from sound trucks advertising the current movies. Brightly painted, horse-drawn carriages resemble flamboyant stage coaches. I noticed the driver of one, a black-bearded character with a roguish grin, who could have doubled for any of Jean Lafitte's pirates.

We drove out to the pagodas and pilgrim hostels around Mandalay Hill. "Every good Buddhist," explained Joe, "is expected to put on the saffron robe, beg for his food and live as a *pongyi*—a monk—at least once in his lifetime."

"How about you?" asked Craig.

"I have done this several times," answered Joe.

The *pongyis* seem especially numerous and influential in Mandalay. They file through the streets in silent columns, protecting their heads from sun or rain with red umbrellas of lacquered paper. Some look quite prosperous in sunglasses and yellow shoulder bags which match their robes. The dozens of local *pongyi tomes* (monasteries) are centers of religious scholarship. The monks have their own ward at the hospital and are responsible for signs throughout town in Burmese and English which read, "Be kind to animals by not eating them."

Joe took us to a nearby village which was celebrating a *Nat* festival. *Nats* are playful household spirits which the Burmese venerate as holdovers from their pre Buddhist animistic religion. To reach the village we drove to the end of a dirt track and were rowed along a canal in a *sampan*. These little boats have high, double-pronged sterns and eyes painted on their bows. The boatman stands in the stern and propels the sampan with two crossed oars.

Peasants in their holiday best flocked into the village and the Burmese love of color and gaiety was much in evidence. The main street was festooned with banners and lined with improvised stalls. Cigar-puffing women bartered and gossiped among stacks of tobacco leaves and piles of bananas and coconuts. Bowls of Chinese noodles and pork were sold from little wagons. Vendors peddled everything from sugar-cane juice to pungent dried fish. I saw several small *pongyis* who could not have been more than eight or nine years old. The *Nat* shrines dripped with flowers and inside the temple worshipers plastered patches of gold foil onto a seated Buddha. This practice of continuously gilding the idol had given it a lumpy, bloated appearance.

That night we joined the promenade outside the palace walls and came upon a feeble one-man band. A withered ancient played his fiddle, sang in a trembling falsetto and banged on cymbals and wood block.

"He claims to be one hundred and three years old," said Joe.

A traditional Burmese theater company was performing in Mandalay and we were allowed to go backstage. Child-like dancing girls wound themselves into their glittering costumes and applied makeup with the help of their mothers. Warriors with drooping mustaches and wooden swords played cards or curled up asleep. A band contributed energetic background music as the huge cast trooped on and off stage. There was a portable Buddhist shrine where actors and actresses prayed before each performance.

The following evening we decided to see the show. Spectators rent deck chairs or floor mats for their seats and settle down for the night. This is literally true since the performance lasts until 6:00 A.M. Anyone feeling tired can lie back and sleep for awhile. The singing, dancing and rambling slapstick do not have to be followed closely or continuously. And the audience knows the traditional show almost by heart. We arrived about 9:30, took a half-hour break at midnight and had enough by 2:30.

En route to Maymyo Joe pointed out pagoda-crowned promontories unsafe to visit because of insurgent activity. Maymyo is a hill station whose solid brick houses retain an air of British colonial days. We inspected a condensed-milk factory, its only problem a shortage of milk to condense, and an unfinished silk-weaving mill where busy little silkworms munched their mulberry leaves.

Mr. Barnes returned to Ragoon while Craig, Waldo and I hopped a bus for Lashio and the Shan States. A Volkswagen half an hour ahead of us was stopped by *dacoits* (bandits) and the passengers were robbed of everything except their shorts. Luckily we had no trouble. Lashio is the beginning of the old Burma Road and the closest I came to China. There are many Chinese residents, some anti-Communist refugees, others illegal immigrants smuggled across the border by the Reds. The Burmese police are too short-handed to effectively patrol the frontier.

Lashio has a marvelous bazaar and it was our good fortune to be there on market day. Indians and Chinese own the shops but the shoppers are mostly Shan villagers and Kachin tribesmen. *Shan* means "Siam" and these people are descendants of Siamese invaders. Their round, flat faces, light skin and wispy mustaches give them a Chinese appearance. They dress in loose, short trousers, open shirts and pointed cartwheel hats made of palm leaves. Each carries a long-handled knife called a *dah* and a gaily striped shoulder bag. Real jungle rustics use bows but no arrows in hunting birds and small game. They fire pellets as from a slingshot. The bodies of the men are covered with blue tattooing, the designs thickly spread over arms, legs and chests. Both men and women wrap white towels around their heads as turbans.

The Kachins are a primitive tribal people from north Burma. Not long ago they were head-hunters. Their women are clad in embroidered red skirts, matching leggings and revealing, low-cut blouses or in voluminous garments of bright blue. They wear a wide metal band or coils of woven horsehair around their waists. These are said to be chastity belts. Their teeth are stained red from betel nut juice. Silver coin jewelry, bare feet and babies in slings on their backs complete the picture. Kachin men carry wicked-looking *dahs* as long as swords.

The bus to Hsipaw came out to the resthouse where we were staying and picked us up.

"This is really good service," commented Waldo but we soon changed our minds. For a full hour the bus called at passengers' homes and cruised all over town looking for more riders. Finally the driver was convinced that no one else could be persuaded to go to Hsipaw and we departed. The family living upstairs in the bus depot invited us to spread our sleeping bags on their floor. After we had crawled under our mosquito nets, they gathered to pray before the flickering candles of a little shrine. Buddhist families devote at least a corner of their home to a place of worship.

At 6:00 A.M. we were awakened by a man who exclaimed urgently, "Your baggage must be aboard in half an hour!"

We stumbled out of bed and hurriedly packed our gear. Four hours later the bus was still rumbling about searching for passengers. Meanwhile we drank coffee with the citizens of Hsipaw and watched militia from outlying villages filing into town. Each man carried an antique rifle and an umbrella hung on his shoulder. Our patience was rewarded about eleven o'clock when the rotund driver of the Peacock Bus Service announced we were leaving. The rival Tiger Bus departed at the same time. During that day and the next we became quite attached to the dilapidated, terribly overloaded Peacock Bus on its laborious journey across the Shan States.

Through wild and tangled jungle, we traveled often for miles without seeing a person. Occasional clusters of bamboo and thatch huts nestled in the bush. A tattooed Shan merchant got off at a jungle clearing and we spent twenty minutes unloading the fantastic assortment of supplies he had brought from Hsipaw. In a tiny hamlet not even shown on our map we slept in a comfortable, deserted house believed to be haunted because of a murder committed there. We continued through pine-clad hills and secluded rice-growing valleys alternating with the unbroken jungle.

"Insurgents only attack buses traveling with military escort," our driver remarked cheerfully. "Peacock Bus is not worth capturing."

We hoped he was right.

Just three miles from Loilem, our destination, old Peacock ran out of gas. We had suffered previous mechanical difficulties and interminable delays but this was a blow so close to the finish. As we sadly wondered what to do, over the hill to the rescue roared old Tiger Bus. Peacock had been ahead in the haphazard turtle race to Loilem but after giving us gas, our friendly rival won the last lap. A young policeman, Jan Say When by name, was aboard the Tiger.

Bubbling over with good will, he insisted that we stay at his home in Loilem. It may have been coincidence but Jan was a Moslem, the son of a Pathan, and this is an unbeatable combination for hospitality.

In the morning Jan took us to Panglong bazaar, a market similar to that of Lashio. But here in the southern Shan States the population is even more diverse. There are Taung-thus (hill people), Palaungs and Badaungs in addition to the dominant Shans. A stylish Taung-thu woman wears a black or dark blue jacket, blouse, skirt and leggings. This somber costume is topped by a length of plaid cloth wrapped loosely around the head like a top-heavy crown. The Palaung lady has rows of red tassels across the front and back of her dress and a black headdress with metal pins stuck in her hair. The Badaungs wear horsehair belts around the hips like the Kachins and bare-midriff jackets. We saw one tribal girl sporting a long horsehair tail.

"When a man pulls the tail," explained Jan, "he is doing the same as putting a ring on her finger."

Old Chinese women hobble about on tiny, bound feet. The southern Shans use colored towels for turbans instead of plain white as in the north. We met one of Jan's friends, a policeman with hand grenades in his belt and a bloody bandage around his head. He had been wounded the night before in a *dacoit* raid on the police post outside Panglong. We watched a truckload of troops armed with rifles and a Bren gun start off on patrol. The atmosphere of Upper Burma is a curious mixture of warlike activity and the placid, age-old routine of village life.

Compared to old Peacock, the bus for Taunggyi was fast and comfortable but it did not have the personality.

The only eccentric behavior was halting out in the middle of nowhere while the driver slowly and carefully collected all fares. The country between Loilem and Taunggyi is a giant mural of hills and valleys painted in greens, blues and purples. Taunggyi itself is a hilltop town justly famed for its pretty Shan girls. In the houses women roll cigars by hand and men fluff cotton with wooden bows similar to single-string harps.

Craig and Waldo decided that they should be back in school and caught a plane for Rangoon. I met an English mining engineer named Aldworth who had tramped the Shan hills for thirty years. A remarkable fellow, he was also an authority on Burmese wild orchids which he exported as a sideline. Aldworth told me about the wealth of minerals lying untapped in the jungles.

"The Shan States," he claimed, "are as rich in lead, zinc, antimony, manganese and gypsum as any area in the world. No capital and these bloody insurgents prevent more than small-scale mining. If things ever quiet down, a chap could make his fortune."

He asked if I would be interested in seeing his lead mines and I jumped at the chance. Along the main road Aldworth pointed out the spot where he had shot a leopard two weeks before. We entered one of the tunnels on his square-mile lease and crawled down a pitch-black shaft. At the bottom three villagers were digging chunks of lead carbonate by candlelight. They dragged the ore to the surface in baskets.

"This vein extends for thirty or forty miles," said my friend. "There is so much lead here that any fool could sink a tunnel into the hillside and strike ore."

The head man of a nearby village was building a big concrete house with the proceeds from his mines. He served us pickled tea, eaten with dried prawns, beans and garlic pearls, and rolls stuffed with chicken, crabmeat and bamboo shoots. Both were delicious. That night we went leopard hunting. There were six of us crammed into a jeep bristling with armament. I was given a rifle and my companions had a shotgun, a U. S. Army carbine and a Sten gun. The mine foreman stood in the back and operated the searchlight. For two hours we bounced over fields and along jungle trails. Did we shoot any leopards? No, but our jeepload of firepower did succeed in bagging one good-sized rabbit.

Next morning I was taken to Heho on an ore truck. The driver, a Karen of my age, had fought as a rebel for three years until he became disillusioned. We passed a farmer riding a buffalo, his wooden plow on his shoulder. Later I saw two peasants bound for market sitting sedately back to back on a buffalo and holding an umbrella for shade. Compared to the Indian variety Burmese buffalo are fatter, have long sweeping horns, and while not exactly scholarly in appearance, seem to be somewhat more intelligent.

From Kalaw I traveled in a road convoy under military escort which rendezvoused with the Mandalay-Rangoon Express. A guard train moved ahead of us pushing an empty flatcar whose purpose was to detonate any mines that might have been laid on the track. All was peaceful except in one village which had been raided by insurgents during the night. The army had rushed belatedly to the rescue and soldiers patrolled the deserted rice fields. At Taungoo an Irish-Burmese river-boat captain and I set up cots together on the station platform when the train "stabled" for the night. No one travels after dark in Burma.

My last few days in Rangoon were spent at the Barnes's house. The air-conditioned bedrooms provided a delicious relief from the humid heat. I read and relaxed and had to be coaxed to come out. The Barneses are certainly on my list of gold-star families. Craig, Waldo and I went to a good party given by a Japanese-American economist and his Hawaiian wife. Two Chinese brothers played guitars, we sang until 4:00 A.M. and it was nostalgically like home. Mr. Barnes took us to lunch at the Strand Hotel, one of the famed "outposts of Empire" during colonial days. Like Raffles' in Singapore the Strand lingers on as a link with the past. At the university I enjoyed a surprise reunion with Bill Rideout, a friend from Stanford. Bill was doing research with a group from Johns Hopkins School of International Relations.

Each year the Shiah Moslems of Rangoon commemorate the martyrdom of Ali, cousin and fourth successor of Mohammed, with a fire-walking ceremony. They parade, garbed in white and holding banner poles, to where a trench has been dug and filled with coals. After much chanting of "Ali, Ali," the leaders trot back and forth through the fire. The other men follow them, some fathers carrying babies in their arms. I stood close enough to feel the heat and see their bare feet sink into the coals. As the fire cools, more men and boys run through the trench.

"Looks easy, doesn't it?" commented a Burmese onlooker. "Last year an Englishman tried it and spent three weeks in hospital."

Since the overland route into Thailand was blocked by a small-scale war between the army and Karen rebels, I decided to fly on Burma Airways. A 30 per cent student discount plus an allowance for publicity purposes reduced the ticket price to about seven dollars. Entering Burma is not especially difficult but trying to leave the country is a frustrating experience. I submitted the last of eight required visa and registration photos to the police. After battling with the authorities over currency regulations, I faced a last-minute demand for an income-tax clearance. This, I discovered later, was completely unnecessary. With Mr. Barnes's help I cut through the red tape and flew off to Bangkok. There was only one other passenger aboard the DC3.

CHAPTER TWENTY

THAILAND
AND CAMBODIA

Mai ben lai means "never mind," the motto of a happy
country. The Thais laugh at themselves and at the world
and nothing seems to bother them. They accept the recent
influx of bustling, impatient, slightly bewildered Americans
with an air of amused tolerance, yet they make good use
of our military and economic aid. The Thais succeed in
blending progress and comparative prosperity with an
ancient and carefree way of life. A clique of army and
police officers controls a benevolent dictatorship and corruption is rampant in high government circles. But Thailand
has no population problem, the peasants grow the best rice
in Asia and most people are indifferent to politics. *Thai*
means "free," and never having been ruled by foreign mas-
ters, the Thais are not troubled by fears and memories of
colonialism. They are not mad at anyone and it is pure
pleasure to be with them.

In Bangkok concrete and glass rub shoulders with bamboo and thatch. There are luxury hotels, flashing neon signs, recent Hollywood films and Chinese night clubs ornamented with lovely girls. Coca Cola is ice-cold and rock 'n' roll blares from jukeboxes. But walk away from the souvenir stores and sleek office buildings and you will find yourself among the bubbling sights, sounds and smells of any Eastern city. Chinese shops sell live ducks, pigeon eggs, herbs and firecrackers alongside Rinso and corn flakes. At portable sidewalk restaurants the customers squat on the curb munching their rice. Small boys have their heads shaved except for a patch of hair in front. Women cook and wash in hidden courtyards while men make wooden furniture and carve decorative coffins. A truckload of pigs travels to market, their heads protruding from wicker baskets as they peer solemnly at the world.

Bangkok is a city of some 300 temples. Largest is Wat Po, the Reclining Buddha, a gigantic gilded statue lying in meditation. Around this central figure are pagodas of brilliantly contrasting mosaics and temples with overlapping roofs of gold, green and red shingles. The latter have symbolic wooden dragon heads extending from the front and back of each roof. Spiral columns represent serpents' tails and stone statues of warriors in tophats guard the gates.

The Royal Palace, enclosed by a mile-square white wall, contains the renowned Temple of the Emerald Buddha. The figure of the Buddha, carved from jade, has three solid-gold costumes which are changed according to season. Encircling the temple is a detailed mural of the *Ramayana*, the Hindu epic. The towering guardian statues in ancient armor have the leering faces of Indian demons. Sections of the palace itself are open to the public but the officials would not let me in without a coat and tie. This seemed ridiculous in the monsoon heat but who was I to argue with the King of Siam?

Bangkok is built on a network of canals called *klongs* which spread out from the Chao Phraya River. Lined with shops and houses on stilts, these muddy *klongs* are busy arteries of city traffic. Peasant families drift to market from upcountry, their tin-roof houseboats loaded with fruits and vegetables. In the early mornings the *klongs* become the scene of a great floating bazaar with food being bought and sold from skiff to sampan. The Thais, extremely clean people, bathe right from their front steps. *Klong* dwellers have school boats instead of buses for their children. The river itself swarms with fat little steamers, junks flying ragged sails and a bewildering collection of barges and lighters. On its bank stands Wat Arun, the Temple of Dawn, whose mosaic spire is the landmark of Bangkok.

I wandered into a swank hotel for a drink of water and threw the dining-room staff into raptures of pure delight. They grinned and giggled while I drank a couple of quarts and then brought me into the kitchen to have lunch with the cooks. On the docks I watched stevedores struggling to load a herd of buffalos aboard a tramp steamer. Buffalos are usually placid but they can be stubborn as camels. The poor, sweating laborers were forced to push, pull and pry each one up the gangway. In spite of almost having to carry some of the dumb beasts, the ever-cheerful Thais kept on smiling.

One evening I saw Siamese boxing which was performed according to an ancient and colorful ritual. The fighters knelt in their corners and prayed for success. Then each shadow-boxed in slow motion, dancing and leaping around the ring, to terrify his opponent. During the bout they kicked with their bare feet as well as punched with their fists while clarinet, drums and xylophone provided appropriate music. In the galleries where I sat, betting among the spectators was fast and furious.

Gordon Allison, an ex-G.I. from Tennessee and friend of a fellow I knew in Rangoon, lived in a small, elevated house outside Bangkok. His wife, Pranee, came from north Thailand where all the girls are pretty. She had a radiant smile, lustrous blue-black hair and skin the color of burnished gold.

"I decided Thailand was the place for me," said Gordon, propping his bare feet on a cushion. "The Army sent me here but couldn't make me leave. I like the people and the easy way they live. We don't have much money—I give English lessons and work at the Argentine Legation—but we don't need much."

"Maybe you have the right idea," I said. "Will you ever go back to Tennessee?"

"Perhaps someday for a visit, but not to stay. You know how the Southerners would treat Pranee."

"Anyway," he added with a grin, "I'm happy in Bangkok."

After spending four relaxed days with Gordon and Pranee, I headed north. The rice fields of the flooded delta are irrigated by damming the *klongs* with bamboo mesh and sod. The villagers fish enthusiastically, using poles, nets and traps. In extreme cases they seal off sections of the *klong,* bail the water out of both ends and collect the stranded fish. Peasant women look identical in dark, drab costumes and lamp-shade hats of palm leaf. The men dress simply in shorts and bandannas or felt hats, and small children are comfortably naked. Riding buffalos is great sport for everyone and boys like to lie on the animals' broad backs while they graze. Every morning the monks beg for food, marching solemnly in single file and carrying their black rice bowls. In front of many homes stand Buddhist shrines which resemble festive birdhouses.

Short rides with a Dutch airplane mechanic and five Thais in a midget car preceded one of my more unusual lifts. A Sherman tank of the Royal Siamese Army took me aboard and I perched on the turret with the boyish lieutenant. We clanked along, chewing up the highway, to the Armored School at Sara Buri. Here the company commander, recently returned from Fort Knox, escorted me on a tour of inspection and invited me to stay awhile. I rode spirited little cavalry ponies with the soldiers, racing bareback and managing not to fall off. That night a monsoon cloudburst threatened to wash away our tents.

Next day I really began to feel like Uncle Sam's official ambassador. I visited a new school, a village clinic and an army hospital where the doctor wore a sword but the medical facilities seemed very modern. Hitchhiking became effortless as my roadside friends made all arrangements, leaving me free to socialize and drink Pepsi Cola. Since there was so little traffic I went wherever anyone was going. This haphazard method of travel gave me a good look at the countryside and I was in no hurry. At one village I sympathized with an old sow harassed by a small boy as she tried to feed her brood. Eventually the pig family escaped its tormentor and settled down, except for one hysterical piglet who missed out on his dinner.

Late the following night I arrived in Siku. I was exhausted and gratefully accepted the hotelkeeper's offer of a couch in the lounge. I noticed vaguely that the rooms looked like cubbyholes and there were no other guests, but I felt too tired to wonder. In the morning several giggling females awakened me by bouncing on my stomach. I discovered that the "hotel" was the house of ill repute. The girls were fat and jolly and there seemed to be no social stigma attached to their profession. My beard fascinated them, since Thais have very little hair on their faces.

Siku is a remote village but I found half a dozen American construction men building a modern highway through the jungle. The contrast between hard-working Yanks and carefree Thais was interesting to watch. At 5:00 A.M. I boarded a truck convoy for the fifteen-hour journey to the base camp. When the new road is finished the same trip will take about two hours. Having eaten nothing but rice for several days, I devoured two whole fried chickens for lunch. The camp was comfortable and efficient, as American quarters always are, and I wallowed happily in hot water and clean sheets.

On the road to Cambodia I drank tea with assorted villagers and noticed that every bridge was being repaired. With a soldier on leave I hitched rides to the border town of Aranyaprathet. My friend's brother was a frontier policeman and we stayed in his barracks. His roommate's English was limited to simple phrases like "hello," "very good" and "take bath." To be obliging I bathed three times during my overnight visit. Whenever the conversation lagged I took a bath.

Cambodia, a lush little kingdom carved from the former French colony of Indo-China, is like Thailand, only more so. The Cambodians are the kind of people who hand you their fat, gurgling babies to play with. At first I misunderstood this gesture and thought they were giving me their children, but soon realized they were simply being sociable. One Cambodian driver not only offered a free bus ride but took up a collection among the passengers for me. I found it impossible to pay for anything in Cambodia except a few bananas.

A snappy police officer and his cute wife drove me through tall-grass country, flat as a board, to Siem Reap. Five kilometers from here stands Angkor Wat, the classic temple in the jungle city of Angkor Thom. The Khmers, a people of Indian origin and Hindu culture, built Angkor between the tenth and twelfth centuries. Its ruins are to the Asian jungle what Petra is to the Arabian desert, an awesome reminder of a little-known civilization.

Angkor Wat itself is the culmination of Khmer artistry, an almost perfectly preserved temple to the god Siva. The approaches are over a causeway of great stone slabs across a broad moat. Courtyards and galleries decorated with reliefs depicting battle victories lead to a squat central tower ringed by steep steps. This was formerly the sanctuary of Siva. Devout Cambodians have added statues of the Buddha festooned with pennants and bright bits of cloth.

Massive stone heads excavated by French archaeologists flank the gateways to Angkor Thom. The numerous towers of Bayon Temple are cut in the form of four human faces, one on each side. Exploring the towers and dark tunnels, I felt an eerie fascination in these brooding giants gazing at me from every angle. I followed jungle trails and stumbled upon more of these faces peering through the undergrowth concealing unrestored temples.

While inspecting Angkor I was a guest of the veterinarian in Siem Reap. My friend, like many educated Cambodians, was studying English with a booklet issued by the United States Information Agency. I proceeded to Kompong Chom, a market town whose yellow plaster walls, wooden shutters, shingle roofs and covered arcades were reminiscent of French colonial architecture in Algeria. Peasant women sold live chickens and fried bananas in the plaza. A medicine man demonstrated his cure-all herbs to the kind of gullible crowd found at any rural American carnival. A blind musician gave a recital, using a five-gallon oil-can cello with wooden neck and two pieces of wire which he scraped with a bow. The music was not the prettiest I have heard.

An eager young student brought me to his family's clothing shop for the night. The local children flocked to stare in open-mouthed wonder at the mysterious bearded creature from another world. I had a rapt audience until the shop doors were closed and they appeared first thing in the morning to look again. A man from Mars could not have excited more curiosity in Kompong Chom.

After breakfast of rice mush, fried dough twists and coffee, I traveled awhile by truck. Then occurred one of those experiences which could only happen to hitchhikers in places like Cambodia. Down the road lumbered an elephant carrying two men. I jokingly stuck up my thumb and was astonished to see them stop. The elephant knelt and they pulled me aboard. I sat on a padded mat and rode with the elegance of a maharaja. My friends eventually turned off into the jungle, and since they spoke only Cambodian, I never discovered where they were going.

I walked to the next village where roadside acquaintances invited me to lunch. We ate rice, fish and aromatic preserved eggs, which taste better than they sound. The houses were raised on piles and had wide cracks between the floor boards, convenient for betel-chewing women to spit through. In another hamlet I saw one of the jungle forts built by the French in their abortive attempt to defeat Communist guerrillas by holding a network of defensive strong points. The old Maginot Line concept was a sad failure. This outpost consisted of entrenchments and barbed wire with a wooden watch tower and a machine-gun nest of logs and earth at each corner. It looked somewhat like an early American stockade. The entire garrison with their women and children appeared to gaze at me. A beret-clad soldier spoke in halting French.

"You must not walk any more. It is very hot. We have a pedicab to take you to Skoun."

The cyclist was very fat but pedaled with surprising energy to the neighboring village. Here the police commandant received me as if I were the king himself. He ordered a magnificent dinner of roast chicken, green salad and two kinds of French wine. Wrapped in a borrowed sarong, I took a bath, Cambodian style, in the front yard of the police station. I dipped water out of a big clay urn, poured it over my head and scrubbed briskly before the fascinated eyes of the populace who watched from across the fence. Suddenly the sarong fell to the ground and there I stood. My audience howled with glee, then turned modestly away as I fumbled to recover my dignity. Everyone, including myself, was hysterical as I hurriedly finished my bath.

En route to Phnom Penh I crossed the outlet of Grand Lake, the rich fishery of Cambodia. The fishermen probe the shallow waters from their boats using large, forked nets. Phnom Penh, the nation's capital, is a slow-moving town of yellow buildings, Buddhist temples and tree-lined avenues. Wherever they colonize, the French love to plant trees. The spire of the Royal Palace has a face on each side like the towers of Angkor. The king's guard is changed with a flourish of bugles and drums. The overlapping roofs and graceful dragon heads of Cambodian temples are similar to those in Thailand. The Mekong River bank bustles with sampans, sailing craft and coastal steamers from Hong Kong and Saigon.

Outside a tiny shrine three bands played in turn as worshipers brought offerings of flowers arranged in coconuts. Using oboelike reed instruments, wooden xylophones, tomtoms, and covered bowls struck with mallets, the musicians were stomping like a Dixieland jam session. In the market, crowded as an Indian railroad station, a father shaved his baby's head with a pocket knife. "Dentists" who file their customers' front teeth and fit on brass caps plied their trade on the sidewalks. A pensive fellow puffed his homemade pipe, a two-foot metal tube from which protruded a cigarette. He produced billowing clouds of smoke which enveloped his head.

The citizens of Phnom Penh play the lottery, take afternoon siestas and love their ex-king Norodom Sihanouk. This clever and energetic leader negotiated independence from France, abdicated and was promptly elected Prime Minister. After being in and out of the government several times, he remains a popular idol, whether the U. S. State Department likes him or not.

I stopped at the American Library to leave my pack and became great friends with the entire Cambodian staff. The messengers, secretaries and assistant librarians were young and so eager to help me that I was overwhelmed with kindness. Their generosity went beyond ordinary limits. Whatever they had was mine because we were friends—as simple as that. They set up a cot for me in the library and the shy, dolllike girls brought sandwiches and worried about my health. Ou Chang, the general handyman, disappeared with my clothes and washed them. Sum Sun, head messenger at the Embassy, appointed himself my official guide.

One evening my friends took me to the theater to see a traditional performance of the struggle between good and evil. Villains in grotesque masks leaped about, roaring fearfully, and the heroine suffered one misfortune after another. The chubby leading man sang his role in a falsetto feminine voice. He seemed quite unheroic in my opinion but the audience loved him. In fact the crowd was uncritically enthusiastic about everyone in the cast. The extremely casual performance featured broad slapstick. Several times the comedian and his small side kick became so carried away with their own antics that they were overcome with laughter. At one point a baby wandered on stage and broke up the show. The scenery was painted on rolled screens. To change the scene someone backstage blew a whistle and a new screen was lowered. Actors waiting for their cues peeked at the audience. I could not remember when I had had more fun at the theater.

A French businessman, one of the few remaining in Phnom Penh, gave me a lift along the Mekong. The river villages sit on stilts and each house has clay pots, the size of wine barrels, for storing water. Men fish from their front porches and paddle over the flooded rice fields in canoes hollowed out of logs. Children play on rafts and occasional seminaked young ladies adorn the landscape.

The Cambodian peasant is a cheerfully serene fellow. His life is uncomplicated and he spends a great deal of time resting in his hammock. Palms, paddies and the river supply all his needs. He lives in a spirit of friendly intimacy with his sway-backed pigs. Here a porker sleeps curled up on the door step, there a sow and her brood frolic in a pen on the front porch. Down the road comes a man leading two piglets on a leash. The pig seems to have replaced the dog in Cambodian affections, yet the peasant doesn't hesitate to eat his porky friend.

Aboard the bus heading toward South Vietnam I told the driver briefly about my travels. He translated for the passengers' benefit and then, much to my embarrassment, collected contributions for me. I tried to explain that I was not entirely destitute but my French was inadequate and he insisted that I take the money. Rather than risk offending him, I accepted.

Rain fell in torrents as I walked the darkened streets of Saigon. "It's too late and wet to search for the police station," I told myself. "Don't be so stubborn, go to a hotel."

As I was about to take my own advice, I spotted a lighted church. Inside a missionary was addressing the congregation in unmistakably American English. I asked if I might sleep in the church but Warren Myers, a fellow Californian, took me home with him instead. Warren had an apartment in Cholon, Saigon's twin city, which is 90 per cent Chinese in population.

"The Chinese," he said, "are the unwanted people of Southeast Asia. They are hard-working and thrifty and control most of the business. These newly independent countries resent them and fear their economic power. The government here has given them an ultimatum—either become Vietnamese citizens or get out."

Saigon is known as the Paris of the Orient with its sidewalk cafés, shaded boulevards, swarms of bicycles and honking, darting Renaults and Citroëns. I think a more accurate comparison would be with some provincial town such as Toulouse. The city is bursting at the seams with refugees from the north and a general influx of population since the end of the Indo-China war. There are so many merchants in business on the sidewalks that it is difficult to thread one's way through the crowds.

The Vietnamese are lighter-complexioned and more Chinese in appearance than their Cambodian neighbors. Black-clad peasants carry food in baskets hanging from bamboo poles. Slender girls make a pretty picture pedaling their bicycles or whizzing along on motor scooters. They wear long dresses over pantaloons and round fiber sun hats tied under the chin with a strip of colored cloth. Large numbers of American-equipped soldiers are reminders of Vietnam's precarious existence as an independent republic. During the spring of 1955 Saigon was the scene of bloody fighting between government forces and the private armies of rebellious war lords. Although Premier Ngo Dinh Diem has restored internal stability, he has outlawed all opposition to his regime. A truly democratic government remains a hope for the future in Vietnam.

Most of the Americans in Saigon live their sheltered lives having as little as possible to do with the "natives." On a Sunday evening Warren took me to a church supper. The guests discussed important things such as their servant difficulties and the shortage of instant coffee at the commissary. They might as well have been in Peoria for all the benefit they were gaining from being in Saigon. But the supper itself was beautiful. I ate as much as I could and seriously considered filling my pockets.

A heavily loaded station wagon squeezed me in for the return trip to Phnom Penh and we rocketed over the flat, rain-soaked countryside. People and animals, except one unlucky dog, scurried out of our path. We breezed through customs and reached Phnom Penh early in the afternoon. Of course I returned to my friends at the library and this time met a few of the Americans in town. Jack Halliday, the assistant public-relations officer, somehow managed to be as harried and distraught as a Madison Avenue advertising man, an almost impossible feat in Cambodia. Joe Belmonte, another Embassy employee, gave me a shirt, replacing one of mine that had disintegrated, and a carton of Chesterfields. Miss Ketchum, the librarian, invited me to a cocktail party. And a tough Marine guard complained about the peaceful local situation.

"I like to fight," he told me. "It's too damn quiet around here. I hope the shooting starts again somewhere and I can get there before it's all over."

This peculiar fellow was the closest I found to an American warmonger.

I hated to leave Phnom Penh, one of my very best stops. Returning to Bangkok by a different route I rode to Battambang on top of a bus, reclining in comfort on a swaying mountain of baggage. Battambang is a pleasant, sleepy provincial town. Along the river bank are moored dozens of wooden houseboats, some with thatched roofs and little porches, others covered with corrugated-iron canopies. The sound of temple drums and gongs floats across the water, canoes drift downstream and men doze in their hammocks. The tranquil scene is disturbed briefly by a pig, squealing in protest, being transported to market on the back of a bicycle.

I stayed with Bill Weeks, director of the U. S. Information Agency, who asked me to speak to the students at the teachers' college. At first I struggled to describe my journey in French but my vocabulary failed and an interpreter mercifully rescued me. Khau Bun Hok, the U.S.I.A.'s jack of all trades, was driving to Aranyaprathet the following morning. He delivered me to his friend, the stationmaster, who arranged a complimentary train ride to Bangkok. Chugging through submerged countryside where roads were under water, our train was the only nonfloating transport. Travelers poled or paddled their canoes to the railroad stations, which were built on raised embankments.

After a brief visit with Gordon and Pranee, I left Bangkok in a jeep. The Thais were celebrating Children's Day and I watched the festivities at Rat Buri. Boys and girls, neatly attired in their school uniforms, sang and recited in the town square. As proud parents stood by a band played boisterously and local officials made pompous speeches. It was reminiscent of an old-fashioned holiday at home.

In Hua Hin, a resort on the Gulf of Siam, the Salesian Fathers welcomed me to their college. The Italian and Thai priests were men of great charm and intelligence. Next morning I swam with several students at a seemingly endless white sand beach, deserted except for us.

That afternoon I waited beside the road but not a single vehicle appeared. The narrow strip of Thailand which extends over 700 kilometers south to the Malayan border is a sparsely populated wilderness. Somewhere below Hua Hin the road simply dissolves into the jungle. This route, if passable at all, might have taken weeks to hitchhike so I decided to catch the evening train. The only noteworthy sights on this twenty-four-hour journey were mountainous rocks rising in isolated splendor from the flat jungle floor.

CHAPTER TWENTY-ONE

MALAYA

"Those Gurkhas are bloody devils in the jungle," said the Cockney soldier as he sipped his cup of tea. "They 'ave bashed more Reds than any other regiment."

"The only ones better," spoke up another Englishman, "are the Sarawak Rangers from North Borneo. Every battalion uses two or three as scouts. And those chaps are so good they can smell a man coming at night and tell you whether he is Chinese, Indian, Malay or European."

My informants were military guards at the mainland terminal for Penang Island. I had been talking with a group of Gurkha soldiers who became very excited when I showed them my kukri and explained that I had been in Nepal. Attracted by this intense discussion, the Englishmen had invited me to their station shack for bully beef, biscuits and tea.

Crossing to Penang on the ferry, the town with its backdrop of green-clad hills comes suddenly into view. The sea is almost artificially blue and the tropical sun glistens on yellow and white buildings. Jungle slopes split by farming valleys seem to have been polished to a sparkling gloss. The harbor is alive with Malay fishing boats, ponderous ocean-going Chinese junks, sampans scooting about like water bugs, oil tankers, rusty tramp steamers and sleek freighters.

Penang is clean and orderly, stamped with the efficiency of British rule. Along Beach Street are located the banks, shipping agencies and trading companies. Chinese shops emblazoned with gaudy signs line the side streets. Here craftsmen weave wicker furniture, sew clothing and carve wooden chests. In the yards hang racks of smoked fish while prawns and split coconuts are spread to dry in the sun. On the docks coolies load sacks of pungent copra, bales of sponge rubber, bars of pure tin and barrels of palm oil. The sarongs and blouses of Malay women are splashes of contrasting color. Their hair is worn in long thick braids and old ladies have small gold rings piercing each ear from top to bottom. A snake charmer, haggling the crowd to buy patent medicines, gets very little co-operation from his bored cobra. There are Indian money changers, Malays in bold sarongs and black caps and Sikh bank guards armed with shotguns.

The Chinese temples are highly ornamental with curving tile roofs topped by undulating dragons and weird images flanking the entrances. The musty interiors contain a jumble of prayer banners, brooding idols, bells, gongs and great leather-bound drums, candles and smoking joss sticks, paintings, flowers and figurines. A procession honoring the

Festival of the Nine Goddesses was forming in one temple courtyard. Assorted musicians, worshipers and onlookers milled around gay floats decked with colored paper. Flags and pennants fluttered from tall poles. Statues of the goddesses were carried by pairs of men who rocked them vigorously to cast out evil spirits lurking within.

The majority of Penang's population, like that of every Malayan town, is Chinese. The native Malays are farmers and fishermen, police and civil servants. Chinese immigrants plus a considerable number of Indians control the business, trade and local industry. British supremacy has insured peace and stability among these three racial groups. But independence for the Malayan Federation raises the problem of Chinese domination. For the time being Singapore Island with its 80 per cent Chinese population will remain a British Crown colony and the Malays will have a slight majority within their own country. But if Singapore is incorporated into the Federation the Chinese will actually outnumber the Malays. With their wealth and numerical superiority they will definitely gain the balance of power. Malaya understandably does not want Singapore and is developing her own smaller seaports. The Federation can live without Singapore but the great harbor will be crippled without the mainland.

To further complicate the problem practically all of the Communist terrorists in the Malayan jungle are Chinese. The prestige of Red China is high, particularly among the younger generation. China has become a world power, the first and only Asian country to successfully defy the West. To proud and sensitive people, bitter about the white man's selfish rule, this is tremendously important.

I met Anton Fernando, a Ceylonese newspaperman, and Hamzah bin Mohammed Salleh who described himself as "not a good Moslem but a good Malay." We painted the town on a very modest scale and discussed the pros and cons of colonialism.

"The British have done good things for Malaya," said Hamzah, "and any fair-minded Malay will admit this. I was in the Navy and went to London for the coronation. I liked the English people in England. But in my country they are so arrogant, and the women are worse than the men.

"Superior white women!" he laughed. "I remember the ones on the streets of London whose price was ten bob."

"The English are like anyone else," said Anton. "A man who is nobody at home comes out here and straightaway he has a big house, servants, an important position. So he and his family begin to think that they are better than you and me."

Each Malay *kompong* (village) along the road south contained a row of ramshackle shops. Houses with steep thatched roofs and carved woodwork were scattered among the coconut palms. Three British soldiers gave me a fast lift to the tin mining town of Taiping. Wide streets, laid out in a neat pattern and flanked by arcaded stores, were deserted in the midday heat. The thunder of drums attracted me to a Chinese club where a boy was practicing the dragon dance. Standing inside a ferocious papier-mâché dragon's head, he had only his feet protruding. With a couple of assistants filling the tail he leaped and wriggled in an amazing display of energy. I became exhausted watching him and was sitting in the park when two Chinese teachers came along. They took me to inspect a tin dredge, a rumbling, clanking monster which scooped ore through torrents of water and wallowed in a lake of its own making. We swam in a pool near the exclusive club for Europeans only. Even at this late date within months of Malayan independence the white men refuse to change their ways.

A Chinese doctor drove me to the camp of the Royal Australian Regiment in Kuala Kangsar. The Diggers were big brash fellows in bush hats with turned-up brims.

One of them predicted, "After you see ol' Aussie you'll never go back to Yankeeland."

I continued to Ipoh with two brothers, one of whom was roly-poly and appropriately named Tong Fatt. They showed me Chinese opencast tin mines on the scarred hills. The ore is washed over the steps of rickety wooden structures built like giant staircases. We joined several friends for a real feast in an Ipoh restaurant. I was becoming quite an expert with chopsticks and managed to eat as much as anyone. This was no mean feat because the Chinese are rapid eaters and a clumsy beginner gets lost in the shuffle. I had learned to pick up pieces of meat and vegetable from platters in the center of the table. I had also practiced the rotating motion for shoveling rice into my mouth from the bowl held under my chin.

In speaking of Red China one of my companions said, "The Communists are firmly in control whether you Americans like it or not. They will not go away like a bad dream simply because America ignores them. Your government deals with Russia and other Communist countries even when it disagrees with them. How can you expect to learn anything about China if you have no diplomatic relations?"

"I agree with you that our attitude is naïve and unrealistic," I said. "But what do you think will happen in China?"

"The Chinese people have the oldest way of life on earth. They have survived many invasions and absorbed many philosophies. China will change Communism to suit itself rather than Communism changing China. But what the result will be I do not know."

After dinner we visited the amusement park, a feature of every Malayan town. The strip-tease show had Chinese girls doing bumps and grinds to rock 'n' roll music in a performance which would have pleased Billy Minsky. My friends arranged for me to stay at their Sports Club. The sports seemed to be limited to frenzied night-long games of mah-jong. The gamblers played fast and furiously, slapping the ivory cubes on the table, whooping delightedly at a clever move and shuffling the pieces with a deafening racket. The uproar finally lulled me to sleep.

Tong Fatt was driving on to Kuala Lumpur, capital and largest town of the Federation. East of the road lay wild mountains where the British Army goes "jungle-bashing" in search of elusive Communists. We passed rubber estates, the trees planted in orderly rows with cups hanging below the slashes in the trunks to catch the dripping latex. Chinese New Villages were surrounded by barbed wire and patrolled by security guards. Peasant families formerly scattered in the jungle have been collected into these New Villages in an effort to stop the smuggling of food to the terrorists. Check points manned by Malay police and Royal Scots Fusiliers searched all road traffic. It is illegal even to carry food through these areas. This starvation campaign has been fairly successful but is a long, slow process.

In Kuala Lumpur a young police lieutenant invited me to his home. Mohammed's small, neat house seemed to strike a balance between Western comfort and Eastern simplicity. Chairs, tables and a telephone combined with mats and cushions on the floor. Both Mohammed and his pretty wife had been educated in British schools and spoke English as well as I. That evening the neighborhood children gathered for their weekly religious lesson. They recited verses from the Koran in Arabic and I reflected how widespread the influence of Islam has been. I also decided that *Mohammed* must be the most popular title on earth. From Morocco to Malaya every third Moslem seems to be named for the Prophet.

The High Courts and government buildings of Kuala Lumpur have been constructed in a peculiar Victorian Moorish style. They are white in color with plentiful spires and arches. The Malay Mosque, its striped minarets and yellow dome framed by coconut palms, is Arabic in mood and design. The stately British Club and its immaculate *padang* (sports field) fairly reek of the "white man's burden." There are large Chinese department stores, venerable English trading companies and ultramodern, glass-fronted office buildings.

I went to the movies and found myself being interviewed and photographed in the theater lobby. Gopi Kumar, a bouncy bright-eyed little Indian reporter for the *Singapore Standard*, took complete charge of my affairs. During the next eighteen hours he became my close friend, adviser and guardian angel. Gopi gave me a sarong and tried to arrange an interview with Tunku Rahman, the Prime Minister. Unfortunately this gentleman was too busy to receive hitch-hikers.

"I belong to Malacca," Gopi told me. "You must not miss this historic city, the oldest in Malaya."

When I agreed, he secured a complimentary bus ticket, made long-distance phone calls and presented me with introductions to half the people in town. Owen Liu, the first of my hosts in Malacca, was waiting to greet me at the bus station. Kumara Das, an Indian teacher at the high school, took time off from classes to be my guide. Together we called on the Surajens, a warmhearted Indo-Chinese family. Mr. Surajen lent Das his car and we were off to find Peter Jones, a British Army corporal. The three of us went to a party in the home of a Portuguese Eurasian family. Later we watched Malay couples dancing without touching each other and ended the evening at a Chinese night club.

I could have spent a month in Malacca. Gopi's introductions were responsible for a royal reception involving more people than I knew what to do with. I tried to contact all his friends but two days were simply not enough time.

The Portuguese came to Malacca early in the sixteenth century. One moldy gate of their fort erected by Alfonso D'Albuquerque is still standing. Upon a hill sits the shell of their church, the oldest European building in Southeast Asia. After fifty years the Dutch captured Malacca and ruled for more than one hundred fifty years until they in turn were driven out by the British. For centuries the city was a center of the spice trade through the Straits of Malacca. Today its shallow port handles only a few coastal sailing ships. On palm-fringed beaches fishing boats are pulled up on the sand and nets hang in the sun. The fishermen take life easy in their flimsy huts.

The old Chinese merchant families live along narrow lanes in yellow and blue houses with richly carved doors and latticework. These people speak the Malay language but still write in Chinese characters. They are a community separate from their recently arrived countrymen. The Dutch have left thick-walled pink buildings with wooden shutters and tile roofs. Their Town Hall is as solid as one of Rembrandt's burghers. Even the countryside around Malacca seems more picturesque than that farther north. The peasants in conical fiber hats, their sarongs tucked up around their waists, plow the waterlogged paddies. Buffalos pull carts whose curving canopies look like the hulls of ships. A Chinese funeral has mourners in sackcloth, a razzle-dazzle band and relatives carrying the ornate coffin.

I rode with a Malay official through rubber estates and pineapple plantations to Johore Bahru. Across the causeway lay Singapore Island, "Gateway to the East." For me it was the exit and I felt sad to be leaving Asia. Having traveled without delay or difficulty, I decided that Malaya was among the best countries for hitchhiking.

Singapore is a bubbling polyglot mixture, one of the world's most fascinating cities. For hours I picked my way along side streets festooned with drying laundry and jammed with carts, pedicabs and surging humanity. I stared at everything, trying to stamp these sights indelibly on my mind. Red-and-yellow-robed Chinese priests presided over a religious ceremony around a roaring bonfire right in the middle of a crowded thoroughfare. At a Hindu temple two sadhus clad only in loin cloths, their heads shaved except for a single long lock of hair, prayed to the gods while drums throbbed and horns wailed. I wandered past the side shows and eating stalls, the shops and cabarets of the Happy World Amusement Park. I admired the shapely Chinese ladies in their tight silk dresses with slit skirts.

The commercial center of Singapore is dominated by the Asia Insurance Building, an eighteen-story skyscraper. In front of the Victoria Memorial Hall stands a statue of the city's founder, Sir Stamford Raffles. Barges so completely clog the river that it is possible to cross by stepping from one to another. Small freighters lie at anchor in the Inner Roads and a fleet of tall-masted, high-boomed sailing ships rides offshore. Along the beach Malay craftsmen pound and saw on wooden hulls. At night the sky is lighted by a multitude of neon signs in English and Chinese.

I left my pack in Raffles Hotel as an excuse to inspect this venerable stronghold of the British Raj. To my disappointment none of the gin-and-tonic drinkers looked at all like Colonel Blimp. I visited the garden estate of the late multimillionaire Tiger Balm King, an unbelievable conglomeration of statues, fountains and shrines. I walked into the exclusive Cricket Club and was politely requested to leave.

Before sailing from New York I had inquired about a visa at the Australian Consulate. The official had talked vaguely of medical examinations and police good-conduct records and had advised me that the easiest way was to immigrate. In Singapore the Australian High Commission issued the visa in thirty seconds flat. The visa officer even waived the usual fee because he was hurrying to a party and could not bother to make out the receipt.

After only two days in Singapore the luck of the vagabond put me aboard a Dutch ship bound for Australia. The *Tjibadak* was an aged passenger freighter with a Chinese crew and Dutch officers. One of the cargo clerks had been taken sick and the company did not have time to bring a replacement from Hong Kong. I helped to inventory the cargo of rubber, tin, tea, rice and oil and was given passage to Brisbane.

CHAPTER TWENTY-TWO

AUSTRALIA
AND
NEW ZEALAND

"I RECKON WE live for leisure and pleasure," mused the salesman as we drove through the gum forests. "They say 'Give an Aussie a few bob for beer and a quid for the races and he's happy.'"

"I've heard that the people believe quite strongly in the welfare state," I said.

"My word," he said in agreement. "Here in Queensland the Labor Party has been in power for almost forty years. The government does everything from running the railroads to paying bonuses for children. Prices are regulated according to the basic wage. Any bloke who wants to work can afford his own home if he can find one to buy. The housing shortage is bloody awful. Except for some of the cattle and sheep station owners, people are not rich. But no one is very poor either. It's a good country with a big future."

The *Tjibadak* had sailed through the Indonesian islands, stopping briefly at Jakarta, and followed the Great Barrier Reef to Brisbane. Having been,in Asia for so long, I thought at first that I was home again. Modern, prosperous Brisbane looked to me like an American city. But I soon began to appreciate the individual character of Australia.

Before World War II this huge island was Anglo-Saxon, agricultural and isolated. The threat of Japanese invasion jarred the Australians into an awareness of their precarious position. "Populate or perish" warned the postwar government and within ten years over a million immigrants were added to a population which today totals about ten million. Many of these New Australians came from Europe bringing different customs and ideas. Although the heritage and culture remains basically British, Australia is becoming a real melting pot. The war and its aftermath also encouraged industrialization so that the country no longer lives exclusively "on the sheep's back."

I spent my first night in Brisbane at St. Vincent's Hostel for Destitute Men. After this auspicious introduction to Australia I set off on a quick tour of southeastern Queensland. My salesman friend drove me up the coast to the run-down mining town of Gympie. We stopped in the bush and listened to the peculiar cry of the whip bird, a whistling crack like that of a bull whip. I rode to Toowoomba with a cattle buyer, an enthusiastic member of the local flying club. He took me for a flight in a Tiger Moth over the Darling Downs, rolling wheat plains stretching far to the west. On the main highway a wiry little Scot in a Volkswagen halted beside me.

"Stow your swag in back and hop in. I'll take you to Sydney."

Jock not only transported me some 750 miles but paid for my meals and hotel as well. We admired the sweeping white sand beaches at Surfer's Paradise and Coolangatta of which the Aussies are so proud. We followed the coastal route through small towns with false-front stores and corrugated iron-roofed houses which all look alike. Friends in Sydney introduced me to John Crawley, a photo engraver newly arrived from London. John and I decided to hitchhike to Melbourne together. In the New South Wales sheep country we watched the activity inside a shearing shed. Using electric clippers the fast-working shearers stripped thick coats of Merino wool from the struggling animals.

The Suez crisis had just begun when we listened to a heated debate in the Parliament at Canberra. The Labor Party was attacking the Conservatives for their unqualified support of the Egyptian invasion. One portly legislator slumped over his desk, sound asleep. The Canberra police put us into a judge's chambers for the night, a cozy spot with soft carpets on the floor.

The Snowy Mountains are the scene of a large-scale hydroelectric and irrigation scheme. Although November is supposed to be the beginning of summer, it was snowing at the Adaminaby Dam construction camp. We hurriedly left the mountains and rode on a logging truck into Victoria. Hitchhiking was slow and the miles of empty bush were bleak and monotonous. At Orbost we slept in a convict-built lockup, a small cell behind the policeman's house. A squatter (farmer) friend of John's took us kangaroo-hunting near Yarragon. We spotted 'roos but our marksmanship was poor.

From November 22 to December 8, Melbourne was the "Capital of the World." The Olympic Games were a spine-tingling spectacle, a fitting climax for my trip. For a week before the Games started John and I worked as dishwashers in the Russian team's kitchen. Since the Olympic Village was off-limits to the public, this gave us a unique opportunity to look behind the scenes. The teams lived in apartments and houses built especially for the occasion. The flag of each nation flew in front of its quarters. In our dining hall a crew of chiefs from half a dozen European countries prepared food that was truly magnificent.

The Russians trooped in solemnly for each meal, ate like horses and filled their pockets with fruit. They seemed particularly fond of bananas, which may have been a new delicacy for them. In contrast to the noise and laughter in other dining halls, ours was silent. The Russian athletes did not socialize, even among themselves, and seemed completely aborbed in the serious business of training. They went everywhere in groups, never alone. As the Games progressed the Russians relaxed somewhat and threw a vodka party for the kitchen staff. The happiest member of their team was Nina Ponomareva, the discus thrower who had caused an international incident by shoplifting some cheap hats in London a few months before. Always smiling, Nina was accompanied by two men in civilian clothes, obviously not athletes. Most of the women were hard and muscular but several pretty gymnasts stood out like rare jewels. I spoke briefly to a couple of Russians but we discussed the Games and avoided politics.

I spent every spare minute watching the activity at the training track. Emil Zatopek, the once invincible Czech, jogged with a pretty Cuban girl. Hal Connolly, the American hammer thrower, gave pointers to an Englishman and a Pakistani. A long-legged Rumanian female high jumper looked so much like a boy that I stood right beside her and still couldn't be certain she was a girl. Indian hockey players, the Sikhs with their hair tied in bows, practiced unceasingly. This method pays off since India has never lost in Olympic hockey. Perry O'Brien warmed up for the shot-put as the Russian coaches studied his every move. They carefully photographed his preliminary routine including the way that he spits. Ron Delaney, the Irish miler, ran like a spastic chicken and looked incapable of beating anyone. His style is so peculiar that he was easy to follow as he won the 1,500-meter race. The voluble Italian coach waved his arms, wrung his hands and clasped his head as he urged on his sprinters. A tall, angular Finn trotted round and round in a funny red hat. Sir William Slim, the Governor General, arrived to shake hands with everyone.

Mary Rao, the lone girl on a forty-man Indian team, I feel certain was brought to Melbourne purely for decorative purposes. She spent her time looking lovely in saris and posing for pictures. In her only appearance at the Stadium she collapsed and was dramatically carried off the field. Russians and British in blue track suits, green-clad Aussies, Poles and Canadians in red combined colorfully on the field. Runners from Kenya had twisted ears and tribal scars on their faces. A giant Fijian weight lifter wore sport coat, tie and lava-lava (sarong). A dolllike fourteen-year-old Filipino girl swimmer was wide-eyed with excitement. There were turbaned Pakistanis, Indonesians in bright jackets and black caps, happy-go-lucky Brazilians and understandably subdued Hungarians.

When the Games started John and I resigned from the kitchen and became spectators. I watched cycling races, gymnastics and Greco-Roman wrestling for the first time. Field hockey, considered a girls' game at home, is rough and skillful as played by barefoot Indians and Pakistanis. Seeing European football teams in action, I could also appreciate the great popularity of soccer. Boxing was like an international Golden Gloves tournament. The Aussies dominated the swimming races in the futuristic Olympic pool. Their radiantly healthy girls and boys were unbeatable.

The American basketball team was so expert it had no real opposition. The players should have staged an exhibition game among themselves to demonstrate the fine points of basketball. In Melbourne I saw for the first time University of San Francisco stars Bill Russell and K. C. Jones. The Russians played fairly good, if slow and awkward, basketball featuring their seven-foot two-inch Latvian center. This massive fellow was a bewildered ox both on and off the court.

But best of all were the track and field events under the shadow of the Olympic torch in the Main Stadium. There were many high lights. American Charlie Dumas and Australian Chilla Porter engaged in a gruelling high jump duel. Vladimir Kuts, the Iron Man of the Russian Navy, became a worthy successor to Zatopek by twice running Britain's Gordon Pirie into the ground. I wondered if the American press would give Kuts the credit he deserved or simply brush him off because of his country. I hoped that the papers were not making the Games into a contest between America and Russia for national supremacy.

After walking 50 kilometers (31 miles) for a gold medal, New Zealander Norm Read trotted an extra lap around the Stadium. At this point the crowd went wild. Texan Bobby Morrow qualified as the world's fastest human by winning the 100- and 200-meter sprints. Betty Cuthbert and Shirley Strickland scored a clean sweep of the women's races to become the toasts of Australia.

After Milt Campbell's great performance in the decathalon, I overheard the caustic remark, "Yanks don't worry about a bloke's color when he wins for Uncle Sam."

Norwegian Egil Davidsen leaped with joy even before his world record-breaking javelin throw touched the ground. Alain Mimoun, an Algerian Frenchman, ran to victory in the killing marathon and the band played the "Marseillaise." Englishman Chris Brasher, disqualified after winning the steeplechase, appealed to the judges and the decision was reversed. Perhaps the finest competitors of all were the persistent little Ethiopians, Koreans, Thais and Japanese who kept running in spite of the marked superiority of their rivals. These men upheld the true Olympic spirit of good sportsmanship.

On the final day the athletes marched onto the field mixed together regardless of nationality. The Olympic torch was extinguished and a long sigh arose from the crowd. Twenty-five pounders fired a salute to the massed flags. The choir sang the "Olympic Hymn" and "Will Ye No Come Back Again." The Games were an unforgettable experience and I could have cried when they ended.

Fortunately for John and me Ben Cocks was the kind of friend who felt personally responsible for our well-being in Melbourne. He was proud of his city and helped more than anyone else to make our visit so memorable. Ben arranged for us to stay successively with his in-laws, his parents and a most generous family named Buttifant. Soon after our arrival he introduced us to a peculiar Victorian phenomenon known as the "six-o'clock swill." This frenzied drinking bout takes place in the hotels, the Australian pubs, every afternoon.

"Aussies are great beer drinkers," explained Ben, "and six o'clock closing is supposed to prevent drunkenness. After work everyone goes flat out with one eye on the clock. At six a bell rings and the hotel shuts for the night."

"It may be uncivilized," he laughed, "but at least a bloke gets home for tea."

After the Games John found a job and I toured Tasmania, the small island south of the mainland. Green and pretty farming country, Tasmania is more solidly British in custom and tradition than other parts of Australia. People who were born here and have never been overseas speak of England as "home." Parts of the island, particularly the northwest coast, look very much like Devon and Cornwall. I traveled to Hobart, the quiet and conservative state capital, through the apple-growing Huon Valley and down the sparsely populated east coast with its fishing and resort villages. Port Arthur, the notorious penal colony to which convicts were transported for many years, is one of the few historical monuments in Australia. I found youth hostels in Tasmania, the first since leaving Trieste.

The three German cyclists with whom I had sailed to Rangoon were working in Melbourne. We met unexpectedly on the street and I spent Christmas with them. Coming as it does in the middle of the summer, the Australian Christmas is national vacation time. Factories shut down, most businesses close and everyone goes on holiday. It seems strange to see so many families leaving rather than homeward bound for Christmas.

"My bloody oath!" exclaimed the bushman, staring at me. "The Yank is a *fair dinkum swagie.*"

This meant simply that I looked like a true Australian hobo. I had been waiting in the sleepy town of Port Augusta for a lift into the outback. The two rugged bushmen in their battered truck were the first travelers I had seen in four hours.

"Me and me cobber are heading for the lead mines at Mount Isa," said the driver as we bounced north over the dirt track.

"That kangaroo guard," he explained, pointing to a framework of iron pipes in front of the grille, "is to stop the bloody 'roos from jumping into our lights at night. If one of them smashes the radiator, then we're in strife. This outback country is no place for a breakdown. That's why the ol' truck is chockablock with extra petrol, water and enough tucker to feed us for days."

We were entering the scorched desert plains of central Australia, the *never-never* land of scrub brush and bare rock, metallic skies and limitless vistas. Here the cattle stations cover hundreds, even thousands, of square miles and precious water is pumped by windmills from deep wells.

This is the home of primitive aborigines, the ostrichlike emus and dingos (wild dogs). The kangaroos run in herds and are so numerous that the stations hire men to shoot them.

In Kingoonya, a handful of houses with a hotel and general store, I met Gil Vaughan, a taciturn Victoria potato farmer. Gil was driving to Alice Springs, the green oasis in the exact center of Australia. We reached Coober Pedy at eight o'clock on New Year's Eve. The local inhabitants, some fifty opal miners and half-caste *abos*, were having a party with a keg of beer and empty oil drums to pound at midnight. Coober Pedy is an unusual settlement where everyone lives underground. To avoid the 120-degree heat in the shade, the miners reside in dugouts cut into the hillsides. These caves are cool and free of the flies which swarm in the open. Two stores at the crossroads are Coober Pedy's only conventional buildings.

One of the miners, an ex-real-estate salesman from Los Angeles, had been bitten by the opal "bug" while vacationing in Australia. Jim and his partner needed help in cleaning tailings from their mine shaft and asked us to work with them for several days. Gil and I took turns filling a forty-gallon drum with loose rock and hoisting it to the surface on a windlass. I did not mind the blistering heat as much as the persistent flies. Jim showed us how to dig through the powdery rock and find the elusive pieces of sparkling, multicolored opal. We lived in his dugout, a cozy two-room cave with a cooking fireplace, chairs, table and radio.

Gil and I drove one night and most of the next day to reach Alice Springs. We were in the Northern Territory, an area of half a million square miles with a population of 16,000. The white-painted houses, flower gardens and trees of the Alice were a refreshing contrast to the surrounding desolation. I visited the headquarters of the Flying Doctor, the unique medical service for outback families. Every isolated station has a two-way radio and a landing field. In case of illness or accident a doctor either flies to the scene or the patient is flown in to the hospital. After emergency calls have been transmitted, the radio network relays telegrams, personal messages and even bets on the next Saturday's races.

In speaking of the aborigines, a local stockman told me, "The black fellows are good *jackaroos*—cowboys to you— but they're not reliable. Every so often they 'go walkabout,' just disappear into the bush, and stay away for weeks at a time. You never know what a black fellow will do next."

I returned to Port Augusta and crossed the wheat and vineyard country of South Australia with a Dutch shark fisherman. En route to Sydney an obliging truckdriver stopped at the game sanctuary in Healesville. I saw wombats, which look like a cross between a pig and a bear, fat little koalas munching eucalyptus leaves, and an entertaining platypus named Peter.

Sydney is a world-ranking city of two million people spread around a superb natural harbor and dominated by an enormous single-span bridge. The residents of Sydney are extremely proud of this bridge and regard it with almost holy veneration. In order to visit several friends in the city I moved around spending a day or two with each. Des De Belle, a lanky sheep shearer with whom I had traveled in Tasmania, helped me secure passage to New Zealand. Aileen and Beryl, girls I had originally met in Spain, took me to the beaches where the waves are excellent for surfing and

life guards watch for sharks. I stayed with Bob Barbour—
our paths had crossed in Afghanistan—and Barbara Everest, the stewardess from the *Tjibadak*. After a busy week
in Sydney I sailed across the Tasman Sea to Auckland.

New Zealand is as close to being a hitchhiker's paradise
as any country I know. The topography ranges from semitropical bush, luxuriant as any equatorial jungle, to snow-
clad peaks laced with glaciers. The roads are narrow and
often rough but there is plentiful traffic on most of them.
And the cars invariably stop even if they are going only a
mile or so. The *Kiwis* (New Zealanders) are as hospitable
to strangers as Middle Eastern and Asian people. This
makes them unexcelled in the Western world. They took
me into their homes and passed me on to their friends. During my first ten days in New Zealand I paid for exactly
two meals and one movie ticket.

While wandering through Auckland I noticed what
looked like a public park with flower gardens and soft
lawns. Deciding that this would be a fine place to sleep,
I settled down for the night. I awoke with a flashlight shining in my eyes.

"You're under arrest," announced the bobbie. "This is
Government House."

Chagrined to discover that I had been reposing on the
equivalent of the White House lawn, I was escorted to the
police station. Here I explained to the sergeant that I was
a newly arrived tourist and had meant no harm. He laughed
and sent me across the street to sleep undisturbed in Albert
Park.

I traveled north to the Bay of Islands, famed for scenery
and deep-sea fishing, and into the forests of redwoodlike

kauri trees. A butcher guided me through the meat-freezing works at Kawakawa. Husky Maoris seized the hapless sheep, cut their throats with one deft stroke and hung the carcasses on a moving chain to be skinned and dressed. Frozen meat and dairy products exported to Britain are the backbone of New Zealand's economy.

In Auckland again, I met a woman named Hilda Drage in a hardware store. This was a fortunate encounter, since Hilda and her husband Denis practically adopted me into their family. Denis repaired my pack, which was falling apart and Hilda sewed my torn clothing. They took me fishing for snappers along the black sand beaches west of Auckland. New Zealand is a great country for sportsmen. The *Kiwis* measure trout in pounds rather than inches and hunt wild pigs with dogs and knives. There are so many deer that the government is obliged to hire professional hunters.

I visited George Pancheri, Hilda's brother-in-law and a former U. S. Navy man, at his dairy farm on the Bay of Plenty. George is one of numerous American servicemen who liked New Zealand well enough to settle there. I proceeded to Rotorua, the center of a thermal area containing geysers, boiling pools and mud volcanoes. It reminded me of Yellowstone on a less spectacular scale.

There are many Maoris, the original New Zealanders, in Rotorua. The ancestors of these Polynesians came, probably from Hawaii, in war canoes six hundred years ago. An intelligent, good-natured and adaptable people, they have prospered side by side with settlers of British descent. Setting an example for the rest of the world to emulate, the Maoris and whites have demonstrated that two races can live together harmoniously. I think that the most important reason for this situation has been mutual respect. In the early days of British colonization, the Maoris tried unsuccessfully to drive out the newcomers. The white settlers in turn were able to defeat but never completely conquer the brave and stubborn natives. Out of this stalemate grew a realization that one group need not rule or destroy the other. And for almost a hundred years there has been little friction between Maori and *Pakeha* (white).

I headed south from Rotorua to Wairakei, where bores are being drilled like oil wells to tap the underground thermal energy. Continuing along the shore of Lake Taupo and past the smoking Ngauruhoe volcano, I rode with a racetrack driver and in a bacon truck to Wellington. The capital of New Zealand, with its wooden houses marching up the hills overlooking the harbor, reminded me of Bergen, Norway. I sailed across Cook Strait from the North to the South Island. On the ferry I met Peter Fraser, a teacher from Port Washington, Long Island, barely three miles from my home town of Manhasset.

We hitchhiked together, riding with an old man who drove continually on the wrong side of the road. Perhaps he thought that with Americans he should keep to the right. The police in the coal-mining town of Greymouth put us up in their very comfortable jail. Our progress down the west coast was slow, but eventually we arrived at Franz Joseph Glacier. This mass of ice has ground its way from high on the slopes of the Southern Alps to a point in the rain forest a few hundred feet above sea level. We could not figure out why it had not melted. We climbed onto the glacier and heard the blue ice creaking around us. A rushing torrent of water poured from a gaping cavern at the bottom of the glacier.

Peter went on to Fox Glacier and I crossed the bare mountains to Christchurch, largest city on the South Island. Following the east coast over the Canterbury plains and through hills alive with sheep, I reached Invercargill. Wind-swept and Scottish, Invercargill boasts the distinction of being the southernmost city in the British Commonwealth. Unless someday I journey to Patagonia or Antarctica, I will never go farther south than this.

With a mountain-climbing law student I drove into Milford Sound, a fiord as awe-inspiring as any in Norway. Peaks rose sheer from the sound, and waterfalls tumbled over the cliffs. I continued to Queenstown, a resort flanked by mountains called the Remarkables, Arrowtown, an old gold-mining center, and the Hermitage, a lodge below Mount Cook, highest mountain in the Southern Alps. In the MacKenzie Country, an area named in honor of an itinerant sheep rustler, I stopped at an army camp. "G'day, g'day and how would you be?" the soldiers greeted me. "Always glad to see the Yanks."

The *Kiwis* wore their distinctive headgear, which look like Boy Scout hats gone to seed. A disgruntled sergeant told me, "Our jokers don't have any decent bloody equip-ment. When the *Pommie* [English] guns wear out, they send them to us."

I sailed from Christchurch back to Wellington and spent a couple of days with the parents of a fellow I had met briefly in Pakistan. Mr. and Mrs. Moar gave me a shirt and a pair of tennis shoes (my faithful boots had finally been ripped to shreds) and treated me with the utmost kindness. I know that they were doing for me

· 285

what they hoped someone else would do for their son.

En route to Auckland, in a place called Te Kuiti I was invited home by a clarinet-playing restaurant owner who loved American jazz. Denis Drage found me a temporary job with the Auckland Gas Company. For a week I was employed in their warehouse as a sorter and counter of pieces of pipe. It was uninspiring, but none of us worked very hard.

I sailed for home via the Fiji Islands and Hawaii, aboard the Orient Lines' steamship *Orion*. During our brief call at Suva I met a Fijian merchant who took me to his village to drink *kava*. This potent beverage, made from ground-up roots mixed with water, is consumed throughout the South Seas. In Honolulu the chromed automobiles with their "dollar grins," swank beach hotels and typical American efficiency seemed almost as strange and exciting to me as to my Australian shipmates. The *Orion* was a painfully slow vessel, but one morning, three weeks after leaving Auckland, she steamed under the Golden Gate Bridge. My 80,000-mile journey was finished.

I had learned that a traveler who is willing to meet people on their own level, with an open mind and a smile, is welcome throughout the world. As a hitchhiker I had demonstrated to others that every American is not wealthy and supercilious, racing from place to place in a huge car. And they had shown me the goodness to be found in men everywhere. To some the Brotherhood of Man may be a faded cliché. But to me it is a vivid reality, because I lived it every day for twenty-six months.